CIVIC CENTER

THE**new** biology

Cancer

Revised Edition

THE **new** biology

Cancer

The Role of Genes, Lifestyle, and Environment
Revised Edition

JOSEPH PANNO, PH.D.

An imprint of Infobase Publishing

CANCER: The Role of Genes, Lifestyle, and Environment, Revised Edition

Copyright © 2010, 2005 by Joseph Panno, Ph.D.

Facts On File, Inc.
An imprint of Infobase Publishing
132 West 31st Street
New York NY 10001

Library of Congress Cataloging-in-Publication Data

Panno, Joseph.
    Cancer: the role of genes, lifestyle, and environment / Joseph Panno.—Rev. ed.
        p. cm.—(The new biology)
    Includes bibliographical references and index.
    ISBN 978-0-8160-6848-7
    1. Cancer—Social aspects. 2. Cancer—Environmental aspects. 3. Cancer—Genetic aspects. I. Title.
    RC262.P35 2011
    616.99'4–dc22   2009050783

Facts On File books are available at special discounts when purchased in bulk quantities for businesses, associations, institutions, or sales promotions. Please call our Special Sales Department in New York at (212) 967-8800 or (800) 322-8755.

You can find Facts On File on the World Wide Web at http://www.factsonfile.com

Text design by Erik Lindstrom
Composition by Hermitage Publishing Services
Illustrations by the Author
Photo research by Diane K. French
Cover printed by Bang Printing, Brainerd, Minn.
Book printed and bound by Bang Printing, Brainerd, Minn.
Date printed: September 2010
Printed in the United States of America

10 9 8 7 6 5 4 3 2 1

This book is printed on acid-free paper.

Contents

Preface   xi
Acknowledgments   xiii
Introduction   xiv

1 Normal Cells   1
   The Origin of Life   1
   The Struggle for Survival   4
   Cell Communication   10
   The Rise of Multicellular Organisms   15

2 Cancer Cells   19
   Cancer Cells Are Immortal   20
   A Damaged Genome   23
   A Failure to Communicate   26
   Cell Division without Controls   27
   One Mutation Is Not Enough   29

3 Cancer Genes   32
   Oncogenes and Proto-oncogenes   33
   Tumor Suppressor Genes   34
   A Dangerous Mix   35
   Cancer Genomes   38

4 Cancer Progression   41
   Cancers Develop from a Single Bad Cell   41

The Switch from Benign to Malignant Tumors   42
The Role of Sex Hormones   44
Aging and the Incidence of Cancer   46

5 Carcinogens   47
Aflatoxins   49
Arsenic Compounds   51
Asbestos   52
Benzene   53
Metals   54
Industrial Emissions   56
Radiation   57
Tobacco Smoke   59

6 Common Types of Cancer   63
Cancer Terminology   65
Bladder Cancer   68
Brain Tumors   69
Breast Cancer   74
Colon Cancer   76
Leukemia   77
Lung Cancer   79
Ovarian Cancer   82
Pancreatic Cancer   83
Prostate Cancer   85
Skin Cancer   87

7 Cancer around the World   91
The Magnitude of the Problem   92
Developed Countries Have the Highest Cancer Rates 98
Cancer and the North American Diet   100
Cancer and Lifestyle   105
Cancer and the Environment   106
Summary   107

8 Cancer Therapies 108

Biotherapy 109

Bone Marrow Transplants 113

Chemotherapy 116

Gene Therapy 122

Radiotherapy 123

Stem Cell Therapy 124

Surgery 125

9 Clinical Trials 128

Bladder Cancer 128

Brain Cancer 129

Breast Cancer 131

Colon Cancer 133

Leukemia 134

Lung Cancer 136

Pancreatic Cancer 138

Prostate Cancer 139

Skin Cancer 140

Concluding Remarks 141

10 Resource Center 143

Cell Biology 143

Biotechnology 166

Gene Therapy 174

Matching Tissues 179

The Human Genome Project 182

Understanding Clinical Trials 186

Gene and Protein Nomenclature 189

Weights and Measures 190

Glossary 191

Further Resources 220

Index 230

Preface

When the first edition of this set was being written, the new biology was just beginning to come into its potential and to experience some of its first failures. Dolly the sheep was alive and well and had just celebrated her fifth birthday. Stem cell researchers, working 12-hour days, were giddy with the prospect of curing every disease known to humankind, but were frustrated by inconsistent results and the limited availability of human embryonic stem cells. Gene therapists, still reeling from the disastrous Gelsinger trial of 1998, were busy trying to figure out what had gone wrong and how to improve the safety of a procedure that many believed would revolutionize medical science. And cancer researchers, while experiencing many successes, hit their own speed bump when a major survey showed only modest improvements in the prognosis for all of the deadliest cancers.

During the 1970s, when the new biology was born, recombinant technology served to reenergize the sagging discipline that biology had become. This same level of excitement reappeared in the 1990s with the emergence of gene therapy, the cloning of Dolly the sheep, and the successful cultivation of stem cells. Recently, great excitement has come with the completion of the human genome project and the genome sequencing of more than 100 animal and plant species. Careful analysis of these genomes has spawned a new branch of biological research known as comparative genomics. The information that scientists can now extract from animal genomes is expected to improve all other branches of biological science. Not to be outdone, stem cell researchers have found a way to produce embryo-like stem cells from ordinary skin cells. This achievement not only marks the end of the great stem cell debate, but it also provides an immensely powerful procedure, known as cellular dedifferentiation, for studying and manipulating the very essence of a cell. This procedure will become a crucial weapon in the fight against cancer and many other diseases.

The new biology, like our expanding universe, has been growing and spreading at an astonishing rate. The amount of information that is now available on these topics is of astronomical proportions. Thus, the problem of deciding what to leave out has become as difficult as the decision of what to include. The guiding principle in writing this set has always been to provide a thorough overview of the topics without overwhelming the reader with a mountain of facts and figures. To be sure, this set contains many facts and figures, but these have been carefully chosen to illustrate only the essential principles.

This edition, in keeping with the expansion of the biological disciplines, has grown to accommodate new material and new areas of research. Four new books have been added that focus on areas of biological research that are reaping the benefits of genome science and modern research technologies. Thus, the New Biology set now consists of the following 10 volumes:

1. *Aging*, Revised Edition
2. *Animal Cloning*, Revised Edition
3. *Cancer*, Revised Edition
4. *The Cell*, Revised Edition
5. *Gene Therapy*, Revised Edition
6. *Stem Cell Research*, Revised Edition
7. *Genome Research*
8. *The Immune System*
9. *Modern Medicine*
10. *Viruses*

Many new chapters have been added to each of the original six volumes, and the remaining chapters have been extensively revised and updated. The number of figures and photos in each book has increased significantly, and all are now rendered in full color. The new volumes, following the same format as the originals, greatly expand the scope of the New Biology set and serve to emphasize the fact that these technologies are not just about finding cures for diseases but are helping scientists understand a wide range of biological processes. Even a partial list of these revelations is impressive: detailed information on every gene and every protein that is needed to build a human being; eventual identification of all cancer genes, stem cell–specific genes, and longevity genes; mapping of safe chromosomal insertion sites for gene therapy; and the identification of genes that control the growth of the human brain, the development of speech, and the maintenance of mental stability. In a stunning achievement, genome researchers have been able to trace the exact route our human ancestors used to emigrate from Africa nearly 65,000 years ago and even to estimate the number of individuals who made up the original group.

In addition to the accelerating pace of discovery, the new biology has made great strides in resolving past mistakes and failures. The Gelsinger trial was a dismal failure that killed a young man in the prime of his life, but gene therapy trials in the next 10 years will be astonishing, both for their success and for their safety. For the past 50 years, cancer researchers have been caught in a desperate struggle as they tried to control the growth and spread of deadly tumors, but many scientists are now confident that cancer will be eliminated by 2020. Viruses, such as HIV or the flu, are resourceful and often deadly adversaries, but genome researchers are about to put the fight on more rational grounds as detailed information is obtained about viral genes, viral life cycles, and viruses' uncanny ability to evade or cripple the human immune system.

These struggles and more are covered in this edition of the New Biology set. I hope the discourse will serve to illustrate both the power of science and the near superhuman effort that has gone into the creation and validation of these technologies.

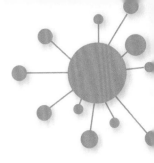

Acknowledgments

I would first like to thank the legions of science graduate students and postdoctoral fellows who have made the new biology a practical reality. They are the unsung heroes of this discipline. The clarity and accuracy of the initial manuscript for this book was much improved by reviews and comments from Diana Dowsley, Michael Panno, Rebecca Lapres, and later by Frank K. Darmstadt, executive editor, and the rest of the Facts On File staff. I am also indebted to Diane K. French and Elizabeth Oakes for their help in securing photographs for the New Biology set. Finally, as always, I would like to thank my wife and daughter for keeping the ship on an even keel.

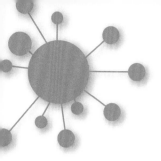

Introduction

Cancers are produced by cells that have gone "mad," whereas normal cells are "sane"—they are polite and enjoy the company of other cells. As a community, they work together for the good of the many, are well organized, hardworking, and content with their lot in life. Heart cells enjoy pumping blood, brain cells would not change places with skin cells for anything under the sun, and no way would any of them do anything that would jeopardize the health of the body they so carefully constructed. Cancer cells do not care about any of this. They do what they want and go where they please. If they decide to build a large tumor in the middle of the brain, well, that is what they are going to do, even if it kills the body they are living in.

Taming a cancer cell is hard to do and usually fails. Normally, surgeons just cut them out or try to kill them in some way. It is a brutal game from start to finish. However, advances in the past

10 years are making it possible to deal with this disease in a more elegant fashion. Scientists know now that a cancer cell's madness is a fever of the genes, a fever that destroys the cell's communication network and its ability to control its own reproduction. Many of the affected genes have been identified, and by restoring them to health we can stop the cancer.

Although cancers have been diagnosed for the past 100 years, physicians were at a loss to explain the underlying causes of the disease. Throughout much of the 1900s, scientists believed that cancer was caused by a microbial infection. Indeed, certain tumors found in chickens, known as sarcomas, were shown to be infected with a virus, but most human cancers showed no such infection. Consequently, the cause remained a mystery for many years, even after the introduction of recombinant DNA technology in the 1970s. Many investigators at that time believed the cell's genes were the main culprit, but there seemed to be no way to identify those genes or even to estimate the number of genes that might be involved.

The breakthrough came in the 1980s when scientists began reexamining the chicken sarcoma and, in particular, the virus that was always associated with it. Using recombinant DNA technology, scientists showed that one of the virus's genes was responsible for inducing the cancer. The identification of this gene, called *Src* (pronounced sark), provided a direct link between a gene and cancer induction. The identification of a cancer-causing gene (now known as an oncogene) was extremely important, but it did not address the fact that most cancers are not associated with a viral infection. The resolution to this puzzle came when investigators searched the chicken genome for a gene similar to *Src*. To their great surprise, they not only found *Src,* but they were able to show that this gene originated in the chicken genome and was picked up by the virus during an infection episode. Researchers subsequently found *Src* in the human genome and the genomes of many other organisms, ranging from single-celled protozoans to primates.

By 2009, investigators around the world had succeeded in identifying more than 200 oncogenes in the human genome. This information provided, for the first time, a comprehensive theory of cancer induction: Cancers are caused by the conversion of normal cellular genes, known as proto-oncogenes, to oncogenes. Oncogenes have the ability to cause cancer because their normal function is concerned with the regulation of especially important cellular processes, such as regulating the synthesis and repair of DNA, as well as being involved in mediating cell-to-cell communication. Now, scientists believe that oncogenes are only part of the story and have begun sequencing the genomes of individual cancer patients in an effort to identify all genetic mutations associated with specific cancers.

Mutations in specific genes are believed to be the fundamental cause of all cancers. These mutations alter the programs that regulate cell division, growth, communication, and differentiation. Collectively, these mutations can destroy the cell's identity, converting it from a well-behaved member of a community to a dangerous outlaw.

As much as we fear and loathe cancer, this disease has been a driving force behind innumerable studies that have not only led to the discovery of oncogenes but have helped us understand the inner world of the cell. This knowledge has provided us with the ammunition we need to fight cancer but, more important, it has paved the way for many powerful therapies that will someday rid the world of other noxious diseases, such as AIDS, Alzheimer's disease, and other infirmities that strike us as we grow old.

This volume, a part of the New Biology set, explores the many facets of cancer research from basic genetic and cellular mechanisms to the danger of carcinogens and the influence of lifestyle. This edition contains updated and revised material throughout, three new chapters (1, 3, and 5), and many new drawings and photos, all of which are now in color. Chapters 1 through 4 now focus on the unique characteristics of normal cells, cancer cells, cancer genes, and cancer progression. These chapters present a cohesive vision of cancer and retain the train of thought established in the introduction, which deals with a comparison between normal cells, cancer cells, and the discovery of oncogenes. These chapters also touch on a recent shift in the scientific community regarding the root cause of cancer. Many scientists now believe that genome instability initiates the transformation, not oncogenes, while others believe that cancers are caused by a special class of stem cells. In the previous edition, carcinogens were discussed briefly within the context of cancer progression. In this edition, the whole of chapter 5 is devoted to these extremely important compounds. This information is often difficult to obtain; presenting it here should prove a useful resource. Chapter 9 (Clinical Trials) chapter 7 in the previous edition, has been rewritten with the inclusion of many recent trials. The final chapter, as before, provides background material on cell biology, biotechnology, and other topics that are relevant to cancer research. The cell biology and biotechnology primers have been extensively revised and condensed to improve the clarity of this important background information.

Normal Cells

Normal cells are marvels of organization, clarity of purpose, and resourcefulness. They acquired these admirable characteristics over millions of years as they climbed out of the primordial ooze to produce the stunning array of creatures that now inhabit the Earth. These simple organisms appeared on Earth at a time when violent storms, volcanic eruptions, noxious atmospheres, and oppressive heat were the rule of the day. All of these obstacles were overcome as cells refined their structure and expanded their communities to such an extent that they tamed the Earth and made its atmosphere fit for modern creatures to breathe.

THE ORIGIN OF LIFE

Life on Earth arose from microscopic bubbles that formed spontaneously in the oceans about 3.5 billion years ago. How these bubble formed and how they evolved into living organisms are the subject of much research and debate. There are of course no fossils from that period that could be used to reconstruct the events that led to the appearance of the first cell, so scientists have had to rely on what is known about the ancient Earth and about cells, alive today, that have retained primitive characteristics.

It is known that the young Earth was hot, with surface temperatures high enough to melt lead. The atmosphere consisted of methane, ammonia, and carbon dioxide, with barely a trace of oxygen. Most of these gases were released into the atmosphere by volcanic eruptions. After 500 million years, Earth's surface temperature dropped considerably, and when it did it began to rain: a deluge that lasted thousands of years leaving most of the planet covered in water, just as it is now. Heat and the electrical activity of the storms converted the atmospheric gases into molecules such as sugar, amino acids, nucleic acids, and fatty acids. The heat fused many of these molecules into macromolecules (chains of molecules) such as protein, deoxyribonucleic acid (DNA), ribonucleic acid (RNA), and a fatty substance called phospholipid. These compounds enriched the water, turning the oceans into a nutrient broth. Phospholipids could not dissolve in water the way the others could but spread out on the surface, producing Earth's first oil slick.

Storms whipped up the surface of the young oceans into thousands of waves that broke on the primeval shores. These waves generated billions of microscopic bubbles, some of which were stabilized by a thin phospholipid coating or membrane. When the bubbles formed, they captured a tiny drop of the nutrient broth that was all around, and for a short time these bubbles were like a billion separate laboratories all experimenting with a unique combination of the materials at hand. When the bubbles burst, they released the fruits of their labor into the water for the next generation to capture. After countless generations, the bubbles reached a point where they could regulate their internal environment and perform some simple chemical reactions that stabilized their membrane and orga-

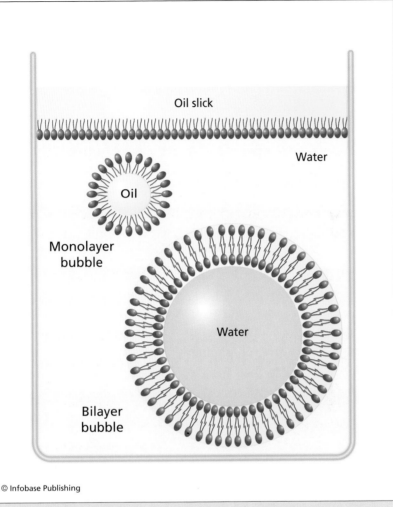

Oil slick

Water

Oil

Monolayer
bubble

Water

Bilayer
bubble

© Infobase Publishing

Phospholipid bubbles. Phospholipid molecules have a hydrophilic head-end (red ovals) and two hydrophobic tails that do not mix with water and will avoid being surrounded by it. In an oil slick, the hydrophobic tails mix with the oil while the heads stay close to the water. In turbulence, phospholipids form two kinds of bubbles: a monolayer that can only capture a drop of oil and a bilayer that can capture a drop of water. The bilayer allows the hydrophobic tails to associate with themselves, while the heads associate with water on both the inside and outside surfaces of the bubble.

nized their internal functions. Eventually they learned how to store information in a primitive genome and began to control their own duplication, rather than depending on ocean waves and turbulence. After 500 million years, simple bubbles evolved into a population of cells, the first life-form to appear on Earth.

THE STRUGGLE FOR SURVIVAL

The first cells are believed to have had an RNA genome that contained a dozen or so genes. These genes coded for very simple proteins that may have been used for structural purposes or as enzymes that could extract energy from the available nutrients. The first cells simply absorbed these ready-made molecules from the water in what is known as a heterotrophic lifestyle. Initially, there was plenty of food to go around. Scientists have estimated that the young biosphere had enough dissolved nutrients to last 500 million years. This is a long time but not nearly long enough to account for the emergence of higher organisms, an event that took 2 billion years.

How did the early cell populations continue on after the original pool of nutrients had been consumed? Scientists believe the biosphere was rescued from certain doom by the evolution of the first cells into the ancestral prokaryotes, which consisted of both heterotrophs and autotrophs. Unlike heterotrophs, autotrophs get their energy directly from the sun in a process called photosynthesis. This transition from heterotrophy to autotrophy was critical to the survival of life on Earth. Dying and decomposing autotrophs replenished the dissolved nutrients that the heterotrophs needed to survive. The heterotrophs, functioning like scavengers, kept the system healthy by minimizing the buildup of decomposed material. Once this simple ecosystem was established, the ancestral prokaryotes evolved into archaea, bacteria, and eukaryotes, the three major divisions of life in the world. The eukaryotes went on to form protozoans, fungi, plants, and animals.

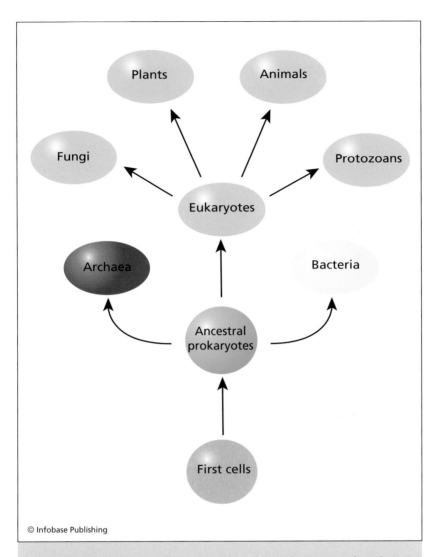

Cell classification. The first cells evolved into the ancestral prokary-otes, which gave rise to the archaea, bacteria, and eukaryotes, the three major divisions of life in the world. The archaea and bacteria are very similar anatomically but differ biochemically. Eukaryotes, anatomically and biochemically distinct from both the archaea and bacteria, gave rise to plants, animals, protozoans, and fungi.

Bacteria and archaea are modern-day prokaryotes that have a relatively simple structure but a complex biochemistry. Typically, these cells have a genome consisting of about 4,000 genes. The archaea, as the name suggests, are the most ancient form of cellular life known to exist on Earth today. These prokaryotes can live in very extreme environments, common to the young Earth, such as volcanic vents where there is little or no oxygen and the temperature may exceed 158°F (70°C). Bacteria, being more advanced than the archaea, are better adapted to environments provided by the Earth today; they are comfortable in the presence of oxygen and generally prefer cooler temperatures ranging from 68°F (20°C) to 104°F (40°C). Bacteria were also the first autotrophs to appear on Earth. These bacteria usually occur as chains and are known as Cyanobacteria or blue-green algae.

Eukaryotes are bigger and much more complex than prokaryotes. These cells are strictly aerobic (require oxygen), generally prefer mild temperatures, and have developed the autotrophic lifestyle to an exquisite degree. The cellular compartment, homogeneous in prokaryotes, is divided into the nucleus and the cytoplasm. The nucleus contains the DNA, which may encode 30,000 genes. The cytoplasm is further divided into a complex set of organelles, which are responsible for most of the cell's biosynthetic activity. All eukaryotes have special cell-surface structures that made the appearance of multicellular organisms possible. The cytoplasm of an autotrophic eukaryote, such as chlamydomonas, is dominated by the green chloroplast, an organelle that is responsible for the cell's photosynthetic activity. Additional information regarding the structure and function of the eukaryotes is provided in chapter 10.

The evolution of the eukaryotes was as important to the survival of the young biosphere as was the appearance of the autotrophs. Prokaryote heterotrophs served a valuable role as scavengers, but they could not limit the size of the autotroph population, and hence the young biosphere was unstable. Single-cell eukaryotes, known as protozoans, stabilized the system by developing the ability to

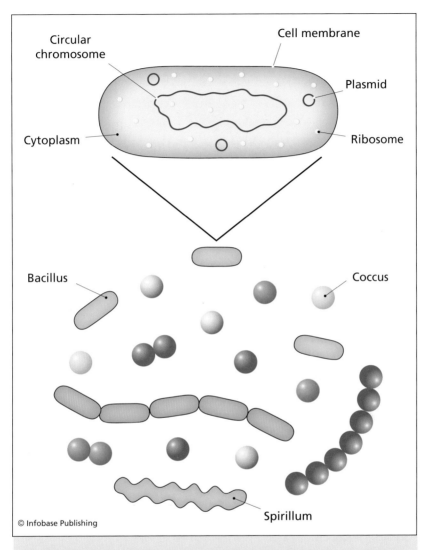

Circular chromosome

Cell membrane

Plasmid

Cytoplasm

Ribosome

Bacillus

Coccus

Spirillum

© Infobase Publishing

Prokaryotes. All prokaryotes have the same basic anatomy consisting of a cell membrane, cytoplasm (or protoplasm), and a circular DNA chromosome. Some bacteria have a second, smaller chromosome called a plasmid, which may be present in multiple copies. The cytoplasm contains a wide assortment of enzymes and molecules, as well as ribosomes, protein-RNA complexes that are involved in protein synthesis. The cells may be spherical (coccus), rod shaped (bacillus), or wavy corkscrews (Spirillum), appearing singly, in pairs, or linked together into chains.

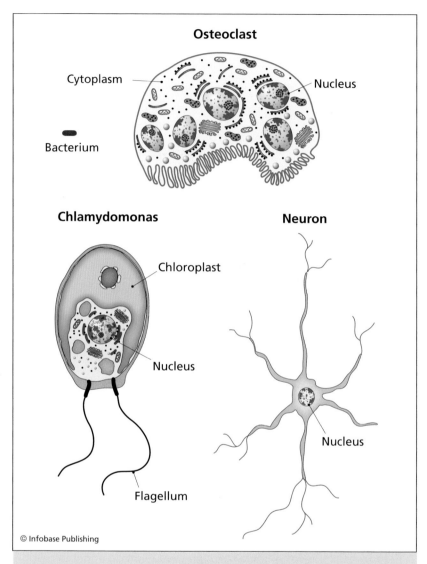

Eukaryotes. The prokaryotes gave rise to large and very complex cells known as eukaryotes. A single bacterium (upper left) is shown for scale. Osteoclasts are multinucleated cells involved in bone re-modeling in humans and other animal species. Neurons are found in all animals, where they form the brain, spinal cord, and nerve fibers. Chlamydomonas is a photosynthetic protozoan, a large group of eu-karyotes that gave rise to all multicellular plants. Non-photosynthetic (heterotrophic) protozoans gave rise to animals.

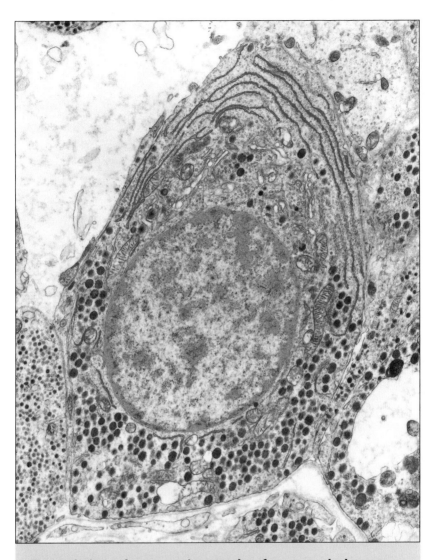

Transmission electron micrograph of a growth hormone–producing cell from the pituitary gland. The pituitary gland is located at the base of the brain. Here, a growth hormone–secreting endocrine cell, known as a somatotroph, is shown. The hormone is in the numerous granules within the cell cytoplasm. Visible cell organelles include mitochondria and the nucleus with its chromatin. There are large amounts of rough endoplasmic reticulum (with the protein-synthesizing ribosomes). Magnification: 12,000×. *(Biophoto Associates/Photo Researchers, Inc.)*

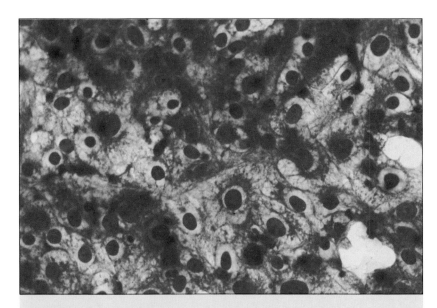

Normal cells growing on a culture plate. Magnification: 128×
(Custom Medical Stock Photo)

hunt autotrophs as a source of food, thus marking the beginning of predator-prey relationships and the stability that such relationships bring to a biosphere. Protozoans developed special cell-surface structures that they used to hunt and capture their prey. These structures made it possible for them to communicate with their environment and with other cells.

CELL COMMUNICATION

An elaborate structure called the glycocalyx contains all of the cell's communication hardware. The glycocalyx is a forest of glycoproteins and glycolipids that covers the surface of every cell like trees on the surface of the Earth. This structure can be found among the prokaryotes, but the eukaryote glycocalyx is much more complex. The earliest eukaryotes hunted bacteria for food, and their single-cell descendents, the protozoans, still make a living in this way.

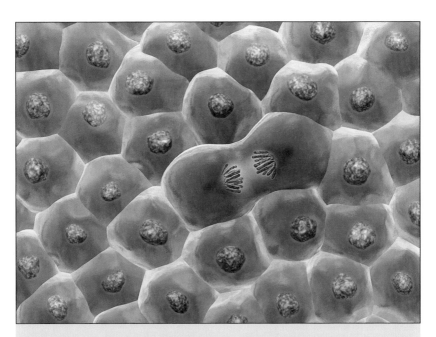

A generic cell in the process of cell division. Magnification: 1,000×. *(Gary Carlson/Photo Researchers, Inc.)*

Scientists believe the glycocalyx evolved over time to meet the demands of this kind of lifestyle. Viewed in this way, the glycocalyx is indeed versatile, providing hardware for communications and for the capture and ingestion of food molecules and cells. In addition, many of the glycoproteins are specially adapted for holding cells together and thus made it possible for multicellular organisms to appear.

The communication hardware, built primarily from the glycoproteins, consists of signaling pathways that relay information from the membrane to the interior of the cell. There are many different kinds of pathways, each designed to detect a different external signal. Bacteria, for example, consume a variety of sugars and thus have different pathways for detecting glucose, lactose, and sucrose. Binding of these food molecules to a receptor activates the

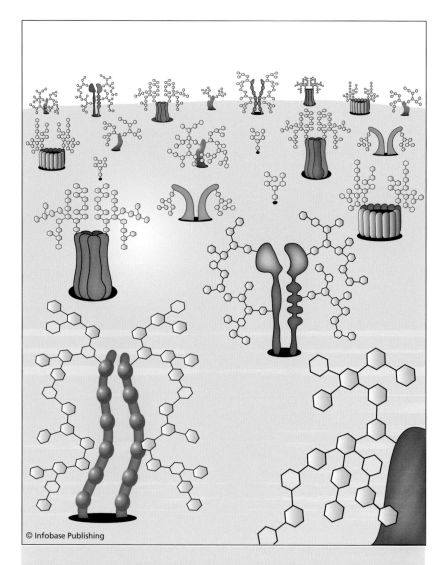

Panoramic view of the glycocalyx. This image is a three-dimensional rendering of the glycoproteins and glycolipids that cover the surface of all cells. The paired glycoproteins in the foreground are cadherin (front left) and integrin (upper right). These structures help hold cells together in animal tissues. The barrel-like structures are part of the cell's communication hardware.

© Infobase Publishing

signaling pathway, which leads to the formation of a cytoplasmic second messenger. The second messenger may activate enzymes in the cytoplasm or might move into the nucleus where it stimulates the expression of one or more genes. The activated cytoplasmic factors and/or the gene products are then directly responsible for initiating the ingestion of the food.

Protozoan hunters evolved cell-surface receptors designed to bind preferred species of bacteria. This is possible because the bacterial glycocalyx, which is species-specific, provides the recognition factors for the hunters. Thus, the ability of one cell to detect the presence of another cell is very ancient, preceding the emergence of multicellular organisms. And yet, this ability is crucial for the survival of all animals, because it is responsible for the phenomenon known as contact inhibition (a property that is lost or damaged in cancer cells) and is used by animal immune systems to distinguish cells of the body from invading microbes, parasites, and cancer cells.

Among multicellular organisms, all of which are made of eukaryote cells, communication between cells is mediated by paracrine (direct cell-to-cell communication) and endocrine (indirect) systems. Both of these systems rely on the release of molecules from one cell or group of cells that are supposed to modify the behavior of other cells. In a paracrine system, cells release signaling molecules into the immediate neighborhood, thus affecting a small, localized population of cells. In an endocrine system, signaling molecules, known as hormones, are released into the blood where they are able to affect the behavior of cells and tissues throughout the body. White blood cells of the human immune system coordinate their attack on invading microbes by signaling each other with molecules known as interleukins. This is an example of a paracrine cell signaling system because the interleukins are released into the local environment and not into the circulatory system. On the other

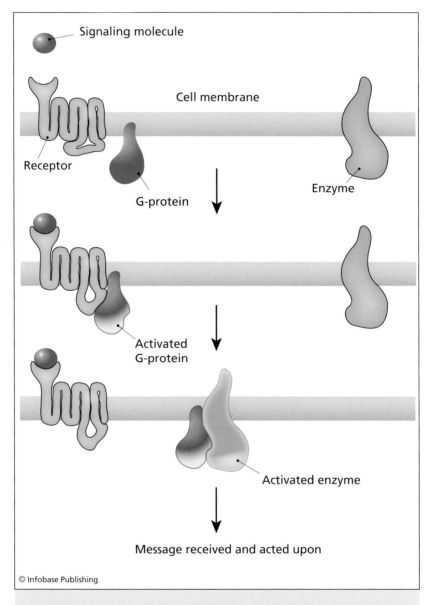

Signaling molecule

Cell membrane

Receptor

G-protein

Enzyme

Activated
G-protein

Activated enzyme

Message received and acted upon

© Infobase Publishing

G-protein-linked receptor. The signaling molecule binds to the receptor, leading to the activation of the G-protein, which in turn activates an enzyme. The enzyme activates secondary messengers, which effect some change in the cell.

hand, the pituitary gland, central to the vertebrate endocrine system, releases hormones into the blood, which affect cells and tissues throughout the body. This kind of communication is intended for the coordination of an animal's physiology.

Paracrine and endocrine signaling are efficient and effective, but higher organisms would never have evolved if there were no other way for cells to communicate. The problem with these systems is that they are relatively slow. If the human brain had to use the endocrine system in order to wiggle a toe it would take several minutes before the order could be received and acted upon. Fortunately, there is a third way for cells to communicate, which depends on the coordination of ion channels. In this system, a ligand or an electrical stimulus opens ion channels, which allows the inward movement of positively charged sodium ions. The inward movement of these charged particles stimulates the cell to release a special kind of paracrine molecule, known as a neurotransmitter. The neurotransmitter binds to other neurons, which activates their ion channels and, subsequently, the release of more neurotransmitter. In this way, the initial signal can pass through an entire circuit in a fraction of a second. Using this system, the human brain can order the big toe to move in less than a millisecond. This form of cell communication was invented by neurons and forms the basis for all neural communications involving the brain, spinal cord, peripheral nerves, and neuromuscular junctions.

THE RISE OF MULTICELLULAR ORGANISMS

The evolution of the glycocalyx made it possible for early eukaryotes to hunt for their food. But it also made it possible for those cells to communicate with each other for the purpose of forming small colonies. Initially, the colonies consisted of about a dozen cells that would associate with each other for brief periods in order to accomplish a specific task, either to enhance their hunting ability or for reproduction.

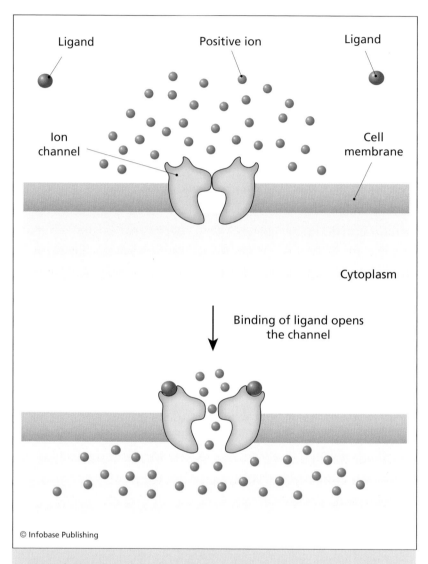

Ligand-gated (Lg) ion channel. The closed channel keeps positively charged ions outside the cell, and in this state the membrane is said to be polarized (i.e., positive on the outside, relative to the inside). The channel opens when bound to a signaling molecule (ligand), allowing the ions to rush inside, thus depolarizing the membrane and initiating an electrical current.

It took almost 2 billion years for the first colonies to evolve into true multicellular organisms. The first of these were similar to modern-day red algae, a very simple form of seaweed. The red algae were followed by the marine sponges, which consist of different kinds of cells, but lack tissues and a nervous system. The next stage of development is represented by the cnidarians (jellyfish and corals), animals that are made from only eight cell types but which possess a mouth, digestive tract, and tissues, such as epithelia and muscles. Echinoderms (sea stars and sea cucumbers) and mollusks (snails, clams, and octopods) introduced many refinements including a central nervous system, a visual system, and enhanced locomotion. All of these innovations were developed to an exquisite degree with the appearance of the vertebrates during the Cambrian period about 530 million years ago.

The evolutionary transition from single cells to multicellular organisms is replayed every time a fertilized egg develops into a multicellular plant or animal. This process, known as embryogenesis, has three distinguishing characteristics:

1. a single cell, the egg, differentiates into many different kinds of cells during embryonic development;
2. the location and behavior of all the cells in the body are carefully regulated; and,
3. some of the cells, such as those making up the nervous system, lose the ability to divide.

All of these characteristics are under genetic control and depend on a healthy genome. Cancer is a genetic disease, being caused by defects in two or more genes. Thus, it is not surprising that this disease can affect all three of the above characteristics. Embryonic development produces the many different kinds of cells that form a body, such as neurons, muscle, or skin. Normally, these cells retain their identity for the life of the individual, but cancer cells, possessing a crippled genome, lose their identity, often reverting back to an embryonic (i.e., undifferentiated) cell type. Once this happens, the cells lose their desire and their ability to remain within their home tissue; at the same time, they regain the ability to divide and to move. In addition, with a corrupted genome, cancer cells can ignore important regulatory signals from the body, and, as a consequence, the body loses its ability to control the behavior of its own cells. Those deranged cells are then free to go where they please and do as they will. With these changes in place, a cancer cell is well on its way to reclaiming the carefree lifestyle of its protozoan ancestors.

2

Cancer Cells

What happens to a cell when it becomes cancerous, when it loses its identity and stops caring about the community that it lives in? When Robert Louis Stevenson wrote *The Strange Case of Dr Jekyll and Mr Hyde* in 1886 he was trying to illustrate the complex nature of the human psyche, which seems to be a mixture of good and bad intentions. Although Dr Jekyll was a good and honest man, his scientific experiments turned him into Mr Hyde, an evil and sadistic man who cared for nothing. Today, scientists know that human insanity can be traced to a disturbance in brain biochemistry. Likewise, the insanity of a cancer cell can now be traced to a corruption of its genome, which leads to a disturbance in the biochemistry of cell division and its ability to communicate with other cells. Paradoxically, these changes can also increase the life span of a cancer cell.

CANCER CELLS ARE IMMORTAL

The difference between cancer cells and normal cells is profound not only because of the way they look and behave, but also because of the radical difference in their life spans. Placed in tissue culture, cancer cells can live forever. Normal cells, on the other hand, die after about 50 generations. The best proof of cancer cell immortality comes from HeLa cells, a cultured cancer cell line that was established in 1951 from a cervical tumor that was isolated from a woman named Henrietta Lacks. The HeLa cell line has been growing well ever since, and cultures of these cells are maintained for research purposes by laboratories around the world. Henrietta Lacks, a native of Baltimore, Maryland, was 31 years old when the tumor was discovered. She died of cervical cancer eight months later.

It may seem odd to think that the achievement of immortality is a bad thing. There is a tendency to believe that if a cell becomes im-

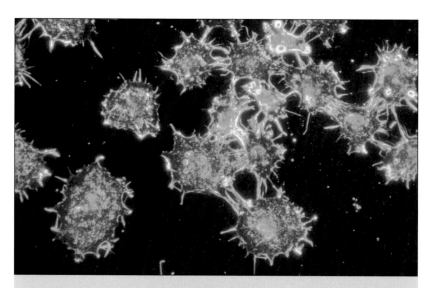

Cultured human carcinoma cells. The details of these cells show the very irregular surface membrane. Magnification: 500×. *(Dr. Cecil H. Fox/Photo Researchers, Inc.)*

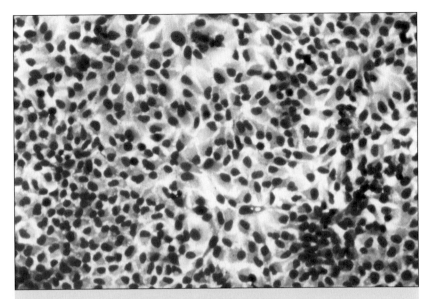

HeLa cells growing on a culture plate. Magnification: 100×. *(Cytographics/Visuals Unlimited)*

mortal it might immortalize the entire organism. But an animal's body is designed around the principle of regulated cell division for the good of the community. Most cells in an adult's body are post-mitotic, a condition that guarantees a stable organ size and shape. Some cells are allowed to divide, such as skin and bone marrow, but only a limited number of times. The only immortal cells in the body are the germ cells (sperm and eggs), although even they will die out if the individual never has children. This is not to say that such an arrangement can never be tampered with. Stem cells can also proliferate for years in culture (although it is not yet known if they are truly immortal), and their use in medical therapies may make it possible to extend the human life span. For now, however, the acquisition of immortality by a somatic cell always leads to trouble.

For 40 years, scientists struggled to understand the mechanism by which cancer cells are immortalized. Throughout the 1990s,

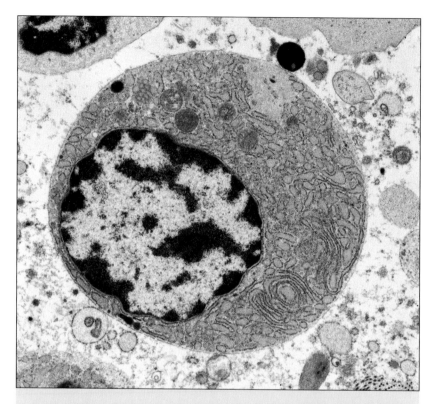

A colored transmission electron micrograph (TEM) of a thyroid cancer cell. The nucleus (black) contains chromatin (green), a complex of DNA and proteins. The nucleus is abnormally large; this is common in cancer cells as they are abnormally active. The cell is also abnormally spherical, another characteristic of cancer cells. The thyroid gland is located at the base of the neck and produces hormones that regulate metabolism. Thyroid cancer is more common in women than men. It can cause swelling and hoarseness. Treatment is with surgical removal of the thyroid gland, often combined with radioactive iodine therapy. Magnification: 4,000×. *(Steve Gschmeissner/Photo Researchers, Inc.)*

attention was drawn to a special DNA sequence called a telomere, located at the tips of the chromosomes. Each time the DNA is replicated during the S phase of the cell cycle, the telomeres shrink, but they are later restored by a special enzyme called telomerase. By carefully studying the mechanics of DNA replication, scientists have been able to conclude that telomeres are essential for the correct duplication of each chromosome. A failure to duplicate the DNA automatically terminates the cell cycle. Normal cells lack telomerase (that is, the gene for telomerase is turned off in adult cells), and for this reason they cannot proliferate indefinitely in the body or in cell culture.

A DAMAGED GENOME

Becoming immortal is only one of many things that must happen before a cell becomes cancerous. A cell that simply divides indefinitely can produce a tumor mass, but as long as it remains benign it can usually be removed surgically. The real danger occurs when some of the cancer cells break away from the original tumor to colonize other parts of the body. Metastasis is a complex process that involves many changes in the cell's biochemistry. The earliest indication that these changes were rooted in the cell's genes came from histological examinations of cancer cells. These studies showed that most cancer cells have an abnormal karyotype that is characterized by the presence of many broken and fragmented chromosomes.

The Philadelphia chromosome (named after the city where it was first discovered) is a striking example of the relationship between genetic abnormality and cancer induction. This chromosomal abnormality involves a translocation between the long arms of chromosomes 9 and 22. This abnormality is associated with chronic myelogenous leukemia and can be found in the leukemic white blood cells of virtually every patient suffering from this form of cancer. The Philadelphia chromosome alters the normal gene expression of the cell and is one example of a somatic mutation, or change in the genome, that can lead to cancer.

An analysis of breast and prostate tumors has shown that specific gene mutations that often occur in cancer cells are the result

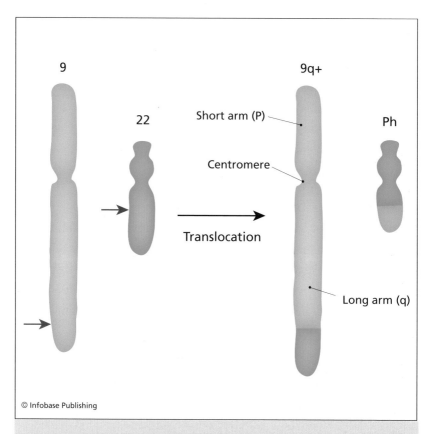

9

22

9q+

Short arm (P)

Centromere

Ph

Translocation

Long arm (q)

© Infobase Publishing

The Philadelphia chromosome (Ph). This chromosome is produced by a translocation between the long arms of chromosomes 9 and 22. Red arrows mark the fragmentation points. The notation "9q+" indicates an addition to the long arm of chromosome 9. The chromosomes are aligned at the centromeres.

of a prior event (or events) that corrupts the entire genome. Consequently, a typical cancer cell karyotype is radically altered. Some of the chromosomes break apart into smaller fragments, some of which fuse with other chromosomes. The fusion process is usually associated with the destruction of genes on the host chromosome, thus amplifying the damage. In addition, whole chromosomes, often

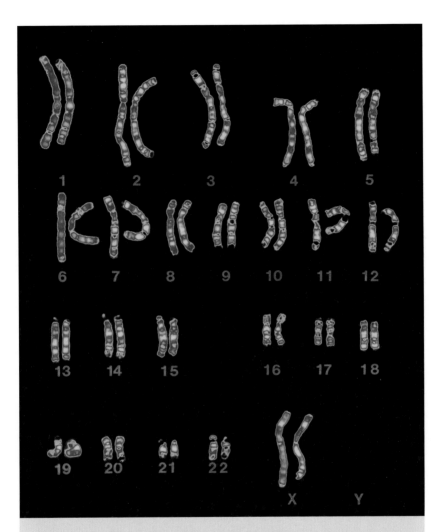

Enhanced light micrograph of a normal human female karyotype. The full complement of chromosomes is arranged in homologous numbered pairs that are similar in length and banding pattern. Male and female sets differ only in the sex chromosomes (bottom right): a male would be labeled XY instead of XX. The nucleus of each human cell contains 46 chromosomes in total, 23 of maternal and 23 of paternal origin. A normal female karyotype is written: 46, XX. *(SPL/ Photo Researchers, Inc.)*

containing more than 1,000 genes, are sometimes lost or duplicated during cell division. These abnormalities, known as aneuploidy, alter the normal gene expression profile of the cell with disastrous consequences. Many scientists now believe that aneuploidy is the root cause of cancer induction: activation of cancer genes and other traits characteristic of cancer cells (discussed below) seem to follow from a global corruption of the genome.

A FAILURE TO COMMUNICATE

When normal cells are placed in culture they can proliferate long enough to cover the bottom of the dish in a single layer, or monolayer, of cells. When the monolayer is established, the cells stop growing due to a phenomenon known as contact inhibition. The cells in the monolayer know they are in contact with other cells and this information is enough to signal an end to proliferation, to ensure that the cells do not pile up on each other. Cancer cells, in culture, do not respond to contact inhibition. Instead, they continue growing, often forming large clumps of cells on the plate.

The failure of contact inhibition in cancer cells is a failure to communicate and is due to an abnormal glycocalyx. In normal cells, the glycocalyx contains many cell surface glycoproteins that act like sensory antennae. When those antennae make contact with the glycocalyx of another cell, the information is relayed to the interior of the cell by a signaling pathway that tells the cell to stop growing. It may also activate other pathways that stimulate the formation of physical connections between the cells. None of this works in cancer cells. The antennae are either gone or are no longer linked to the proper signaling pathway. As a consequence, cancer cells grow over the top of one another, and the only thing that limits their growth, in vivo and in vitro, is the availability of oxygen and nutrients. As they pile up, forming a large clump, the cells in the middle stop dividing and may even die for want of food and air.

The corrupted communication channels that are characteristic of cancer cells account for their apparent lack of manners and their tendency to crowd each other when grown in culture; it also accounts for the ability of cancer cells to colonize tissues that are normally reserved for other cells. A normal heart cell would never try to colonize the brain or the liver. Conversely, brain cells would never try to invade the skin, bone, or any other type of tissue.

If a normal cell should accidentally break loose from its parent tissue or organ and find itself in foreign territory, it would quickly receive and process signals from the surrounding cells that would cause it to commit suicide. Cell suicide is called apoptosis and is regulated by specific communication pathways. Cancer cells will not commit suicide. They either ignore the signals from cells around them, or the pathways regulating apoptosis are dysfunctional. In either case, the loss of the death signal makes it possible for cancer cells to grow in any environment.

The ability to ignore an order to commit suicide, however, is only one element in the complex process known as metastasis. In order for cancer cells to invade other territory, they must break loose from the tumor mass, travel through the tissue or organ until they reach a blood vessel, penetrate the vessel wall, and then, after being carried along in the circulating blood, exit the vessel in some other part of the body. Once they have colonized fresh territory and begin to form a tumor, they must activate angiogenesis, the growth of blood vessels into the tumor, in order to receive oxygen and nutrients. This may appear to be an unlikely scenario, depending as it does on so many processes, but cancer cells are capable of coordinating all of these events, and when they do they are free to go where they please.

CELL DIVISION WITHOUT CONTROLS

Oncogenesis (cancer development) is an unfortunate legacy of the free-living, carefree lifestyle that was typical of our single-cell protozoan ancestry. Paradoxically, cancer does not affect modern-day protozoans. If any of those cells becomes abnormal, it is of no great consequence; that crazy cell, with a mangled genome, simply dies because of its weirdness, without taking a virtual universe of cells with it. Perhaps this is why our protozoan ancestors never found a way to fully protect themselves from cancer: It simply did not matter to them. Abnormal cells occurred, but they never threatened the survival of other cells.

Protozoans are not only free-living, but, like economists, they are firm believers in the principle of continual growth. These cells never became post-mitotic but divide every half hour or so and keep it up for as long as they can. To this extent, protozoans and their bacterial ancestors are immortal creatures that have existed for millions of years. But in order to produce multicellular organisms, protozoans had to come to some kind of mutual understanding that limited the reproductive ability of some of the cells, forcing them to become post-mitotic, while allowing others to divide for the life of the organism. For the post-mitotic crowd, the arrangement may have seemed impossible, as they were being asked to do something that went against their very nature. Genes that regulated their reproduction, which had undergone millions of years of adaptive evolution to ensure the cells could divide rapidly, were now being asked to shut down and remain silent. For the mitotic crowd, the agreement meant that each cell division had to be tightly controlled; no variation in the daughter cells would be allowed as it might have been with their free-living ancestors.

The ancient need for rapid and unlimited growth versus the restraint that is required for the construction of a multicellular creature is at the heart of the problem. When a normal cell becomes cancerous, it is simply reawakening its ancestral urge for unlimited growth and the carefree attitude that comes with it. The immortal lifestyle of protozoans depends on special genes that regulate the cell cycle and communication with the outside world. In that context, those genes are the cell's most prized possession, but when a cell in an animal's body becomes cancerous, those same cherished genes begin to fail and ultimately become a liability.

Typically, cancer cells lose one or more of their cell cycle checkpoint monitors, so they divide whether things are right or not (see page 160). This is the reason cancer cells develop an abnormal genome and physical appearance. Corrupting the genome in this way may seem to spell certain death for a cell, but it is really the means by which cancer cells reinvent themselves. The checkpoints are intended to maintain the status quo; without them the genetic profile of a cell, including which genes are on or off and which are mutated, can change very quickly and radically. The T-cells of our immune system can detect abnormal, potentially dangerous cells, and when they do they order those cells to commit suicide. The gross changes in a cancer cell's genetic structure, however, often knock out its ability to respond to those signals. When this happens, the cancer cell has gained immunity to apoptosis and is well on its way to fulfilling its quest for immortality and assuming the lifestyle enjoyed by its protozoan ancestors.

ONE MUTATION IS NOT ENOUGH

Cancer cells are genetic mutants; this is clear from their abnormal karyotype and the apparent distortions in their communication pathways. These changes produce a standard behavior pattern for cancer cells that consists of the following:

- ► cancer cells ignore signals that regulate proliferation;
- ► they sidestep built-in limitations to their own reproduction;
- ► they are genetically unstable;
- ► they escape their parent tissue;
- ► they colonize foreign tissue, and
- ► they avoid suicide.

This list is a good indication that more than one defective gene is required to produce a cancer cell. The actual number of genetic mutations that must occur to produce a cancer cell is unknown but may involve dozens of genes. The mutations occur slowly over time in a sequential fashion and may account for the age-related onset of brain tumors, breast cancer, and prostate cancer. This fits with many observations over the past 10 years concerning tumor progression, whereby a mildly abnormal cell gives rise to a colony of cells that gradually evolves into metastatic cancer.

The driving force behind the evolution of a cancer appears to be the genetic instability that is characteristic of these cells. Normal cells are vigilant and constantly check the accuracy of their products by monitoring the behavior of their own machinery. When the DNA is duplicated in preparation for cell division, regulators, monitors, and repair enzymes are on guard to make sure no mistakes occurred when the daughter strand was made. If an error is detected, the cell does not divide until the damage is repaired. If the damage cannot be repaired, the cell will either commit suicide voluntarily or be forced to do so by the immune system. Repair enzymes and monitors also check to ensure the chromosomes segregate properly (i.e., are portioned out equally to the daughter cells). If segregation is abnormal, one daughter cell will end up with too many chromosomes, while the other cell will have too few. When this happens, apoptosis is activated by the monitoring system, so that both cells commit suicide.

Cancer cells behave as though they have an absolute disdain for quality control. If an error is made during DNA synthesis, they do not bother making repairs before continuing through the cell cycle. If chromosomes fail to segregate normally or develop an abnormal karyotype, the two daughter cells do not commit suicide. In this way, the abnormal cell line accumulates many genetic abnormalities until it becomes malignant, or until it is destroyed by the immune system. In a bizarre sense, cancer cells are trying to establish a situation in which genetic variability is maximized, with a subsequent increase in the rate at which they evolve.

The accumulation of mutations through genetic instability is acted upon by natural selection. Most of the cells in the original tumor will be so abnormal they will be incapable of providing for themselves and will eventually die out. In many cases this will lead to the disappearance of the entire tumor mass. But it can also happen that an abnormal cell will appear within the original tumor that has just the right combination of mutated genes, mutations that switch a benign tumor to a malignant cancer.

3

Cancer Genes

Cancer is a disease of the genes. It may seem odd that one's genes can make one sick and even kill, for they are in a sense one's most trusted ally. Their evolution, stretching back 3.5 billion years, made life what it is today: vigorous, diverse, and perfectly adapted to Earth's many environments. At the cellular level, dozens of enzymes devote themselves to tending to the chromosomes and the genes they contain, like worker bees tending to their queen. When genes are damaged, the enzymes repair them; when the genes need to divide, the enzymes carefully copy each chromosome into an exact duplicate; and when it is time for the cell to divide, the enzyme attendants move the chromosomes into position, attach them to the spindle, and gently send them on their way.

A gene that gives someone cancer is like a queen bee stinging a caretaker drone to death. When a tumor forms, some of our genes cross the line from a good gene that codes for an important cellular protein to a bad gene that produces a protein capable of sending us to an early grave. Fortunately for us, the number of cancer-causing genes is small compared with the 30,000 in the human genome, but it is still a large number. Genes that cause cancer do so by gaining a new function or by losing their normal function. The gain-of-function cancer genes are called oncogenes, and their normal counterparts are called proto-oncogenes. The loss-of-function cancer genes are called tumor suppressor genes (TSGs), because their normal job is to keep the cell from dividing inappropriately.

ONCOGENES AND PROTO-ONCOGENES

Cancers are caused by oncogenes, which are produced when their normal counterparts, the proto-oncogenes, are altered in some way. Research in many laboratories over the past 20 years has shown that the conversion of proto-oncogenes to oncogenes (a PO conversion) occurs by essentially two methods: a point mutation (a change affecting a single nucleotide) and insertional mutagenesis. If the mutation occurs within the gene's promoter (the genetic element that turns a gene on or off), the protein product will be the same before and after the conversion but the amount of the protein will be different. More commonly, the mutation occurs within the coding region, in which case the protein still functions, but it does its job in a much different way. It is for this reason that oncogenes are referred to as gain-of-function cancer genes. In the second method of PO conversion, insertional mutagenesis, a retrovirus inserts itself into a chromosome as part of its own life cycle. Some scientists believe that point mutations and insertional mutagenesis act indirectly by initiating aneuploidy, which is then responsible for the PO conversion.

Oncogenes have names that are derived from the type of cancer they induce or are associated with (see table on page 35). For example, the *Ras* (rhymes with gas) oncogene was originally isolated from a rat sarcoma; *Myc* (pronounced mick) is often expressed in a leukemia, called myelocytoma; and *Src* (pronounced sark), the first oncogene to be discovered, was isolated from a chicken sarcoma. For convenience, oncogenes and proto-oncogenes have the same name; that is the *Myc* oncogene is also the *Myc* proto-oncogene. It is usually clear from the context of the discussion which one is being referred to. Many oncogenes, including *Ras, Myc,* and *Src,* stimulate proliferation-signaling pathways, forcing the cell to divide uncontrollably. Gene and protein naming conventions are discussed in chapter 10. The cellular origin to retroviral oncogenes was discovered in the 1980s by Drs. J. Michael Bishop and Harold Varmus, for which they shared the Nobel Prize in physiology or medicine in 1989.

TUMOR SUPPRESSOR GENES

Three genes, called *Rb, P53,* and *P21,* code for proteins (Rb, P53, and P21) that act as TSGs, and all of them are required for the G1 checkpoint to work properly (see table on page 35). By convention, gene names are italicized, whereas the gene product is not (see "Gene and Protein Nomenclature" in chapter 10). The *Rb* gene, the first TSG to be identified, was discovered in a study of retinoblastoma, a rare childhood cancer of the eye. Subsequent studies have shown that *Rb* codes for a protein that is involved in blocking DNA synthesis when the G1 checkpoint detects a problem and is expressed in all cells of the body. The function of this gene is now known to be abnormal, or simply lost, in many kinds of cancers, including carcinomas of lung, breast, and bladder.

The *P53* gene (named after the weight of the gene's protein product) may be the most important cancer-causing gene known, as its loss of function is associated with more than half of all known cancers. This gene, like *Rb,* blocks progression through S-phase when DNA damage is detected. It does this indirectly by activating the synthesis of P21, which binds to the DNA to block replication. In addition, *P53* mediates external requests (primarily from T-cells) for the cell to commit suicide. Consequently, cancer cells lacking a

EXAMPLES OF CANCER GENES

GENE	TYPE	FUNCTION	TUMOR
P53	Tumor suppressor	G1 checkpoint/ apoptosis	Carcinoma
Rb	Tumor suppressor	G1 checkpoint	Carcinoma
P21	Tumor suppressor	G1 checkpoint	Carcinoma
Ras	Oncogene	G-protein	Sarcoma
Src	Oncogene	Tyrosine kinase	Sarcoma
Myc	Oncogene	Transcription factor	Carcinoma

Note: Cancers are caused by loss-of-function TSGs and gain-of-function oncogenes. The P53 gene may be the most important cancer-causing gene of all, as it is associated with half of all known cancers. Oncogenes generally overstimulate signaling pathways that promote cell proliferation, leading to uncontrolled cell division. By convention, gene names are italicized.

functional P53 gene can divide without restraint, and they are no longer under the control of the immune system or inhibiting signals from neighboring cells, meaning they are immune to apoptosis.

TSGs lose their normal function as a consequence of a point mutation, leading to a defective protein. The mutation may occur spontaneously, or it may be induced by radiation, such as UV light, X-rays, or radioactivity, or noxious chemicals, such as pesticides, industrial pollutants, or tobacco smoke.

A DANGEROUS MIX

A potential cancer cell that activates one or two oncogenes may be able to grow inappropriately, but it will produce only a harmless benign tumor. Cancer cells become deadly when they simultaneously activate two oncogenes and telomerase (Tm) while deactivating a TSG.

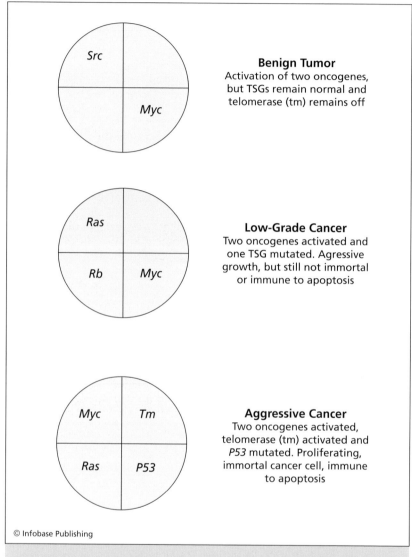

Benign Tumor
Activation of two oncogenes, but TSGs remain normal and telomerase (tm) remains off

Low-Grade Cancer
Two oncogenes activated and one TSG mutated. Agressive growth, but still not immortal or immune to apoptosis

Aggressive Cancer
Two oncogenes activated, telomerase (tm) activated and *P53* mutated. Proliferating, immortal cancer cell, immune to apoptosis

© Infobase Publishing

A dangerous mix of genes. The deadliness of a cancer cell depends on the mix of genes it can turn on or off. Activating two oncogenes, while telomerase remains off and tumor suppressor genes remain normal, leads to cell growth but not immortality or metastasis. Activating two oncogenes, telomerase, and mutating P53 leads to the formation of an aggressive metastatic cancer.

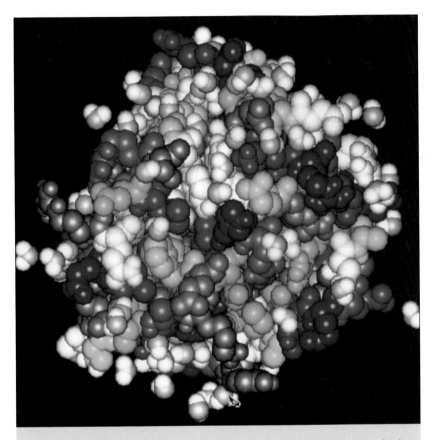

Cancer protein. This is a computer model of a Ras protein, which is involved in cancer cell formation. *(James King-Holmes/Photo Researchers, Inc.)*

Cancer induction and treatment becomes very complex when aneuploidy is considered, because it could affect the behavior of hundreds of cancer-causing genes and TSGs. Scientists know that the cell cycle is central to cancer induction and have identified the major components of the G1 checkpoint, but very little is known about the proteins that manage the G2 and metaphase checkpoints. Many cancer cells are undoubtedly mutating genes controlling these checkpoints in order to acquire immortality and the power of metastasis.

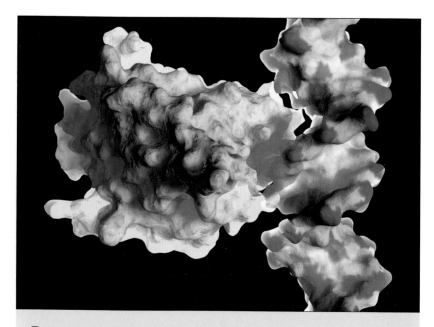

Tumor suppressor protein. Computer artwork of the tumor suppressor protein p53 (yellow) bound to a molecule of DNA (pink). P53 plays a very important role in preventing the replication of cancerous cells, so much so that it is found to be inactive in 50 percent of all cancers. *(Phantatomix/Photo Researchers, Inc.)*

The completion of the human genome project has brought renewed hope to the field of cancer research. Scientists will now be able to identify every genetic defect in every known type of cancer. Such work has already identified the molecular events that lead to some of the deadliest forms of cancer, such as those affecting the pancreas, liver, and colon. Perhaps for the first time in almost 40 years, since the war on cancer began, one may feel confident that cures for these terrible diseases are close at hand.

CANCER GENOMES

One of the earliest attempts to study the genome of cancer cells occurred in the early 1980s when total genomic DNA from cancer cells was injected into normal cells. The transfer converted the normal cells into cancer cells, and subsequent studies showed that the transformation was caused by a point mutation in the *Hras* gene. Thus began the almost feverish search for other abnormal genes that are responsible for the development of human cancers.

Cancer cells, isolated from a single individual, are closely related but not genetically identical. This is due to the genetic instability of a cancer cell (discussed above), which gives it a high mutation rate. Consequently, any group of cancer cells may contain a wide variety of genetic mutations. These include single base substitutions, or point mutations; insertions or deletions of segments of DNA; rearrangements, in which a piece of DNA moves from one location to another; gene amplification, whereby a piece of DNA is duplicated many times over; and copy number reductions, which may result in the complete loss of a specific piece of DNA. Cancer genomes may also contain pieces of foreign DNA, in particular viral DNA sequences (or entire viral genomes) that are known to cause a variety of human cancers.

The acquisition of all this genetic damage occurs slowly over many years and will vary from one individual to the next, depending on ancestry, lifestyle, diet, and environmental influences. Needless to say, scientists are eager to identify and to characterize all of the mutations that are associated with human cancers. With the recent development of ultrafast DNA sequencers, scientists are now able to sequence the genomes of individual cancer patients. This effort has led to the identification of more than 100,000 cancer-related mutations, but only a few of these, the so-called driver mutations, are directly responsible for cancer induction. The rest, known as passenger mutations, are the result of genomic instability, but they do not have the power to convert a normal cell into a cancer cell.

Separating the driver mutations from the passengers is a major challenge. So far, driver mutations seem to cluster among certain types of genes, for example, those that code for protein kinases and components of signaling pathways. In addition, driver mutations are often specific to different kinds of cancers. Passenger mutations, on the other hand, are more or less randomly distributed throughout the genome and are not associated with a particular form of cancer.

Cataloging the mutations and identifying the drivers and passengers will not be easy. Scientists will have to sequence each cancer genome 20 times, which amounts to about 100 billion base pairs of DNA sequence. To cover all possible variations, between individuals and between 50 different types of cancer, it may be necessary to sequence 20,000 cancer genomes. This is truly a monumental task that could never be finished by a single lab or even a single country. Consequently, scientists have established the International Cancer Genome Consortium (ICGC), so that the sequencing can be worked on in parallel by hundreds of research groups around the world.

4

Cancer Progression

Cancers usually take a long time to develop. This is because, as pointed out in the previous chapter, it takes a defect in more than one gene before a cell can make the switch. Potential cancer cells appear continuously throughout an individual's life, but most are destroyed by the immune system, and still others never manage to develop a lethal genetic profile. For a cancer to develop, all the "right" conditions must exist simultaneously in the same cell. This is the reason a tumor appears originally in only one part of the body and over the years spreads to other areas.

CANCERS DEVELOP FROM A SINGLE BAD CELL

Cancer cells within a tumor are like any other living community in that they are subject to the same laws of natural selection. Most cancer cells die spontaneously because their genome has been so badly corrupted they are incapable of maintaining basic housekeeping functions. Of those that survive, one may have a genetic profile that favors rapid growth, so much so that it quickly becomes the only cell type within the tumor. This scenario has been confirmed experimentally by examining characteristics of cancer cells isolated from different regions of a single individual's body. For example, certain forms of leukemia are associated with the presence of the Philadelphia chromosome, created by a translocation between the long arms of chromosomes 9 and 22 (described in chapter 2). Detailed sequence analysis of the DNA spanning the break site shows it is identical in all leukemic cells from a single patient, confirming a common ancestry. In other words, the leukemia cells in that particular patient are all derived from a single cancerous founder cell.

THE SWITCH FROM BENIGN TO MALIGNANT TUMORS

Malignant cancer cells are those that have acquired the ability to leave the tumor of their origin and migrate throughout the body where they initiate the formation of new tumors. This process called metastasis requires the following conditions:

- ▶ first, the cancer cell must be able to break away from the tumor mass;
- ▶ second, once it has broken free, it must be able to migrate throughout the intercellular space until it contacts a blood vessel (at this stage the cancer is locally invasive); and,
- ▶ third, the cancer cell must be able to penetrate a blood vessel in order to enter general circulation, which carries the cell to a new location where it forms new tumors.

Scientists believe each step in the development of invasiveness and metastasis is controlled by a separate group of genes, but so far no such genes have been identified.

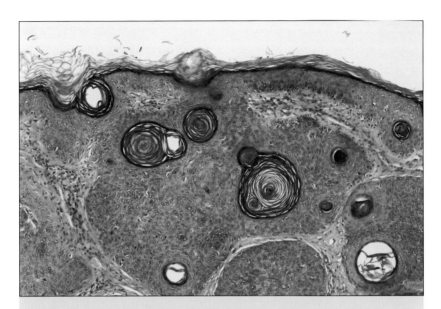

Light micrograph of a section through a wart in human skin. This is a common benign (noncancerous) skin tumor also known as basal cell papilloma or seborrheic keratosis. It arises from the epidermal layer of the skin. Within the wart are a number of cysts (round), within which are concentric layers of keratin, a tough skin protein. These warts become more common with age. They are harmless but may be removed by freezing (cryotherapy) for cosmetic reasons. Magnification: 570×. *(Dr. E. Walker/Photo Researchers, Inc.)*

It is possible, however, to infer the identities of some of the genes, based on the requirements at each step. Separation of a cancer cell from the rest of the tumor requires the breaking of chemical bonds that normally hold cells together. The most important of these bonds are mediated by cell surface proteins called cadherins, which project from every cell allowing two or more cells to make physical connections. Disruption of these bonds may occur in cancer cells when the gene coding for a cadherin mutates, thus producing a defective protein. Metastasis, invasiveness, and penetration of blood vessels require the activation of genes that make it possible for the cell to move, much like an amoeba or a macrophage of the immune

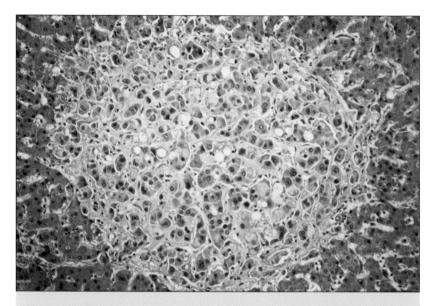

Liver cancer. The cancer cells are the large pale-stained cells form-ing a nodule among the darker healthy liver cells. This cancer spread from a primary site in a breast. The spread of cancer throughout the body is known as metastasis. Once a cancer has spread beyond its initial site, the prognosis is poor. *(CNRI/Photo Researchers, Inc.)*

system. Since more than 80 percent of all human cancers are car-cinomas (i.e., cancers of stationary epithelial cells), the acquisition of motility is a crucial step. If it were possible to block this step, all cancers could be reduced to harmless benign tumors. One gene, called *Rho,* shows increased expression in aggressively metastatic cancers, and it is known that this gene is involved in regulating cell motility in protozoans and macrophages. It is hoped that with the sequencing of cancer genomes it will soon be possible to identify other genes involved in metastasis.

THE ROLE OF SEX HORMONES

Hormones, such as estrogen, progesterone, and testosterone, prepare the human body for reproduction and stimulate the development of sexual characteristics as each individual passes through puberty. For women, estrogen stimulates development of the breasts, ovaries, uterus, and the general shape of the body. The cells of the uterine lining are stimulated to grow and divide every month as part of the woman's menstrual cycle. If a pregnancy occurs, progesterone, along with estrogen, helps maintain the uterine lining to support development of the fetus. In men, testosterone stimulates development of the testes, sperm production, and growth of facial hair and musculature.

The sex hormones exert their varied effects by promoting cell growth and cell division. As long as the cells in the target organs are healthy, with checkpoint monitors intact, there is no problem. But if a crucial gene or set of genes is defective, and the cell is being bombarded with signals to proliferate, the situation can become serious very quickly. This is the reason why cancers of the breast, uterus, ovaries, and prostate are so common and so dangerous. Cancers such as these are a natural consequence of reproductive physiology, and treatments often try to reduce the levels of sex hormones to withdraw the stimulus to the tumor cells. As discussed more fully in the next chapter, this approach is not a pleasant experience, involving as it often does the removal of the ovaries, to eliminate the synthesis of estrogen, or the testes, to block production of testosterone.

The relationship between steroid hormones and cancer production introduces serious concerns regarding hormone replacement therapy (HRT), particularly for women, to minimize bone loss in the elderly. HRT can alleviate some of the symptoms of osteoporosis in men and women, but it may do so at the risk of developing cancer. Similar concerns exist in the sporting world, where steroids are used to enhance performance. While such treatments do seem to be effective, the athlete who uses hormone supplements will likely pay a heavy price for it in later life by developing prostate, breast, or uterine cancer.

AGING AND THE INCIDENCE OF CANCER

Human cancer is primarily an age-related disease that strikes when an individual is 50 years of age or older. The age of the individual and the time element are important largely because the formation of a tumor is a multistep process that takes many years to complete. There are, however, many exceptions to the age-cancer relationship. Lung cancer, brought on by cigarette smoke, and childhood leukemias are the most notable examples. The chemicals in cigarette smoke are known to accelerate tumor formation, but the factors responsible for cancer acceleration in children are still unclear.

Cancers are age related because our cells change with time, becoming more susceptible to genetic damage and less capable of dealing with the damage when it does occur. This problem is believed to be due, in large measure, to a reduction in the ability of our immune system to track down and destroy abnormal cells as they appear; the body's diminished immune response gives those cells time to evolve into a potentially lethal cancer.

The increased incidence of cancer in those aged 50 and over is also coincidental with the onset of sexual senescence in both men and women. It is quite possible that the hormonal changes that occur during this period contribute to our increased susceptibility to cancer. Age-related hormonal changes are primarily concerned with a shift in the ratio of estrogen to testosterone (ET ratio) in both men and women. Young women have a high estrogen/testosterone ratio (a lot of estrogen, very little testosterone), whereas young men have a low estrogen/testosterone ratio (a lot of testosterone, very little estrogen). Estrogen levels drop dramatically in women after menopause, and men show a similar decline in the level of testosterone at a corresponding age. As a consequence, men and women approach a similar ET ratio between the ages of 50 and 80, which is thought to influence the rate at which genetic instability occurs. In addition, many scientists believe the shift in the ET ratio is largely responsible for the weakening of our immune systems, leading to the increased occurrence not only of cancer but also of many other diseases.

Carcinogens

Many cancers are an unfortunate consequence of our physiology, biochemistry, and cellular ancestry, but an even greater number may be caused by chemicals or radiation in our environment. Cancer-causing agents such as these are called carcinogens. In 1978, the U.S. Congress, in response to public concerns over environmental carcinogens, instructed the Department of Health, Education, and Welfare (now the Department of Health and Human Services [HHS]), to publish a Report on Carcinogens (RoC) every two years that lists substances known to be or suspected of being carcinogens. The First Annual Report on Carcinogens was published in 1981. The report provides the following information: a detailed description of the nature of each substance and an estimate of the number of persons exposed to dangerous chemicals; the risk to public health from exposure to environmental carcinogens; and a discussion of requests received each year for the evaluation of potential carcinogens.

New substances are added to the RoC only after a lengthy evaluation of their suspected dangers. This information is obtained by government research agencies, such as the National Toxicology Program (NTP), academia, industries, and other research organizations. Many listed substances have been reviewed by organizations such as the International Agency for Research on Cancer, part of the World Health Organization, in Lyon, France, and the California Environmental Protection Agency (Cal/EPA). The final decision as to whether a substance is added to or removed from the list is made at a public hearing convened by HHS after extensive consultation with the NTP.

The current RoC, published in 2007 as the 12th report on carcinogens, contains 246 entries, 17 of which are new to this report. Of the total, 58 substances are known to be carcinogens. The remaining 188 substances are suspected of being carcinogenic and are currently under investigation. The investigations may be epidemiological, that is, scientists try to determine the factors affecting the occurrence of a specific disease in a human population. Laboratory studies may also be conducted in which animals are exposed to a suspected carcinogen. Estimating the extent to which listing a substance in the RoC protects public health is perhaps the most difficult task in preparing the RoC. The carcinogenic risk, or the probability of developing cancer, depends on many things, including the intensity and duration of exposure to a carcinogen. People may respond differently to similar exposures, depending on their age, sex, overall health, and many other factors. Only rarely can risk for cancer be estimated with high confidence, and these estimations usually require long-term human exposure studies, which are often unavailable.

The nature of carcinogens is highly variable, appearing as radiation, industrial emissions, tobacco smoke, certain metals, and even the cooking grease used in fast-food restaurants. The discussion in this chapter will be limited to known carcinogens that have had the greatest impact on public health.

AFLATOXINS

Aflatoxins are compounds that are produced by mold that grows on stored wheat and peanuts. Early evidence for the carcinogenicity of these substances came from descriptive studies correlating geographic variation of aflatoxins with the incidence of liver cancer. Studies in China and several African countries showed a strong correlation between exposure to aflatoxins and the incidence of liver cancer. In the United States, exposure to aflatoxins, which is common in the Southeast, was shown to increase the incidence of liver cancer by 10 percent. The epidemiological studies are supported by studies on animals. Rats, hamsters, and monkeys exposed to aflatoxins developed tumors in the liver, lungs, and colon.

Aflatoxins come from fungi from the genus *Aspergillus*. The high ambient temperature found in Africa, parts of China, and the American Southeast favors the growth of this organism on peanuts and grain. It is also found growing on bread that is stored at normal room temperatures throughout Europe and North America. *Aspergillus* produces four kinds of aflatoxin, referred to as B_1, B_2, G_2, and M_1. Aflatoxin B_1 is metabolized by the liver to yield a highly reactive compound, aflatoxin-8, 9-epoxide, that is capable of forming DNA adducts, which can cause cancer by decreasing the accuracy of DNA replication. This aflatoxin epoxide can be neutralized by a cellular protein known as glutathione in a reaction mediated by the enzyme glutathione S-transferase (GST). Animals that are resistant to the aflatoxins, such as mice and some fish, show high GST activity levels, much higher than those observed in humans.

Exposure to aflatoxins can be minimized by avoiding moldy bread and corn. Occupational exposure to these toxins, however, remains a serious problem. Farmers and agricultural workers have the greatest risk of exposure. For example, of 45 animal-feed production plant workers, 17 were found to have high levels of aflatoxin B1 in their blood after working for only four weeks.

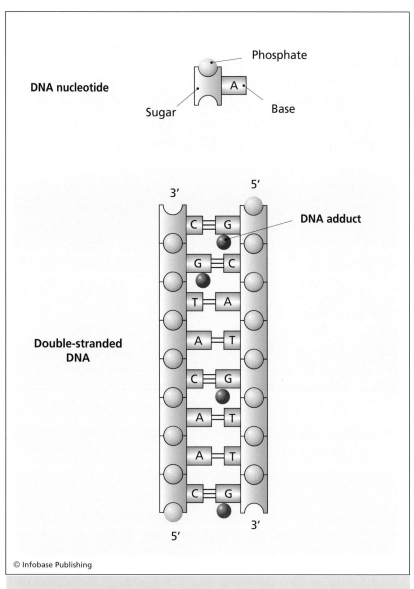

DNA adducts. Carcinogens can bind directly to the DNA, forming a carcinogen-nucleotide base complex known as an adduct. The adducts can interfere with the accuracy of replication, thus accelerating the mutation rate. The adducts shown here are formed by benzopyrene (gray spheres), a compound that binds to guanine (G).

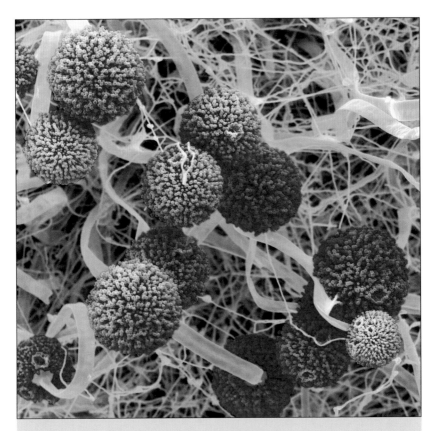

A scanning electron micrograph (SEM) of the fungus *Aspergillus niger.* Magnification: 220×. *(Dr. Fred Hossler/Visuals Unlimited)*

ARSENIC COMPOUNDS

Many studies have shown a clear association between exposure to arsenic and the occurrence of a wide range of cancers involving the skin, lung, kidney, liver, bladder, digestive tract, lymph nodes, and bone marrow. Epidemiological studies in Taiwan found that exposure to drinking water containing arsenic (0.35 mg per liter) increased the risk of all of the cancers noted above. Occupational exposure to arsenic in mining and smelting communities is consistently associated with increased risk of lung, kidney, and colon cancers. Other workers exposed to arsenic, such as those in the glass and pesticide industries, develop lung and skin cancers at a higher rate than the general public.

A variety of arsenic compounds have been tested on animals. Mice or rats exposed by oral administration (added to their water), dermal application, inhalation, and intravenous injection developed cancers of the stomach and lungs. In one study, subcutaneous injections of arsenic in pregnant mice led to the development of leukemia in the adults and their offspring. The effects of arsenic compounds on animals are, however, inconclusive as several other studies failed to find a link between exposure and cancer induction.

Arsenic is a naturally occurring semimetallic element that in nature is usually bound to other elements. Common arsenic compounds are arsenic trioxide, lead arsenate, calcium arsenate, and potassium arsenate. Arsenic compounds have been used by industry and the medical sciences for many years. Inorganic arsenic compounds were used as pesticides in the late 1800s and were used to treat leukemia, psoriasis, and asthma in the mid-1900s. During the 1980s, arsenic trioxide was used extensively as a wood preservative and can still be found, as chromated copper arsenate, in pressure-treated wood that is intended for outdoor structures (e.g., utility poles, fence poles, and building lumber). Since 1990, wood preservation has accounted for almost 90 percent of U.S. arsenic consumption. Arsenic is also used in lead solder, solar cells, lasers, light-emitting diodes, and integrated circuits. The mechanism by which arsenic compounds induce cancer is unknown.

ASBESTOS

Asbestos is a generic name given to a group of six naturally occurring fibrous silicate minerals (chrysotile, the most abundant form, actinolite, amosite, anthophyllite, crocidolite, and tremolite). Asbestos minerals possess a number of desirable properties that are useful in commercial applications, including heat stability and thermal and electrical insulation. Although asbestos use dates back at least 2,000 years, modern industrial use began around 1880, reaching a peak in the late 1960s and early 1970s when more than 3,000 industrial applications or products were listed. This material has been used primarily in roofing, production of plastics, and thermal and electrical insulation.

Many studies have shown that asbestos causes cancers of the respiratory tract and abdominal cavity (mesothelioma). Shipyard workers, chrysotile miners, and insulation workers are six times more likely to develop lung cancer. People living near asbestos factories or mines or living with an asbestos worker are at an increased risk of developing mesothelioma. Smokers exposed to asbestos are known to experience an increased risk of cancer that is synergistic (i.e., the effects are multiplicative, rather than additive).

All commercial forms of asbestos have been shown to cause cancer in animals. Inhalation exposure to chrysotile and other forms of asbestos caused lung cancer in rats. The incidence of abdominal cancers was increased by injections of crocidolite in hamsters and actinolite or tremolite in rats. Asbestos fibers vary in length and diameter. Fibers longer than eight μm with a diameter of 1.5 μm are known to be the most carcinogenic.

Production of asbestos in the United States has declined greatly since the 1980s when health and liability issues associated with this substance became apparent. By the 1990s, most of the asbestos mines and factories in the United States had closed. But the material is still being used. As of 2009, U.S. manufacturers had imported more than 30 million pounds (about 13,000 metric tons) of asbestos, most of it from Canada.

BENZENE

Many epidemiological studies have shown that exposure to benzene can cause all forms of leukemia. Increased risk of death from leukemia was very high in groups with the highest exposure. These conclusions were reported in 18 community-based and 16 industry-based studies. Benzene has also been shown to cause cancer in experiments on animals. When administered orally, benzene caused lymphoma, oral-cavity tumors, skin cancer, mammary gland tumors, and lung cancer in male and female rats. When administered by inhalation, benzene caused cancers throughout the body in rats, with a tendency toward lymphomas in mice.

Benzene is an aromatic hydrocarbon derived from coal tar and petroleum, that is used primarily as a solvent in the chemical and pharmaceutical industries and as a starting material in the synthesis of many chemicals, such as phenol, ethyl benzene (used to make styrene), and acetone. Benzene occurs naturally in crude oil and thus is present in gasoline. Benzene is present in the atmosphere both from natural sources, which include oil seeps and forest fires, and from industrial sources such as automobile exhaust, gas evaporation at filling stations, and industrial emissions. Thus, the primary source of human exposure is the atmosphere. Exposure can also come from tobacco smoke and from drinking contaminated food and water. Nearly half of the total exposure in the United States comes from cigarette smoke. Exposures range from 0.06 μg per cubic meter of air (m^3) in rural areas to nearly 400 μg per m^3 in urban areas (0.02 parts per billion to 112 ppb).

METALS

Earth contains a large number of elements known as metals: cadmium, cobalt, iron, copper, lead, mercury, tin, zinc, and nickel, to name a few. Some of these metals, such as copper, iron, and zinc, are essential for normal cellular metabolism. Others, such as lead and mercury, are toxic substances, but only two, cadmium and nickel, are known to be carcinogenic.

Cadmium exposure in an industrial setting is known to increase the risk of lung, prostate, kidney, and bladder cancer. Animals exposed to cadmium and cadmium compounds in a variety of ways develop a wide range of cancers. Inhalation exposure was shown to cause lung cancer in rats and mice; the tumor incidence increased with increasing exposure. Oral exposure caused dose-related increases in the incidences of leukemia and testicular tumors in rats. Subcutaneous injections of cadmium compounds caused cancer at multiple tissue sites, including the prostate gland, testes, lymph nodes, adrenal glands, lungs, and liver. These studies also determined that it is the ionic form of cadmium that is carcinogenic. Thus, the carcinogenic potential of a given cadmium compound depends on the degree to which the compound releases cadmium ions.

Cadmium ions exert their effect by binding to DNA, chromosomes, and nuclear proteins. Increased frequencies of chromosomal aberrations, typified by the number of broken chromosomes and disrupted DNA repair, have been observed in factory workers who process cadmium or use it in a manufacturing process. Cells produce a protective protein, called metallothionein (MT) that binds to and inactivates ionic cadmium (and other ionic metals). Rats and mice are not equally sensitive to cadmium. Mice are more resistant to cadmium as a lung carcinogen, which is due to differential expression of the MT gene in lung tissue following exposure by inhalation. In general, tissues in which cadmium causes cancer (in rodents or humans) show minimal expression of the MT gene or limited activation of MT in response to cadmium.

The carcinogenic profile of nickel is very similar to that of cadmium. Epidemiological studies involving workers in the nickel-refining industry have shown that exposure to this metal can cause lung and nasal cancers. Rats and mice, exposed in various ways, develop lung cancer and tumors in many different tissues. Some nickel compounds can pass through the placenta and cause malignant pituitary tumors in offspring.

Nickel and cadmium have many industrial applications. Nickel is used in the production of stainless steel, copper-nickel alloys, coins, alkaline batteries, spark plugs, and in surgical and dental prostheses. Nickel salts, such as nickel acetate, are used as a dye fixative in the textile industry, in electroplating, and as a sealer for anodized aluminum. Cadmium is used in paint pigments, batteries (the common Ni-Cad battery), alloys, stabilizers for plastics, and in reagents used in photocopying.

Large amounts of nickel and cadmium are released into the environment by mines and manufacturers. Workers and the general public can be exposed to these metals by breathing contaminated air or by consuming contaminated food or water. The U.S. Environmental Protection Agency (EPA) has estimated that releases of cadmium compounds (in the United States) since 1998 have ranged from 8.9 million pounds (about four metric tons) to 15 million pounds (ca. 6.8 metric tons). By contrast, the amounts of nickel and nickel compounds released in 2008 was more than seven metric tons. As discussed above, cadmium and nickel induce cancer in a dose-dependent manner. Consequently, of these two metals, nickel may pose the greatest threat to public safety, since so much of it is being released into the environment.

INDUSTRIAL EMISSIONS

Gases and residues released into the atmosphere by coke ovens are serious industrial emissions. Coke is produced by blending and heating coal in the absence of oxygen. Tars and light oils are distilled out of the coal, and, during this process, gases are generated. Coke oven emissions are complex mixtures of dust, vapors, and gases that include known carcinogens such as benzene, cadmium, and arsenic as well as a large number of organic molecules. More than 60 organic compounds, including more than 40 polycyclic aromatic hydrocarbons (PAHs), have been identified in air samples collected near coke plants.

Many studies, dating back to the 1950s, have linked employment in coke plants with cancers of the skin, bladder, and respiratory tract. Recent studies, conducted in the United States, the United

Industrial smokestacks *(Luis Castro/Shutterstock)*

Kingdom, Japan, and Sweden have found an increased risk of lung cancer in human populations exposed to coke oven emissions. Other studies of coke plant workers have reported an increased risk for cancers of the kidney, prostate, large intestine, and pancreas. The carcinogenicity of coke emissions has been confirmed in experiments on animals.

Coke is used primarily to manufacture iron, graphite, and electrodes. By-products of coke production are used to produce benzene, toluene, sulfur, and many other products. More than 33 trillion pounds (ca. 15 million metric tons) of coke and more than 3.5 million pounds (ca. 1.6 metric tons) of coke oven emissions are produced in the United States every year.

RADIATION

There are two forms of radiation that are known to be carcinogenic: ultraviolet radiation (UVR) and ionizing radiation. UVR is a natural component of sunlight and is also produced by sunlamps used in tanning salons and by sterilization lamps used in research laboratories and operating rooms. Ionizing radiation occurs as photons, which includes X-rays and gamma rays, and as atomic particles such as neutrons and alpha and beta particles. X-rays and gamma rays have essentially the same properties but differ in origin. X-rays originate outside the nucleus and involve transitional states of the electrons. Gamma rays originate inside the nucleus, being produced by the decay of radioactive atoms. Radioactive decay is also the origin of atomic particles. The detonation of a thermonuclear device is known to produce all forms of ionizing radiation.

UVR is high-energy radiation that has wavelengths ranging from 100 to 400 nanometers (nm). This type of radiation is divided into three components known as UVA (315 to 400 nm), UVB (280 to 315 nm), and UVC (100 to 280 nm). Of the solar radiation reaching the Earth (as measured at the equator), 95 percent is UVA and 5 percent is UVB. UVC, having the shortest wavelength, is completely filtered out by the atmosphere and does not reach the surface. Thus the carcinogenicity of UVR is due primarily to UVA. UVB and UVC are produced by sunlamps and thus pose a hazard to those who use a tanning bed. But while the carcinogenicity of UVR is well established, data on UVB and UVC are not conclusive. Many epidemiological studies have shown that exposure to UVR causes skin cancer in humans. These studies have been confirmed in experiments on animals. Mice, rats, and hamsters all develop skin or eye tumors when exposed to UVR.

Humans are exposed to high levels of UVR when they spend the day at the beach, work outdoors, or visit tanning salons. UVR is carcinogenic because it damages DNA, leading to gene mutations. Skin cancer is commonly associated with mutations in the *P53* gene, which is known to code for a tumor suppressor. The danger associated with exposure to UVR can be minimized through the use of an effective sunscreen and by avoiding suntan parlors.

Ionizing radiation can cause more extensive cellular damage, involving both the nucleus and the cytoplasm, than UVR. X-rays and gamma rays have been shown to induce gene mutations and extensive chromosomal damage (DNA strand breaks and chromosome fragmentation). Some of the damage is indirect. This can occur when the radiation destroys DNA repair enzymes or cripples components of the translation machinery.

Although ionizing radiation is more dangerous than UVR, the risk of exposure is much less. Humans encounter this type of radiation primarily during medical therapies, such as radiotherapy, positron emission tomography (PET) scan, and standard diagnostic X-rays. In such cases, the intensity of the radiation is so low that the risk is considered to be negligible or acceptable (i.e., the disease being treated poses a greater risk than the radiation). In rare cases, human populations have been exposed to lethal levels of ionizing radiation. This happened in 1945 when atomic bombs were dropped on Hiroshima and Nagasaki, Japan. Subsequent atmospheric tests of nuclear weapons, carried out between 1945 and 1980, have exposed human populations to dangerous levels of ionizing radiation. In one 10-year period, between 1952 and 1962, 520 such tests were conducted. Accidents at nuclear reactors have also been a source of exposure. The worst incident of this kind occurred at the Chernobyl nuclear power plant, located in the former Soviet Union, on April 26, 1986. The explosion released a plume of radioactive fallout that drifted for thousands of miles, eventually reaching the United Kingdom and eastern North America.

TOBACCO SMOKE

The deadliest carcinogens by far are found in cigarette smoke, and among the 50 or so that have been identified, the best studied is a compound called benzopyrene. This molecule, when intact, is not dangerous, but when a cigarette is smoked the benzopyrene enters the blood and travels to the liver where it is inadvertently activated.

Smoking cigarette *(Wallenrock/ Shutterstock)*

An important function of the liver is to detoxify the blood, by break-ing down a wide variety of compounds from alcohol to aspirin. A special set of liver enzymes, called mixed-function oxidases, breaks the toxins down and either stores or eliminates the pieces. In the case of benzopyrene, the oxidases activate the molecule in such a way that it gains the ability to bind to guanine, thus forming DNA adducts.

The binding of benzopyrene to DNA, in itself, is not a problem as long as the cell is post-mitotic. However, DNA adducts greatly in-crease the error frequency associated with DNA replication. Cells in the lung are not post-mitotic but divide frequently, and if those cells contain DNA adducts, errors will be introduced into their genome with each round of the cell cycle. Making the situation worse, other ingredients in tobacco smoke stimulate proliferation-signaling pathways, much as certain oncogenes do, forcing the cells to divide more frequently than normal. The carcinogens' combined ability to form DNA adducts and to force a cell to divide when it should not accelerates the mutation rate and onset of cancers. An accelerated mutation rate increases the risk of damaging a tumor suppressor gene or of activating an oncogene. These changes set the stage for serious trouble to come.

Lung cancer and other cancers caused by tobacco smoke kill more than 400,000 men and women every year in the United States alone and account for nearly 30 percent of the country's annual cancer deaths. Smokers are 22 times more likely to die of cancer than nonsmokers. Worldwide, 4 million people die every year of cancers caused by tobacco smoke. In China, where two-thirds of the adult male population smokes tobacco, more than 1 million die each year of tobacco-related cancers. Lung cancer alone is so prevalent that it has obscured the incidence of all other cancers. Many people have

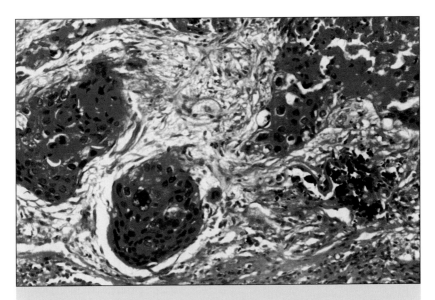

A light micrograph of cancer in a smoker's lung. The round neoplasms are cancer tumors, carcinomas, caused by cigarette or tobacco smoking. The black objects are pockets of embedded tars from the smoke. *(Kent Wood/Photo Researchers, Inc.)*

the impression that the incidence of cancer cases has been increasing over the years, and if all cancers are simply grouped together and plotted against time this does appear to be the case. But if lung cancer is subtracted from the data, the incidence of other major cancers (plotted as deaths per 100,000 people) including colon, breast, and prostate cancer has changed very little since 1930.

It is quite possible that the elimination of tobacco carcinogens would lower the rates for other cancers as well, since it is likely that compounds such as benzopyrene are contributing to the onset of cancers in other organs of the body. Smoking tobacco is associated with an increased risk for cancers of the mouth, throat, stomach, pancreas (the deadliest of all cancers), liver, uterus, kidney, and bladder. It may also be responsible for the increased prevalence of leukemia in adults and children, the latter presumably caused by secondary smoke inhalation. Indeed, laboratory rats and mice, forced to smoke the equivalent of a pack of cigarettes a day, develop benzopyrene DNA adducts in virtually every tissue of the body. If tobacco carcinogens are ever removed from our daily lives, it may well turn out that cancer is more a consequence of *our* lifestyle, than that of our protozoan ancestors.

6

Common Types of Cancer

In 2009, the American Cancer Society estimated that nearly 1.5 million new cancer cases were diagnosed in the United States alone and, in that same year, more than half a million Americans died of cancer. The total number of Americans now living with cancer stands at more than 10 million. Cancer can strike anyone, but the risk increases with age, certain lifestyles, and the quality of our environment. Nearly 80 percent of all cancers are diagnosed at age 55 and older, and smokers are 20 times more likely to develop lung cancer than nonsmokers. Cancers can appear in any of our tissues and organs, but there are some tissues that are more susceptible than others: Skin and the epithelial cells lining the lungs and digestive tract are prominent members in this group. These tissues and organs are at the interphase between the external environment and our internal organs and, like a sailor on the mast, take the full force of the storm when it hits. (See the table on page 65.)

The skin is exposed to daily doses of ultraviolet radiation (UVR) and a variety of chemicals in the environment. The lungs, while providing us with oxygen, are exposed to many other gases, such as smoke and pollutants that happen to be in the air. Our digestive tract is in direct contact with the food and water that is consumed, some of which contains known carcinogens and mutagens.

Some cancers, such as those affecting the brain, breasts, or prostate gland, do not have clear connections to lifestyle or the environment but appear to be a consequence of normal physiology and cellular biochemistry. Our bodies, complex machines that they are, simply start to break down after many years of running, and cancer is one of the regrettable consequences.

The deadliness of a cancer varies depending on the tissue that is affected. Prostate cancer struck more than 190,000 American men in 2009, but the mortality was only 14 percent (that is, nearly 28,000 men died of prostate cancer in that same year). By contrast, brain tumors have a mortality of 59 percent, and lung cancer is even worse, with a mortality of 73 percent. But the deadliest of all cancers are those that appear in the pancreas, where the mortality is a numbing 83 percent. The cancers shown in the tables that follow are covered in greater detail later in this chapter and kill millions of people worldwide every year. Brain tumors are described in this chapter, not because they are numerically common, but because of their notoriety, mortality, and the devastating effects they have on the patient's mental faculties.

Although the total number of cancer cases has increased in the United States since 2000, the mortality rate has declined for all but one: one ovarian cancer. (See the tables on pages 65 and 66.) In 2000, the mortality rate associated with brain cancer was 79 percent but dropped to 59 percent in 2009. Even more impressive is the 23 percent drop in the mortality rate for lung cancer. This encouraging trend is a testament to the improved diagnostics and therapies that have been developed over the past 10 years.

NEW CANCER CASES AND DEATHS FOR 2009

SITE	NEW CASES	DEATHS	MORTALITY (%)	PERCENT CHANGE
all sites	1,479,350	562,340	38	–7
bladder	70,980	14,330	20	–3
brain	22,070	12,920	59	–20
breast	194,280	40,610	21	–1
colon	106,100	49,920	47	–4
leukemia	44,790	21,870	49	–21
liver	22,620	18,160	80	–10
lung	219,440	159,390	73	–23
lymphoma	74,490	20,790	28	–16
ovary	21,550	14,600	68	+7
pancreas	42,470	35,240	83	–16
prostate	192,280	27,360	14	–4
skin (melanoma)	68,720	8,650	13	–3

Note: Data is for the United States and was compiled from information provided by the American Cancer Society. Mortality is the number of deaths divided by new cases times 100. The values are rounded off to the nearest percentage point. "Percent change" is the mortality for 2009 minus the mortality for 2000 (shown in the table on page 66). A negative number indicates a drop in mortality since 2000; a positive number indicates an increase. "All sites" refers to all known cancers.

CANCER TERMINOLOGY

Normal cells become cancerous through a process called transformation, leading to the uncontrolled growth of the cancer cells, which produces a tumor or neoplasm. As long as the tumor remains intact and the cells do not try to invade other parts of the body, the tumor is called benign and can be treated by surgical removal. Tumors become dangerous and potentially deadly when some of

NEW CANCER CASES AND DEATHS FOR 2000

SITE	NEW CASES	DEATHS	MORTALITY (%)
all sites	1,220,100	552,200	45
bladder	53,200	12,200	23
brain	16,500	13,000	79
breast	184,200	41,200	22
colon	93,800	47,700	51
leukemia	30,800	21,700	70
liver	15,300	13,800	90
lung	164,100	156,900	96
lymphoma	62,300	27,500	44
ovary	23,100	14,000	61
pancreas	28,300	28,200	99
prostate	180,400	31,900	18
skin (melanoma)	47,700	7,700	16

Note: Data is for the United States and was compiled from information provided by the American Cancer Society. Mortality is the number of deaths divided by new cases times 100. The values are rounded off to the nearest percentage point. "All sites" refers to all known cancers.

the cells develop the ability to leave the main tumor mass and migrate to other parts of the body where they form new tumors; such tumors are malignant, spreading the cancer by a process known as metastasis. Malignant cancers can be very difficult, if not impossible, to treat. The danger associated with all tumors is that they will switch from benign to malignant before being detected.

Cancers are classified according to the tissue and cell type from which they arise. Cancers that develop from epithelial cells are called carcinomas; those arising from connective tissue or muscles are called sarcomas; and those arising from blood-forming tissue, such as the bone marrow, are known as leukemias. More than 90 percent of all human cancers are carcinomas.

Cancer names are derived from their cell type, the specific tissue being affected, and whether the tumor is benign or malignant. An adenoma, for example, is a benign tumor originating in the adenoid gland, or other glandular tissue, that consists of epithelial cells. A malignant tumor from the same source is called an adenocarcinoma. A chondroma is a benign tumor of cartilage, whereas a chondrosarcoma is a malignant cartilage tumor. Some cancer names can be real tongue twisters: A type of leukemia that affects blood-forming cells is called myelocytomatosis.

Cancers generally retain characteristics that reflect their origin. One type of skin cancer, called basal cell carcinoma, is derived from keratinocytes and will continue to synthesize keratin, the protein of hair and nails. Another form of skin cancer, called melanoma, is derived from pigment cells and is associated with overproduction of the skin pigment melanin. It is for this reason that these tumors are usually very dark in color. Cancers of the pituitary gland, which produces growth hormone, can lead to production of excessive amounts of this hormone, the effects of which can be more damaging than the cancer itself.

Cancer progression is divided into the following five stages:

- ► Stage 0 is noninvasive; that is, it has not begun to spread.
- ► Stage I marks the period when the cancer becomes malignant and begins to spread. The tumor is no more than an inch across, and the cancer cells have not spread beyond the organ or tissue in which they first appeared.
- ► Stage II tumors are still small (one inch or less) but have begun to spread to nearby tissues. A tumor that

has increased in size to two inches but has not begun to spread is still at stage II.

- ▶ Stage III is a locally advanced cancer. In this stage, the tumor is large (more than 2 inches across) and the cancer has spread to nearby tissues.
- ▶ Stage IV is metastatic cancer. The cancer has spread to many other tissues and organs of the body. Correct staging is crucial for application of the appropriate therapy.

In the descriptions that follow, each cancer is described with respect to the basic anatomy of the affected tissue, risk factors that increase a person's chance of developing the disease, disease symptoms, diagnosis, and staging.

BLADDER CANCER

The bladder is a saclike organ that stores urine from the kidneys. Cancer cells appear in the epithelial cells that line the inside surface of the organ. In 2008, this cancer was diagnosed in more than 68,000 Americans and has a moderate mortality of 20 percent and appears to be especially sensitive to diet and the environment.

Bladder cancer is associated with several risk factors: age, tobacco, occupation, infections, race, and sex. People under 40 rarely get this disease, but the chance of getting bladder cancer increases dramatically with age. Cigarette smokers are six times more likely than non-smokers to get bladder cancer. Pipe and cigar smokers are also at increased risk. Workers in the rubber, chemical, and leather industries have a higher risk of getting bladder cancer because of carcinogens in the workplace. So are hairdressers, machinists, metalworkers, printers, painters, textile workers, and truck drivers. Being infected with certain tropical parasites increases the risk of developing bladder cancer. Whites get bladder cancer twice as often as African Americans and Hispanics. The lowest rates are among Asians. Men are two to three times more likely than women to get bladder cancer.

Common symptoms of bladder cancer include blood in the urine, pain during urination, and frequent urination or feeling the need to urinate without results. These are not sure signs of bladder cancer, since other problems, such as bladder stones, can produce similar symptoms. This cancer is diagnosed with a simple physical exam to check for obvious tumor growths; a urine test to check for the presence of blood or cancer cells in the urine; X-ray photography of the bladder; and cystoscopy, whereby a lighted tube is inserted through the urethra to examine the lining of the bladder.

At stage 0, the cancer cells are found only on the surface of the inner lining of the bladder. This is called superficial cancer or carcinoma in situ. At stage I, the cancer cells are deep in the inner lining of the bladder and by stage II have spread to the underlying muscle tissue. By stage III, the cancer cells have spread through the muscular wall of the bladder to the layer of tissue surrounding the bladder. The cancer cells may have spread to the prostate gland (in men) or to the uterus or vagina (in women). By stage IV, the cancer extends to the wall of the abdomen or to the wall of the pelvis. The cancer cells may have spread to lymph nodes, the lungs, and many other parts of the body.

BRAIN TUMORS

The brain is divided into three major regions: the cerebrum, the cerebellum (a smaller area located at the lower back of the brain), and the brain stem, which is continuous with the spinal cord. The brain, along with the spinal cord, is called the central nervous system (CNS) and is constructed of three types of cells: the neurons, the astrocytes (star-shaped), and the oligodendrocytes. The astrocytes and oligodendrocytes form a tissue, known as glia, that supports the neurons.

Brain tumors usually originate in the glia tissue as astrocytomas (from the astrocytes) or oligodendrogliomas (from the oligodendrocytes). These cancers are known collectively as gliomas.

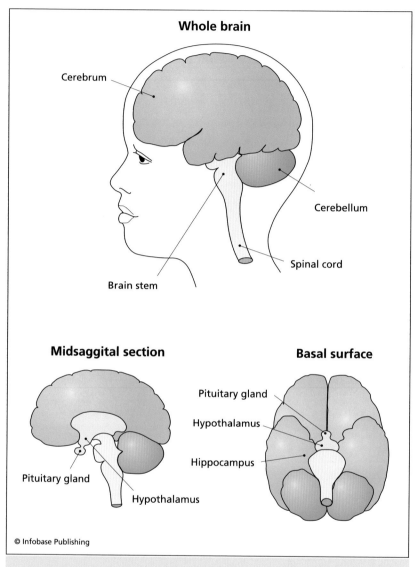

Whole brain

Cerebrum

Cerebellum

Spinal cord

Brain stem

Midsaggital section

Basal surface

Pituitary gland

Hypothalamus

Hippocampus

Pituitary gland

Hypothalamus

© Infobase Publishing

Human central nervous system. The human brain consists of the cerebrum, the cerebellum, and the brain stem, which is continuous with the spinal cord. The brain and spinal cord are called the central nervous system (CNS). The pituitary gland, a crucial part of the neuroendocrine system, is connected to the hypothalamus at the base of the brain (midsagittal section). The hippocampus, located on the basal surface of the brain, coordinates memory functions.

Astrocytomas may grow anywhere in the brain or spinal cord. In adults, these tumors usually arise in the cerebrum. In children, they occur in the brain stem, the cerebrum, and the cerebellum. Brain stem astrocytomas occur in the lowest part of the brain where they are difficult, if not impossible, to remove. Oligodendrogliomas arise in the glia cells that produce myelin; the fatty covering that protects and insulates nerves. These tumors usually arise in the cerebrum, grow slowly, and usually do not spread into surrounding brain tissue.

The most important risk factor associated with this disease is the patient's age. There is no clear link with lifestyle or environmental pollutants. Some people have suspected exposure to cell phone radiation, but this has not been proven, and several attempts to do so have met with failure. Brain tumors occur most often in middle-aged adults and are frequently secondary tumors; that is, tumors that originated in some other part of the body. Secondary tumors are named after the tissue of their origin. For example, a brain tumor that originated in the lung is called metastatic lung cancer, and the cells from such a tumor will resemble lung tissue, not neurons or glia cells.

In 2009, brain cancer was diagnosed in more than 22,000 Americans. Although the number of people affected is small compared with other forms of cancer, brain cancer is included here because of its high mortality (more than 59 percent) and because it exacts an especially heavy toll on those who survive. Damage to virtually any area of the brain will leave its mark. Even if the tumor is removed or destroyed, the patient is often left with a lifelong disability.

The effect that tumors have upon the brain depends primarily on size and location. Growing tumors may put pressure on surrounding tissue, damaging neurons and the many connections they make with other cells. Damage to the brain is also caused by swelling and a buildup of fluid around the tumor, a condition called edema. Tumors can also block the flow of cerebrospinal fluid, causing it to build up inside the brain, producing a condition known as hydrocephalus.

Common symptoms of brain tumors include the following: headaches that tend to be worse in the morning and ease during the day; seizures (convulsions); nausea or vomiting; weakness or loss of feeling in the arms or legs; stumbling or lack of coordination in walking;

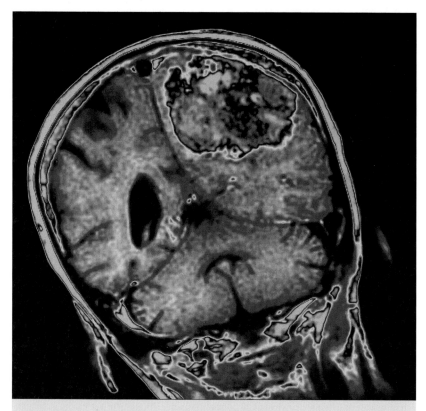

A colored magnetic resonance imaging (MRI) scan of a coronal section through the brain of a 74-year-old woman, showing a large tumor. At upper center is the tumor (blue) within one cerebral hemisphere (orange) of the brain; the other cerebral hemisphere (at center left) is normal containing a dark ventricle or cavity. The cerebellum of the brain is seen at lower center. Brain tumors may be primary tumors arising in the brain first or they may be spread from cancer elsewhere in the body. A large tumor such as this may cause brain compression and nerve damage. *(Simon Fraser/RNC, Newcastle upon Tyne/Photo Researchers, Inc.)*

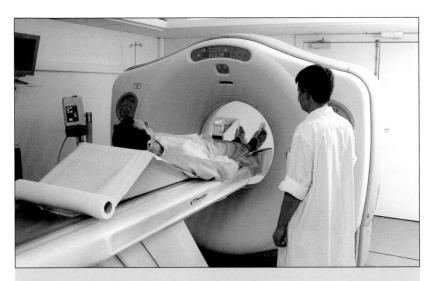

A magnetic resonance imaging (MRI) facility *(AJ Photos/Photo Researchers, Inc.)*

abnormal eye movements or changes in vision; persistent drowsiness; changes in personality, memory, or speech habits.

Brain tumors are diagnosed primarily with a computed tomography (CT) scan or with magnetic resonance imaging (MRI). A CT scan is a series of detailed pictures of the brain that are created by a computer linked to an X-ray machine. In some cases, a special dye is injected into a vein before the scan, which increases tissue contrast. MRI produces computerized pictures of the brain that are based on the magnetic properties of the molecules that are in the tissue. A special dye may be used to enhance the likelihood of detecting a brain tumor.

These cancers rarely metastasize to other tissues or organs but simply grow at their point of origin. Since damage to any part of the CNS is likely to have serious consequences, the main concern with a brain tumor is how fast it is growing. For these reasons, standard staging is not used. Instead, brain tumors are referred to as low, intermediate, or high grade, with respect to their growth rate.

BREAST CANCER

Each breast has 15 to 20 sections called lobes: Within each lobe are many smaller lobules, which end in dozens of tiny bulbs that can produce milk. Thin tubes, called ducts, link all the lobes, lobules, and bulbs. These ducts lead to the nipple in the center of a dark area of skin called the areola. There are no muscles in the breast, but muscles lie under each breast and cover the ribs. The breasts also contain blood vessels and vessels for the lymphatic system, which consists of many lymph nodes occurring near the breast, under the arm, above the collarbone, in the chest, and many other areas of the body.

The most common type of breast cancer is ductal carcinoma, which begins in the lining of the ducts. The second type occurs in the lobes and is called lobular carcinoma. Other than skin cancer (melanoma plus squamous cell carcinoma), breast cancer is the

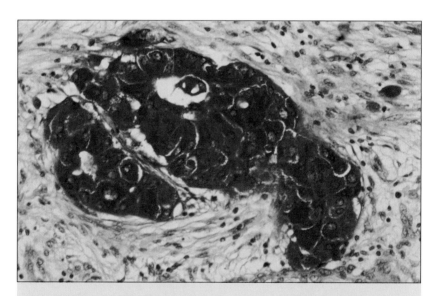

Light micrograph of a carcinoma in breast tissue using an antibody labeling technique. An antibody-linked stain has bound to the cancerous cells and stained them pink. The carcinoma is surrounded by healthy breast tissue (purple). Magnification: 80×. *(Michael Abbey/ Photo Researchers, Inc.)*

most common type of cancer among women in North America, where nearly 200,000 cases are diagnosed each year. Breast cancer also affects more than 2,000 men each year. Despite the emphasis on breast exams as a preventative measure, the incidence of breast cancer and its associated mortality have not changed since 2000.

There are three factors associated with both forms of breast cancer: mutations in two genes (*Brca1* and *Brca2*), estrogen exposure, and late childbearing. *Brca1* and *Brca2* code for proteins that are needed to correct errors in DNA synthesis during the cell cycle. Estrogen is responsible for stimulating the breasts as part of normal reproductive physiology but over time may lead to the transformation of the duct cells. There are those who claim that late childbearing increases the risk of breast cancer, but the relationship has not been established.

There is no pain or discomfort associated with the early stages of breast cancer, which may produce a lump or thickening in or near the breast or in the underarm area; a change in the size or shape of the breast; nipple discharge or tenderness; or swelling redness or scaling of the skin of the breast, areola, or nipple.

Breast cancers are diagnosed with clinical breast exams, mammography, ultrasonography, and biopsies. The clinical exam is used to locate obvious lumps in the breast. It is often possible to tell if a lump is benign or malignant by the way it feels, how easily it moves, and its texture. Mammography uses X-rays to obtain a picture of the breast and any lumps that may be present. Ultrasonography uses high-frequency sound waves to determine whether a lump is a fluid-filled cyst (not cancer) or a solid mass (which may or may not be cancer). This exam may be used along with mammography. In some cases, samples of a suspected tumor are obtained so the cells may be examined under a microscope. This procedure is referred to as a biopsy, and the tissue sample is usually collected with a hypodermic needle.

At Stage 0, the cancer is a noninvasive carcinoma. By stage I or II, the cancer has spread beyond the lobe or duct and invaded nearby tissue. At stage I the tumor is no more than an inch across, and the cancer cells are still inside the breast. Cancer cells begin to spread to underarm (axillary) lymph nodes by stage II. If the tumor increases in size to two inches but has not spread, it is still at stage II. Stage III is locally advanced cancer. The tumor is more than two inches across and the cancer has spread to the axillary lymph nodes and other nearby tissues. By stage IV, the cancer has spread beyond the breast to many other parts of the body.

COLON CANCER

The colon, or large intestine, is part of the digestive tract, which also includes the esophagus, stomach, small intestine, and the rectum. The colon is a muscular tube that is about five feet (150 cm) long. Absorption of digested food is carried out by the intestinal mucosa, which consist of several layers of cells lining the inner surface of the intestinal tract. All of these cells are highly active metabolically and divide at regular intervals, two facts that predispose the cells to cancerous transformation. This predisposition to cancer is compounded by the fact that the intestinal mucosa is exposed to a daily barrage of potentially dangerous chemicals that are found in many kinds of food and beverages.

Colon cancer develops slowly over many years and often begins as a noncancerous polyp. Adenomatous polyps or adenomas often give rise to colon cancer, whereas hyperplastic and inflammatory polyps do not. The occurrence of many hyperplastic polyps, however, increases the likelihood that an adenoma will appear. More than 95 percent of colon cancers are adenocarcinomas, which means they are cancers of glandular cells that line the wall of the colon. Although the incidence of colon cancer has increased from 93,800 cases in 2000 to 106,100 cases in 2009, mortality has dropped by 4 percent. (See the preceding tables on pages 65 and 66.)

The main risk factors for colon cancer are age, ethnic, and racial background (Jews of Eastern Europe and African Americans have the highest rates of colon cancer), a diet high in meat, physical inactivity, obesity, diabetes, and smoking. Studies have shown that smokers are nearly 40 percent more likely than nonsmokers to die of colon cancer. Although most of the smoke is taken into the lungs, it is believed that a portion of it is swallowed where it can affect the cells of the digestive tract. Absorption of the carcinogens in cigarette smoke may be responsible for cancer in the kidneys, bladder, cervix, and other organs. Exposure to secondary smoke can also increase the risk of developing these cancers.

Symptoms of colon cancer include recurring diarrhea or constipation, a constant feeling that a bowel movement is necessary, rectal bleeding or blood in the stool (although the stool may look normal), cramping or a chronic stomachache, weakness, and fatigue. All of these symptoms can occur for other reasons. For example, blood can occur in the stool after the consumption of a rare steak. A thorough diagnosis may include a blood test, biopsy, ultrasound, CT scan, or MRI. Each of these procedures is able to locate suspect polyps that can then be removed and examined for the presence of cancerous cells. If cancerous polyps are detected, the patient may receive a chest X-ray to determine whether the cancer has metastasized to the lungs.

At stage 0, the cancer has not grown beyond the inner layer of the colon. This stage is also known as carcinoma in situ. The cancer has progressed to stage I when the cells invade the muscle layer of the colon. By stage II, the cells have moved through the wall of the colon and at stage III begin to invade nearby lymph nodes. At stage IV, the cells have metastasized to distant sites such as the liver, lungs, and the lining of the abdominal cavity. The five-year survival rate for stage I colon cancer is 93 percent. This drops to 64 percent at stage III and 8 percent at stage IV.

LEUKEMIA

This cancer affects white blood cells (WBC), or leukocytes. Other blood cells, such as red blood cells (RBCs) and platelets (thrombocytes) are not affected. Red blood cells contain hemoglobin and use it to carry oxygen from the lungs to the tissues. Platelets are not complete cells but are fragments of certain kinds of leukocytes. These fragments provide factors necessary for blood clotting. White blood cells are part of the body's immune system. These cells occur as two distinct populations: lymphocytes, which spend much of their time in the lymphatic system, and myeloid cells, which spend much of their time in the bone marrow or general circulation.

Leukemia can arise in either lymphoid cells (lymphocytic leukemia) or myeloid cells (myelogenous leukemia). This disease may be acute or chronic. Acute leukemia is a devastating disease that progresses very quickly, destroying the patient's immune system. Chronic leukemia progresses much more slowly, and even though the leukocytes are transforming they retain some of their normal functions, so the immune system is not destroyed as quickly or as completely. Although the incidence of leukemia has increased over the years, from 30,800 cases in 2000 to 44,790 in 2009, the mortality has dropped by an impressive 21 percent.

The primary risk factor associated with leukemia is the patient's age. Acute lymphocytic leukemia is the most common type of leukemia in young children and in adults who are 65 and older. Acute myeloid leukemia (also called acute nonlymphocytic leukemia) occurs in both adults and children. Chronic lymphocytic leukemia most often affects adults over the age of 55. It sometimes occurs in younger adults but rarely affects children. Chronic myeloid leukemia occurs mainly in adults. Very few children ever develop this form of leukemia.

Some symptoms of leukemia are fever, chills, and other flulike symptoms; weakness and fatigue; frequent infections; loss of appetite and/or weight; swollen or tender lymph nodes, liver, or spleen; easy bleeding or bruising; tiny red spots under the skin; swollen or bleeding gums; sweating, especially at night; and/or bone or joint pain. Leukemia metastasizing to the brain may cause headaches, vomiting, confusion, loss of muscle control, and seizures. Leukemia cells can also colonize the testicles where they cause pain and swelling; the skin and eyes where they produce sores; and many other organs and tissues of the body.

The initial diagnosis for leukemia is based on a simple physical examination, blood analysis, and biopsies. The patient is examined for swelling in the liver, the spleen, and the lymph nodes under the arms, in the groin, and in the neck. A blood sample is examined under the microscope to check for abnormal WBCs. The most definitive test is the microscopic examination of a bone marrow biopsy, which is obtained by inserting a needle into the hip and removing a small amount of bone marrow. If cancer cells are found, X-rays are taken to evaluate the spread of the disease.

Staging is difficult to determine with this form of cancer, since the leukocytes normally travel throughout the body. Consequently, transformation and metastasis may occur simultaneously.

LUNG CANCER

The lungs are a pair of cone-shaped organs that are part of the respiratory system. The right lung has three sections, called lobes, and is a little larger than the left lung, which has two lobes. The lungs extract oxygen from the atmosphere, which our cells need to live and carry out their normal functions, and they expel carbon dioxide, a cellular waste product.

Most lung cancers start in the epithelial lining of the bronchi and occasionally in the trachea, bronchioles, or alveoli. All forms of lung cancer, being derived from epithelial cells, are carcinomas. These cancers are very common and very deadly. In 2009, more than 200,000 cases were diagnosed in the United States alone, and, of these, 73 percent die of the disease. This mortality is an improvement over the shocking 96 percent observed in 2000. Although it is one of the most deadly of all cancers, it is also the most preventable.

Scientists have identified several risk factors for lung cancer. Most of these are due to atmospheric pollutants and the use of tobacco. The smoke from cigarettes, cigars, and pipes contains many compounds,

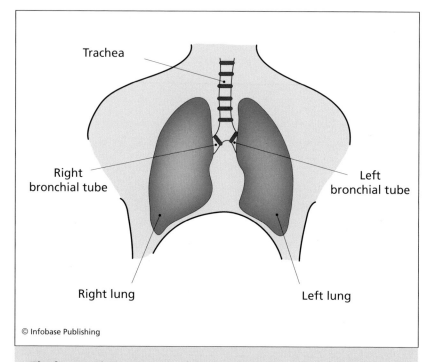

The lungs. These are part of the respiratory system and fill most of the thoracic cavity. The trachea divides into two bronchial tubes, each of which begin branching like a tree once inside the lung. The branches are called bronchioles and terminate in grapelike clusters of alveoli, where gas exchange occurs between the air and the blood.

called carcinogens, that can damage cells, leading to the formation of cancer. The likelihood that a smoker will develop lung cancer is affected by the age at which smoking began, how long the person has smoked, the number of cigarettes smoked per day, and how deeply the smoker inhales. Giving up smoking greatly reduces a person's risk for developing lung cancer. Environmental tobacco smoke, or secondhand smoke, is just as dangerous. Work-related exposure to radioactive gases, such as radon, and to asbestos dust is also known

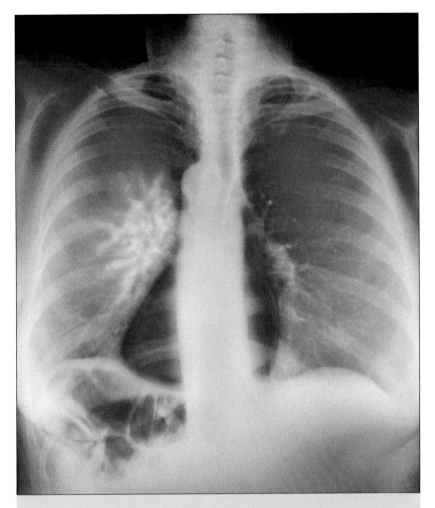

A color-enhanced X-ray of the chest. This shows cancer in the right lung. *(Chris Bjornberg/Photo Researchers, Inc.)*

to cause lung cancer. Atmospheric pollutants contributed by industrial emissions and by car and truck exhaust are also believed to be risk factors, and many are now classified as carcinogens.

The symptoms of lung cancer are complex and severe: a cough that does not go away and gets worse over time, constant chest pain, coughing up blood, shortness of breath, wheezing or hoarseness, repeated problems with pneumonia or bronchitis, swelling of the neck and face, loss of appetite, weight loss, and chronic fatigue.

Lung cancers are diagnosed with a chest X-ray to visualize possible tumors, followed by a lung biopsy to confirm the cancerous state of the tissue at the microscopic level. If the diagnosis is positive, further tests are made to determine the extent of metastasis. Lung cancers often spread to the brain and bones. CT scans and MRI are the most common methods for determining the stage of this type of cancer.

OVARIAN CANCER

Ovaries are the female organs that produce germ cells known as eggs, ova, or oocytes. In mature women, one or more ovum is released from the ovary into the fallopian tubes, eventually coming to rest in the uterus where they have a chance of being fertilized. The ovary consists of three types of cells: the germ cells, stroma cells, and epithelial cells. The stroma cells surround the developing ova, give the organ its shape, and produce the female hormones estrogen and progesterone. The epithelial cells cover the outer surface of the organ. About 85 percent of all ovarian cancers originate in the epithelial layer, 10 percent occur in the stroma cells, and the rest are germ cell tumors.

Risk factors for ovarian cancer include age, obesity, fertility drugs, and estrogen replacement therapy. About 10 percent of ovarian cancers are the result of an inherited genetic predisposition for the disease. Most ovarian cancers develop after menopause and more than half occur in women over the age of 60. A study by the American Cancer Society showed that obesity could increase the risk of ovarian cancer by 50 percent. Other researchers have found that the use of the fertility drug clomiphene citrate may increase the risk of ovarian cancer, but the magnitude is unknown. Results from the Women's Health Initiative, conducted by the National Institutes of Health for 15 years, beginning in 1991, show that estrogen replacement therapy increases the risk of ovarian cancer, but the results are controversial and the magnitude of the risk is uncertain. Although the incidence of this cancer has remained steady over the years, the mortality has increased by 7 percent.

Ovarian cancer is associated with vague symptoms such as abdominal swelling (due to fluid accumulation), unusual vaginal bleeding, pelvic pressure, leg and back pain, stomach pain, and problems with digestion. Screening tests for ovarian cancer are still in the development stage. Transvaginal sonography or CT scans can detect an ovarian growth but cannot distinguish between benign and malignant tumors. Positive imaging results are followed by a biopsy of the suspected tumor, which is examined under a microscope. The vagueness of the symptoms is the main reason this cancer has a high mortality rate: By the time it is detected, it has already spread throughout the body.

Stage I ovarian cancer is still located within one or both ovaries. At stage II the cancer has spread to the uterus, fallopian tubes, and possibly into the abdominal cavity. A stage III tumor is about 0.75 inch in diameter (two cm) and can be found in the lining of the upper abdomen and in local lymph nodes. At stage IV, the cancer has spread to many organs including the liver and the lungs. The five-year survival rate at stage I is 88 percent; this drops to 42 percent at stage III and 17 percent at stage IV. Only 20 percent of ovarian cancers are found at an early stage.

PANCREATIC CANCER

The pancreas is a gland that is part of the digestive system and also plays an important role in the endocrine system. This gland, shaped like a feather, is about six inches long and two inches wide (15 cm by five cm). It is attached to the small intestine, just below the stomach, by way of a common duct that it shares with the liver. The pancreas is both an exocrine and an endocrine gland. The exocrine function involves the secretion of digestive enzymes into the small intestine. These enzymes are released by the pancreatic cells into a treelike network of small ducts that join a central pancreatic duct. More than 95 percent of the gland consists of the exocrine cells and the ducts. The endocrine cells are located in small clusters distributed throughout the gland. These clusters are called the islets of Langerhans. The endocrine cells are of two types, known simply as α (alpha) and β (beta) cells. The α cells produce glucagon, a hormone that triggers the release of glucose from stored deposits throughout the body. The β cells produce insulin, a hormone that activates the uptake of glucose by all of the cells in the body. Thus, hypoglycemia (low blood sugar) stimulates the release of glucagon, whereas hyperglycemia (high blood sugar) inhibits glucagon but stimulates the release of insulin. In this way, these two hormones work to keep the blood glucose at an optimum level.

The most common type of pancreatic cancer develops in the exocrine portion of the gland. Most of the exocrine tumors are malignant, and since they derive from glandular tissue are classified as adenocarcinomas. These cancers usually begin in the ducts but can also develop from the exocrine cells. About two-thirds of the exocrine tumors occur at the head of the pancreas near the main duct. Endocrine tumors, from the α and β cells, are rare and are usually benign; if they become malignant, they are called islet cell carcinomas.

The main risk factors for pancreatic cancer are age, gender, race, cigarette smoking, diet, and obesity. Most patients suffering from this cancer are more than 50 and nearly 90 percent are older than 55. Men have a 20 percent greater chance of developing pancreatic cancer than women and African Americans are almost 50 percent more likely to develop it than whites. Obesity and a diet high in saturated fats can increase one's risk by 20 percent. These factors pale in comparison to cigarette smoke, which can increase one's risk by 300 percent. The incidence of this cancer has increased noticeably since 2000, but its mortality has decreased by 8 percent.

Jaundice is a common symptom of pancreatic cancer. Exocrine tumors often block the common duct, which prevents liver bile from reaching the intestine. One component of bile is a pigmented substance called bilirubin. When the common duct is blocked, bilirubin tends to collect in the blood and in the tissues, which darkens the skin and causes the whites of the eyes to turn yellow. Although pancreatic cancer can lead to jaundice, liver diseases such as hepatitis or gallstones are more common causes. Other symptoms associated with pancreatic cancer are abdominal pain, weight loss, digestive problems, and gallbladder enlargement.

Cancer of the pancreas is usually diagnosed with imaging technologies, such as CT scans, PET scans, ultrasonography, and endoscopic ultrasound. An endoscope is a thin fiber optic tube that can be inserted into the body cavity for a direct image of the pancreas. A biopsy of the gland can be obtained at the same time. Blood tests are also performed to determine whether the patient's jaundice is due to pancreatic cancer or liver disease.

Staging of pancreatic cancer is not usually performed until surgery is performed. At that time the surgeon decides if the cancer is resectable (localized and easy to remove), locally advanced, or metastatic. In the latter cases, the surgeon might try to relieve symptoms stemming from a blocked bile duct, but no attempt would be made to remove the tumors. As indicated in the table on page 65, the mortality associated with pancreatic cancer is extremely high. Only 5 percent of all patients suffering from this disease will survive for five years after the diagnosis.

PROSTATE CANCER

The prostate gland is part of the male reproductive system. It makes and stores portions of the seminal fluid, a fluid that is mixed with sperm to produce semen. The gland is about the size of a walnut and is located below the bladder near the base of the penis. It surrounds the upper part of the urethra, the tube that empties urine from the bladder. Because of its location, abnormal growth of the prostate can pinch the urethra, blocking the flow of urine. The prostate gland is regulated by the male sex hormone, testosterone.

Prostate cancer is the most common type of cancer in North American men other than skin cancer. The number of men affected by prostate cancer is nearly equal to the number of women affected by breast cancer, but the mortality of prostate cancer is lower (see the table on page 65). Age, family history, and diet are the main risk factors. Prostate cancer usually occurs in men over the age of 55. The average age of patients at the time of diagnosis is 70. A man's risk of developing prostate cancer is higher if his father or brother has had the disease. This disease is much more common in African Americans than in whites and is less common in Asians and American Indians. Some evidence suggests that a diet high in animal fat may increase the risk of prostate cancer and a diet high in fruits and vegetables may decrease the risk. Studies are in progress to learn whether men can reduce their risk of prostate cancer by modifying their diet.

Common symptoms of prostate cancer are a need to urinate frequently, especially at night; difficulty starting urination or holding back urine; inability to urinate; weak or interrupted flow of urine; painful or burning urination; difficulty in having an erection; painful ejaculation; blood in urine or semen; or, in advanced stages, frequent pain or stiffness in the lower back, hips, or upper thighs.

The diagnosis of prostate cancer usually begins with a digital rectal exam (DRE) and a blood test for prostate-specific antigen (PSA). The DRE sounds high tech but is not. The patient's doctor inserts a lubricated, gloved finger into the rectum and feels the prostate through the rectal wall to check for hard or lumpy areas. The diagnosis, based on this simple procedure, is surprisingly accurate and informative. Confirmation of cancer, based on the DRE, is obtained by testing the patient's blood for the presence of PSA, a semen protein produced by the prostate, which under normal circumstances should never appear in the blood. Blood that is positive for PSA is strong evidence of prostate cancer. This test is sometimes followed up with a biopsy and ultrasonography.

A stage I prostatic tumor cannot be felt during a rectal exam and there is usually no evidence that it has spread beyond the prostate. At stage II, the tumor is large enough to be felt during a rectal exam but is still noninvasive. By stage III, the cancer has spread outside the prostate to nearby tissues, and at stage IV cancer cells have colonized the lymph nodes and many other parts of the body.

SKIN CANCER

The skin protects us against heat, light, injury, and infection. It helps regulate body temperature and stores water, fat, and vitamin D. This tissue is made up of two main layers: the outer epidermis and the inner dermis. The epidermis (outer layer of the skin) is mostly made up of flat, scalelike cells called squamous cells. Under the squamous cells are round cells called basal cells. The deepest part of the epidermis also contains melanocytes, cells that produce melanin, which gives the skin its color. The dermis (just below the epidermis) contains blood and lymph vessels, hair follicles, and glands. These glands produce sweat to regulate body temperature and sebum, an oily substance that helps keep the skin from drying out. Sweat and sebum reach the skin's surface through tiny openings called pores.

This is the most common type of cancer in North America, with 1 million cases being diagnosed each year. Nearly half of the North American population will develop some form of skin cancer by the time they reach 65. The two most common kinds of skin cancer are basal cell carcinoma and squamous cell carcinoma. Basal cell carcinoma accounts for more than 90 percent of all skin cancers in North America. It is a slow-growing cancer that seldom spreads to other parts of the body. Squamous cell carcinoma also rarely spreads, but it does so more often than basal cell carcinoma. Another type of cancer that occurs in the skin is melanoma, which

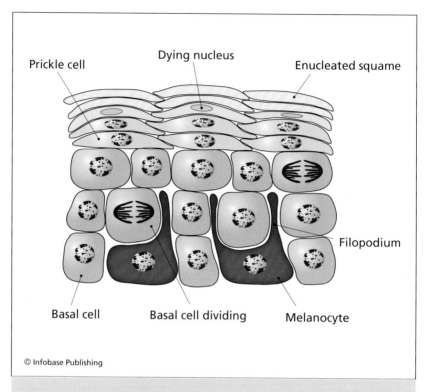

Prickle cell

Dying nucleus

Enucleated squame

Filopodium

Basal cell

Basal cell dividing

Melanocyte

© Infobase Publishing

Structure of the epidermis. The epidermis is a stratified epithelium that forms the outer layer of the skin. It consists of three cell populations: squamous cells (the enucleated squames and the prickle cells), the cuboidal basal cells, and, at the deepest layers, pigment-containing melanocytes. The basal and squamous cell layers are in a constant state of change. Division of a basal cell is followed by keratinization, a process by which the daughter cells are transformed into prickle cells. Keratin is a tough protein that makes the outer cell layer resistant to abrasion. In the final stage of keratinization, the prickle cell loses its nucleus. The now dead and fully keratinized squame eventually flakes off from the surface. Keratinized squames from the scalp are called dandruff.

begins in the melanocytes. Melanomas are quick to metastasize and are often deadly. Basal cell carcinoma and squamous cell carcinoma are sometimes called non-melanoma skin cancer. The incidence of melanoma has increased over the years with a mortality rate of 13 to 16 percent.

Although anyone can get skin cancer, the risk is greatest for people who have fair skin that freckles easily, often those with red or blond hair and blue or light-colored eyes. The primary risk factor is excessive exposure to ultraviolet radiation. The use of sunscreens (particularly on children), hats, and protective clothing is strongly recommended for lengthy outdoor excursions.

The most common warning sign of skin cancer is a growth or a sore that does not heal. Skin cancers vary considerably in the way they look. Some begin as a pale waxy lump, whereas others first appear as a firm red lump. Sometimes the lump bleeds or develops a crust. Skin cancer can also start as a flat, red spot that is rough, dry,

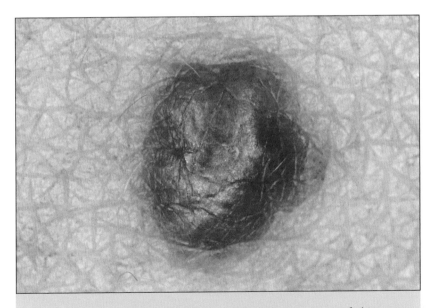

Juvenile melanoma. A malignant melanoma is a type of skin cancer caused by tumors of pigment-producing cells in the epidermis. Malignant melanomas usually start in moles and are caused by mutations induced by ultraviolet radiation in sunlight. They can be fatal if not treated early. *(Biophoto Associates/Photo Researchers, Inc.)*

or scaly. Both basal and squamous cell cancers are found on areas of the skin that are exposed to the sun: the face, neck, hands, and arms. Actinic keratosis, which appears as rough, red or brown scaly patches on the skin, is known as a precancerous condition because it sometimes develops into squamous cell cancer.

Basal and squamous cell carcinomas are generally diagnosed and treated in the same way. When an area of skin does not look normal, all or part of the growth is removed and a portion of the biopsy will be examined under a microscope. Basal and squamous cell carcinoma rarely spread beyond the skin. Melanoma, however, can metastasize to other tissues and organs. CT and MRI are commonly used to assess the invasiveness of malignant melanoma.

7

Cancer around the World

Cancer has become one of the most devastating diseases worldwide—every year about 10 million people are diagnosed with cancer and, of these, more than 7 million will die of this disease. Currently, there are more than 12 million cancer cases worldwide. Every family, in every country of the world, has at least one member afflicted with this disease. The disease burden is immense, not only for the victims and their families, but for the medical establishments that struggle to meet the demand for care and treatment.

In 1948, the United Nations established the World Health Organization (WHO) to help people around the world attain the highest level of health. As part of the fight against cancer, the WHO has collected data on the incidence of cancer worldwide to give governing bodies an estimate of the magnitude of the problem. This information, published every five years in the *World Cancer Report,* provides crucial insights into the causes of cancer and possibilities for treatment and prevention.

THE MAGNITUDE OF THE PROBLEM

Although there are more than 100 different forms of cancer, more than 80 percent of cases involve just 14 types of cancers. WHO has collected detailed information on each of these cancers, for nearly every country in the world.

The most prominent types of cancer in North America are those affecting the breast, colon, lungs, and prostate, accounting for more than 800,000 cases in 2008. Sex-specific cancers, such as those of the breast, prostate, ovaries, and testes, are either very common (breast and prostate cancer) or relatively rare (ovarian and testicular cancers). Other cancers, such as leukemia or those of the lungs and colon, affect both sexes with roughly equal frequencies. A notable exception to this trend is bladder cancer, which affects almost three times as many males as females. In general, males suffer a greater number of cancers than females.

The general trend in South America is similar to that of North America, except that stomach cancer is much more prevalent. While lung cancer affects both sexes almost equally in North America, there is a clear difference in South America where male cases outnumber female cases by two to one. This is also true for stomach and bladder cancer.

The most prominent cancers in Europe are those affecting the bladder, breast, colon, lung, prostate gland, and the stomach. This is similar to what has been observed in North and South America, except that lung cancer is almost four times more prevalent among the males. Although the magnitude of these cancers seems higher in Europe than in North and South America, when corrected for population size the incidence is similar in all of these locations. Africa shows a similar pattern to that observed in Europe and the Americas, except that lung cancer is not as common, whereas liver

(continues on page 98)

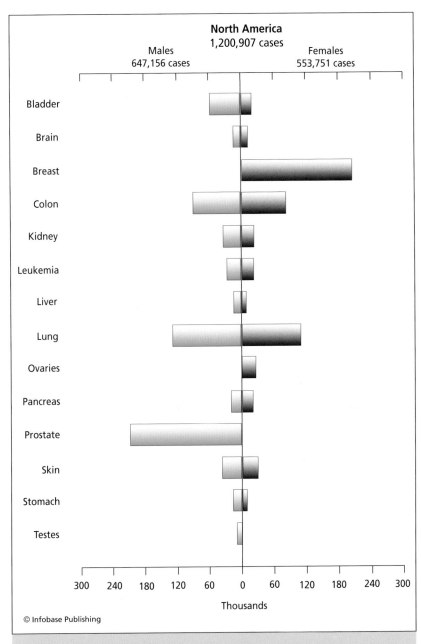

North America
1,200,907 cases

Males
647,156 cases

Females
553,751 cases

Bladder

Brain

Breast

Colon

Kidney

Leukemia

Liver

Lung

Ovaries

Pancreas

Prostate

Skin

Stomach

Testes

300 240 180 120 60   0   60 120 180 240 300

Thousands

© Infobase Publishing

Cancer cases in North America. The data was compiled from information provided by the *World Cancer Report 2008* and the American Cancer Society.

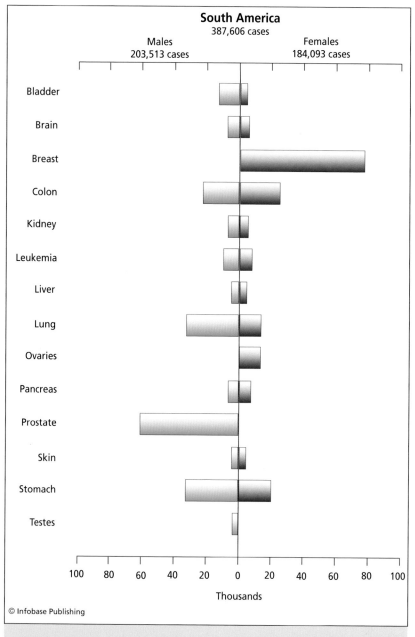

Cancer cases in South America. The data was compiled from information provided by the *World Cancer Report 2008* and the American Cancer Society.

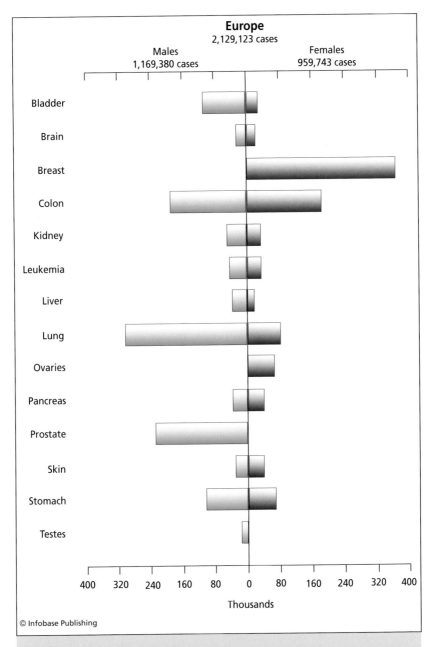

Cancer cases in Europe. The data was compiled from information provided by the *World Cancer Report 2008* and the American Cancer Society.

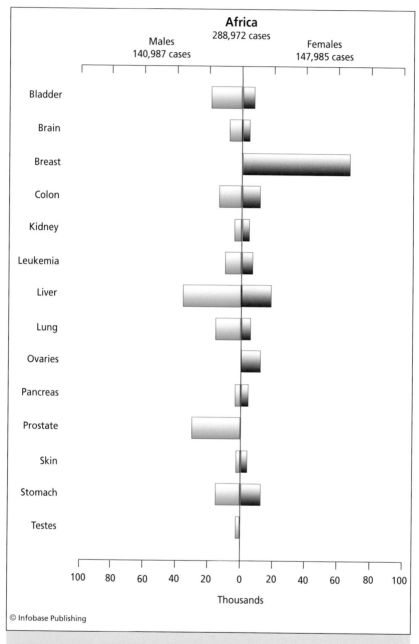

Cancer cases in Africa. The data was compiled from information provided by the *World Cancer Report 2008* and the American Cancer Society.

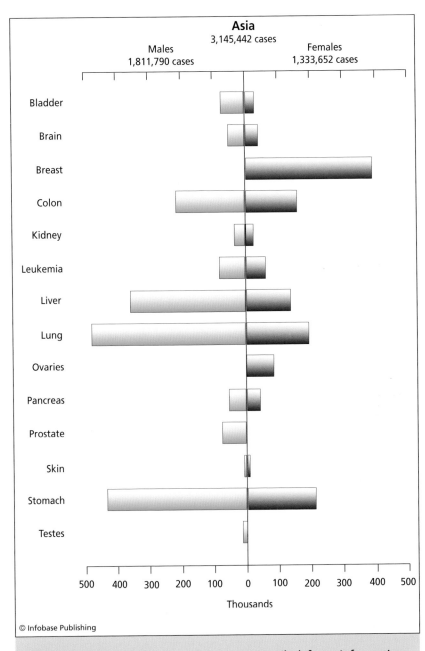

Cancer cases in Asia. The data was compiled from information provided by the *World Cancer Report 2008* and the American Cancer Society.

(continued from page 92)
cancer is prominent. In addition, contrary to other countries, African females have a greater number of cancers than the males.

The cancer profile in Asia is strikingly different than that of other countries. Whereas liver cancer is fairly prominent in Africa, it is relatively rare in the Americas and in Europe. On the other hand, lung cancer is very common in these countries but rare in Africa. In Asia, both lung and liver cancers are very prominent, as is stomach cancer. In Asia, males are much more prone to cancers of the colon, liver, lung, and stomach, than are females.

Africa and South America are the only major regions of the world that record fewer than 1 million cases each year, while North America, Europe, and Asia have between 1 million and just more than 3 million cases each year. The combined total for these countries is just more than 7 million cases in 2008. When other regions of the world are included, such as the Philippines, Australia, and New Zealand, the combined total exceeds 12 million new cancer cases worldwide. The relatively low number of cases recorded in Africa and South America is partly due to inadequate diagnostic facilities, but it may also reflect a regional variation in cancer incidence. The WHO has estimated that the global cancer burden will increase to more than 25 million cases by 2030.

The magnitude of the cancer epidemic defies the medical capabilities of most places in the world. Treatment in North America alone exceeds $1 billion each year, and for the millions of cancer patients who live in poorer countries the treatments are unavailable or too expensive for the local population to afford. Wealthier countries can better afford cancer treatment; this is fortunate for them, since the highest incidence of nearly all cancers occurs in developed countries.

DEVELOPED COUNTRIES HAVE THE HIGHEST CANCER RATES

Of the 14 cancers shown in the accompanying figures, all but two occur with a higher incidence in developed countries (located in

North America, Europe, and parts of Asia). The difference is often profound. Prostate cancer, at the top of the list, is nearly six times more prevalent in developed countries than it is in undeveloped, or less developed, countries (located in South America, Africa, and large parts of Asia). Skin cancer, specifically melanoma, is seven times more prevalent in developed countries, while the remaining cancers are two to three times more prevalent in developed countries. There are two exceptions to this trend: stomach cancer, which occurs with about the same incidence in developed and undeveloped countries, and liver cancer, which is more common in undeveloped countries. The equal incidence of stomach cancer may point to the ingestion of environmental carcinogens that are present throughout the world. (This possibility will be discussed in a later section.) The elevated incidence of liver cancer in less developed countries is likely due to grain storage in equatorial countries, which promotes the growth of a powerful fungal toxin that is known to cause liver cancer. (See the table on page 100.)

Individual comparisons between specific locations, for each type of cancer, show a striking trend. Again, cancers tend to be more prevalent in developed countries. However, in a specific comparison, the magnitude of the difference is staggering. The incidence of prostate cancer in the United States is more than 90 times greater than it is in China. Liver cancer in Mongolia is nearly 30 times more prevalent than it is in Northern Europe, and stomach cancer in Japan is 14 times more common than it is in Africa. These differences are not due to genetic predispositions or resistance to cancers. Chinese who move to the United States develop prostate cancer at a rate typical for the location. Similarly, West Africans develop colon cancer at a higher rate when they move to North America. Scientists interpret the worldwide variation in cancer rates as an indication that most cancers are caused by diet and lifestyle and are therefore avoidable.

THE INCIDENCE OF
COMMON CANCERS WORLDWIDE

CANCER	HIGH INCIDENCE		LOW INCIDENCE	
	LOCATION	INCIDENCE*	LOCATION	INCIDENCE*
Prostate	United States	161.4	China	1.7
Breast	United States	132.5	Mongolia	6.6
Liver	Mongolia	98.9	Northern Europe	3.4
Lung	Japan	76.5	Iran	7.2
Colon	United States	66.5	West Africa	3.4
Stomach	Japan	62.0	North Africa	4.4
Skin	Australia	38.5	China	0.2
Bladder	Egypt	37.1	India	3.2
Ovary	Denmark	14.2	North Africa	2.6
Kidney	Germany	12.3	South Central Asia	1.3
Leukemia	United States	11.2	India	3.1
Brain	Greece	10.5	South Central Asia	2.5
Testes	Denmark	10.3	China	0.4
Pancreas	Japan	9.2	India	1.4

Note: * Incidence is the number of cases per year, per 100,000 population, adjusted for age, thus eliminating effects of population size and age distribution. Cancers for breast and ovary are for women; other figures are for men. Data was compiled from information provided by the World Health Organization and the American Cancer Society for 2008.

CANCER AND THE NORTH AMERICAN DIET

According to the U.S. Centers for Disease Control (CDC), more than 60 percent of American adults are overweight. The typical American diet is high in fat and calories, with insufficient quantities of whole grains, fresh fruits, and vegetables. Whole grain breads and cereals, along with fresh fruit and vegetables, are known to reduce the risk of cancer development, particularly colon cancer. The issue of high- versus low-fat diets has traditionally focused on improving an individual's resistance to cardiovascular disease and diabetes. But recently it has become clear that a high-fat diet is directly responsible for the high incidence of many cancers in developed countries.

Fat is normally thought of as a harmless substance intended for the storage of energy, and historically this has been the case. When human society was based on hunting and gathering, there were periods of the year when individuals would deposit fat as a reserve for the winter months. During other periods of the year, when food was scarce, the fat reserves were depleted and the individual returned to a slimmer physique. Women, during their reproductive years, store fat in preparation for childbirth, but again this deposit was transitory, so that men and women cycled between robust and lean physiques. In recent times, however, there has been a clear trend toward the deposition of permanent body fat, and research has shown a direct link between increased cancer rates and obesity.

Adipocytes, the cells that store fat, increase or decrease in number, depending on the amount of fat being consumed and used. The fat in high-fat diets cannot be metabolized at the rate that it is being ingested, and yet the digestive system is programmed to absorb as much as it can. Consequently, the unused portion is stored in adipocytes, which are capable of proliferating to meet the demand. In other words, development of obesity involves storage of fat and an increase in the number of fat-storing cells. Adipocytes were first identified around the turn of the 20th century, and for more than 90 years these cells were thought of as simple fat-storage depots. This perception changed dramatically in 1995 when several research groups in the United States and Europe discovered that adipocytes synthesize and secrete several growth factors, one of which is called leptin. Leptin has since been shown to be a potent growth factor, capable of stimulating the proliferation of many kinds of cells, including those of the pancreas, liver, lung, stomach, skin, and mammary glands. Even more remarkable is the observation that leptin stimulates the synthesis and secretion of estrogens by adipocytes and by other cells throughout the body, particularly in the ovaries and testes.

The realization that fat cells have an endocrine function came as a surprise to physiologists and endocrinologists. Normally, hormone production is regulated by an area in the brain called the hypothalamus, which in turn, controls the pituitary gland, the so-called master gland of the body. Stimulation of the pituitary gland by the hypothalamus leads to the production and release of pituitary hormones that regulate the activity of secondary glands and tissues throughout the body.

A specific example is the control of the ovaries and the reproductive cycle. In this case, the pituitary gland releases follicle-stimulating hormone (FSH), resulting in the growth and development of ovarian follicle cells. These cells, under the influence of FSH, begin to synthesize and secrete large amounts of the hormone estrogen. The physiological role of estrogen is to stimulate the growth and development of the mammary glands for eventual lactation and of the uterine lining in preparation for fertilization, implantation, and development of the fetus. The ovarian reproductive cycle is characterized by monthly fluctuations in the amount of estrogen released into the blood. After menopause, when the ovaries stop responding to FSH, the level of estrogen in the blood decreases and remains low thereafter. However, because of the endocrine function of adipocytes, obese women have chronically high levels of estrogen in their blood throughout their lives. The constant stimulation of cells in the breast, uterus, and other areas by estrogen and possibly leptin is believed to be the single most important cause of cancer development in these tissues.

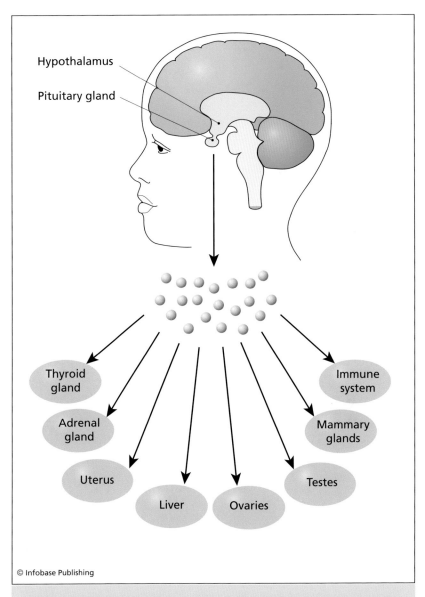

Human endocrine system. This system is controlled by the hypothalamus, which regulates the production and release of various hormones from the pituitary gland. The pituitary hormones, in turn, regulate other glands, tissues, and organs of the body.

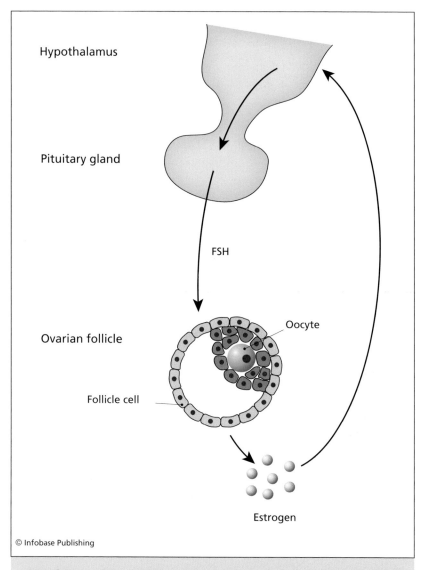

Hypothalamus

Pituitary gland

FSH

Ovarian follicle

Oocyte

Follicle cell

Estrogen

© Infobase Publishing

Regulation of the ovarian cycle. The hypothalamus instructs the pituitary gland to release follicle-stimulating hormone (FSH), promoting maturation of ovarian follicle cells, which in turn begin synthesizing and releasing estrogen. Low estrogen levels stimulate FSH release. High levels of estrogen inhibit the release of FSH but stimulate the release of a pituitary hormone (not shown) that initiates ovulation.

Scientists have shown that obese women have much higher levels of estrogen (130 percent more) than do thinner women. A similar relationship is believed to influence the incidence of prostate cancer in men. In this case, the estrogen produced by the adipocytes over-stimulates the cells in the prostate gland, thus increasing the risk of cancer development. The discovery of leptin and the endocrine function of fat cells provides a direct link between obesity and the high incidence of cancer in the developed world. Breast and prostate cancers are only two of the many cancers that are likely to be induced by a high-fat diet. Additional cancers of the pancreas, liver, lung, stomach, and skin may be attributable to both the elevated levels of sex steroids and to the growth factor leptin.

High fat content is only one element in the North American diet that predisposes people to cancer. A second, and very important, element is insufficient fiber in the diet. Dietary fiber is thought to protect against cancers in general, but most particularly colorectal cancer. Two epidemiological studies examined the relationship between dietary fiber and colon cancer. These studies, involving 519,978 Europeans and 33,971 Americans, are unprecedented for their size and scope. Participants in the study completed a dietary questionnaire and were followed up for cancer incidence. The results showed a clear, inverse relationship between the incidence of colon cancer and intake of dietary fiber. In other words, high fiber intake is associated with a low incidence of cancer. No food source of fiber was more protective than others. That is, the fiber could come from bread, vegetables, or breakfast cereal. The authors of the studies concluded that in populations with low-fiber diets an approximate doubling of total fiber intake from foods could reduce the risk of colorectal cancer by 40 percent.

CANCER AND LIFESTYLE

Although cancer risk increases with obesity and with lack of dietary fiber, many people who are not overweight and eat a healthy diet still develop cancer. A striking example is lung cancer induced by cigarette smoke. This type of cancer is the product of a lifestyle that counteracts the beneficial effects of a healthy diet and slim physique. Another lifestyle variable, excessive alcohol consumption, is associated with increased risk of various cancers, particularly liver cancer. Frequent sunbathing without an effective sunscreen is the greatest single cause of skin cancer (melanoma).

The impact of lifestyle is, of course, exacerbated when poor diet, excessive alcohol consumption, and smoking are combined as is common in North America and Europe. This particular combination almost invariably spells trouble. In rare cases, smokers, for example, have lived long, cancer-free lives, but there are usually compensating elements to their lifestyles. For example, they may not be overweight, or they may have a diet consisting of anticancer foods, such as olive oil, moderate amounts of red wine, and plenty of fruits and vegetables. Such individuals may also have an unusually effective immune system that destroys all cancer cells before they develop into a serious problem.

CANCER AND THE ENVIRONMENT

There are many agents in the environment that can induce cancers in people who are otherwise healthy and careful about what they eat and drink. Two examples of such carcinogens were described in chapter 5: The first involved a fungal carcinogen that causes liver cancer in people living in the Tropics, and the second was asbestos, which damaged the lungs of British factory workers in the 1950s. The incidence of stomach cancer among the Japanese, shown in the table on page 100, may be due to the consumption of fish containing high pesticide or mercury residues.

Food additives, pesticides, and herbicides are believed to be responsible for causing cancers. While many of these compounds have been shown to be mutagens in vitro, there is very little evidence thus far to support their role as carcinogens. Much of the difficulty associated with confirming such a link stems from the problem of distinguishing the effects of a specific pesticide or herbicide from other factors, such as obesity or cigarette smoke. While food additives and pesticides may cause cancer, the number of cases resulting from these carcinogens is believed to be very small compared to the quantity arising from dietary practices (i.e., fat and fiber intake) and lifestyle.

SUMMARY

Cancer is a disease of the genes, but the incidence of this disease is greatly influenced by one's diet and lifestyle. DNA, though a stable molecule, can be damaged by environmental compounds, radiation, and errors in replication that occur during the cell cycle. The cell has very efficient DNA repair systems, but they can only do so much.

A detailed comparison of cancer rates around the world has shown that most cancers are avoidable. DNA damage, at the heart of cancer induction, can be minimized with careful attention to diet and lifestyle. A cancer-resistant diet is low in fat and high in fiber, fruits, and vegetables. A cancer-resistant lifestyle includes regular exercise, no smoking, regular use of a sunscreen, and moderate consumption of alcohol. Studies have shown that these simple measures can reduce the incidence of cancer by almost 40 percent, or 4 million fewer cancer cases worldwide each year.

8

Cancer Therapies

The versatility, adaptability, and extreme hardiness of cancer cells have made it very difficult for scientists to develop methods to either contain or eradicate this disease. Treatment is complicated by the exact nature of the cancer cells, the tissue they arose from, and the tissue or tissues they end up colonizing. Many cancers, such as those affecting the colon or liver, remain tucked away in the darker recesses of the body, where they are hard to detect and even harder to treat. Other cancers, such as melanoma or retinoblastoma, are at or near the surface of the body, and thus are more accessible to observation and treatment. All cancer therapies try to target characteristics that are peculiar to cancer cells so as not to damage normal cells. This could be a mutated protein, a peculiar behavior pattern, such as an increased rate of cell division, or an elevated demand for oxygen to support the cancer cell's high metabolic activity. In some cases, the therapy is followed by an adjuvant therapy to ensure destruction of residual cancer cells. Neoadjuvent therapy, such as surgical reduction of the tumor mass before the main therapy, is also common. Cancer therapies may be divided into seven categories: biotherapy, bone marrow transplants, chemotherapy, gene therapy, radiotherapy, stem cell therapy, and surgery.

BIOTHERAPY

The use of biomolecules, such as antibodies, vaccines, or cell-signaling molecules, to fight cancer cells is known as biotherapy or immunotherapy. Biotherapy may also exploit the properties of the adaptive immune system, which involves the white blood cells (WBCs) called T and B lymphocytes. B lymphocytes produce antibodies tailored for microbe antigens. T lymphocytes, or T cells, are activated by other white blood cells, called monocytes, in a way that alerts the T cell to specific invader antigens. The T cell uses this information to hunt down and destroy those invaders. T cells enlist the aid of other lymphocytes by secreting small signaling molecules called cytokines. A special kind of T cell, called a natural killer (NK) lymphocyte, is activated by the release of cytokines but focuses its attention on attacking and killing infected cells rather than the invading microbe. (See chapter 10 for additional information.) The immune system also attacks cancer cells because they usually contain mutated proteins, displayed on the cell surface, that are treated as being of foreign origin. Biotherapy involves the use of cytokines, bone marrow stimulants, antibodies and vaccines, and angiogenesis blockers.

Cytokines

The first successful biotherapy came with the isolation of a cytokine known as interferon, which stimulates NK cells and seems to have a direct effect on some cancer cells by slowing their growth rate and stimulating more normal behavior. The U.S. Food and Drug

Administration (FDA) has approved the use of interferon to treat kidney cancers, lymphoma, and Kaposi's sarcoma. Other cytokines, called interleukins, have been used to specifically boost the response of T lymphocytes. There are more than 30 known interleukins, but the most promising so far is interleukin-2 (IL-2), which has been approved for the treatment of kidney carcinomas and melanoma. In addition, clinical trials are underway to test the effectiveness of IL-2 as a treatment for cancers of the colon, ovaries, lung, brain, breast, prostate, and bone marrow (leukemia).

Bone Marrow Stimulants

Biotherapies sometimes take a more generalized approach to treating cancer. One such effort involves the use of colony-stimulating factor (CSF) to stimulate cell growth in the bone marrow. Its presence increases the number of WBCs, thus augmenting the immune response, but it also increases the number of red blood cells (RBCs) to improve the overall health and vitality of the patient. RBCs contain the oxygen-carrying pigment hemoglobin and have the very important job of delivering oxygen to all of the cells. Thus, CSF helps ensure that all cells are receiving an adequate supply of oxygen and that the patient does not become anemic. This is an important consideration since the patient may also be receiving chemotherapy or radiotherapy, both of which can damage the bone marrow, leading to an increased incidence of secondary infections and anemia. Administration of CSF can help counteract this effect and, indeed, makes it possible for a patient to tolerate levels of chemotherapy or radiotherapy that would not be possible otherwise.

Antibodies and Vaccines

Special antibodies, known as monoclonal antibodies (MAbs), can be designed to target a specific type of cancer cell or molecules that the cancer cell needs to grow and divide. A single type of B cell, grown in culture, produces these antibodies, which are specific for a single antigen. All the cells in the culture originate from a single founder cell that produces the desired antibody. The cells are thus clones of the original cell, so the antibody they make is said to be monoclonal. MAbs are produced by injecting a single kind of human cancer cell into mice to stimulate the production of antibodies. The mouse cells producing the antibodies are isolated and fused with a culture of immortalized human cells to produce a hybridoma. The hybridomas are also an immortalized cell line and thus can produce a very large quantity of the antibody. Production of MAbs maximizes the specificity of the antibody to ensure that it will not react with, or damage, antigens on normal cells. MAbs can be designed to attack cancer cells directly, or they can be linked to cytotoxic substances that destroy the cancer cell after it encounters the MAb.

Usually, the MAbs are designed to attack cell receptors. Breast cancer may be caused by the lifelong exposure of breast cells to the growth-stimulating effects of the female steroid hormone estrogen. A drug called tamoxifen has been shown to be an estrogen antagonist; it binds to the estrogen receptor, thus blocking the hormone's normal functions. The male counterpart to this strategy involves the use of anti-androgen drugs, specifically to block testosterone receptors, in order to treat prostate cancer. Other MAbs that are used to block cell receptors or their associated enzymes are Avastin (bevacizumab), Erbitux (cetuximab), Herceptin (trastuzumab), and Rituxan. (See the table on page 115.)

In some cases, it is better to have the immune system create the necessary antibodies to fight a specific cancer. This strategy has been used to treat cervical cancer, which is known to be caused by the papillomavirus (PMV). Characterization of PMV proteins has made it possible for scientists to produce a vaccine, which destroys the virus, thus curing the cancer. The anti-PMV vaccine is called Gardasil and was approved for medical use in 2006.

Angiogenesis Blockers

All cells, whether they are cancerous or not, need to be vascularized in order to receive the oxygen and nutrients required to support metabolic activity. Blood vessels also carry away metabolic waste products, such as carbon dioxide, which is expelled from the body at the lungs, and urea, expelled by the kidneys. The circulatory system, consisting of an extensive collection of arteries, veins, and capillaries, provides these essential services. Installing this system requires the formation of new blood vessels, a process that is called angiogenesis.

Angiogenesis is, of course, extremely important during embryogenesis when the circulatory system is being formed and during growth to adulthood. Vascularization during development is so efficient that virtually every cell in the body is less than 4/10,000 inch (100 μm) away from the nearest capillary. Angiogenesis also has many important roles to play during adulthood, such as wound healing, formation of the corpus luteum after ovulation, formation of new endometrium after menstruation, and remodeling the vasculature of skeletal muscle after long periods of exercise.

There are many factors involved in the formation of blood vessels, but the best understood are a tyrosine kinase called vascular endothelial growth factor (VEGF) and a gene regulatory protein called hypoxia-inducible factor 1 (HIF-1). A shortage of oxygen in any cell of the body activates HIF-1, which in turn stimulates production and secretion of VEGF. The VEGF protein induces proliferation of endothelial cells (cells that make up blood vessels) that sprout from the nearest capillary and following the VEGF concentration gradient grow toward the hypoxic cells. Once the cells are vascularized and begin receiving an adequate oxygen supply, HIF-1 is inactivated and production of VEGF drops off, thus terminating angiogenesis.

Tumors, like normal tissue, cannot grow to more than a millimeter or two in diameter without being vascularized, and, consequently, angiogenesis is a prime target for cancer therapy. Clinical trials are currently in progress to test angiogenesis inhibitors on cancers of the breast, prostate, brain, pancreas, lung, stomach, ovary, and cervix, as well as leukemia and lymphomas. So far the studies have had limited success. Endostatin, a widely studied drug that is toxic to endothelial cells, showed great promise in preliminary studies. While it is safe to administer, it has failed to demonstrate antitumor effects. An extract from the oriental fruit *Gleditsia sinensis* (GSE) has been shown to be an effective blocker of VEGF transcription but has yet to progress beyond the basic research stage. Another compound extracted from green tea (GTE) is known to be a powerful blocker of endothelial cell proliferation, but, like GSE, it is still at the preclinical stage of development.

The most successful angiogenesis blocker so far tested is an anti-VEGF antibody called Avastin. This drug has been shown to be effective in clinical trials and was approved by the FDA for routine medical use in 2004. It is used primarily as a treatment for metastatic colorectal cancer. Overall, patients given Avastin survive about five months longer. In addition, the average time before tumors began growing again or new tumors appeared was four months longer than patients who did not receive Avastin. (See the table on page 115.)

BONE MARROW TRANSPLANTS

Transplanting bone marrow (BM) is a common method for treating leukemia and lymphoma. It is also required when radiotherapy is used to treat other forms of cancer, because this therapy often destroys or damages the patient's bone marrow. There are three types of BM transplants, each defined in terms of the donor tissue: autogeneic transplants in which patients receive their own bone marrow, syngeneic transplants in which patients receive BM from an identical twin, and allogeneic transplants in which patients receive BM from unrelated individuals. Autogeneic transplants are most commonly used when chemotherapy or radiotherapy has damaged the patient's bone marrow. Patients suffering from leukemia or lymphoma generally receive syngeneic or allogeneic transplants. Syngeneic transplants are preferred, in order to avoid immune rejection. However, very few patients have identical twins; consequently, the great majority of BM transplants are allogeneic. Allogeneic transplants will be attacked by the immune system, giving rise to a condition known as graft-versus-host disease (GVHD), making it necessary for these patients to take immunosuppressant drugs for the remainder of their lives.

The immune system's decision to accept or reject a given tissue is based on the exact nature of the glycocalyx, the molecular forest covering the surface of each cell in the grafted tissue. The glycocalyx consists of millions of different kinds of glycoproteins that protrude from the cell surface. Immunologists call these glycoproteins cell-surface antigens. Members of the immune system, particularly T lymphocytes, can tell if a cell is foreign or not by examining these glycoproteins. Immunologists have identified many of these glycoproteins and use this information to match donated BM to prospective patients. Given that there are so many different kinds of antigens it may seem like an impossible task. However, some glycoproteins seem to be more important than others, when it comes to invoking GVHD, so immunologists have obtained good results by matching just five or six strong antigens (see chapter 10 for details). Matching BM for a few antigens still leaves many that are unmatched and consequently the grafted tissue will be rejected over time. However, a partial match can still reduce the amount of immunosuppressants the patient must take over a lifetime while improving the long-term survival of the transplanted tissue.

The administration of a bone marrow transplant follows whole-body irradiation to destroy the patient's cancerous bone marrow.

BIOTHERAPY DRUGS

NAME	DESCRIPTION
Avastin	A monoclonal antibody that inactivates the vascular endothelial growth factor receptor. This drug is made by Genentech and was approved by the FDA on February 26, 2004. The active ingredient is *bevacizumab*.
Erbitux	A monoclonal antibody that blocks the human epidermal growth factor receptor. This drug is produced by ImClone and was approved on February 12, 2004. The active ingredient is *cetuximab*.
Evista	An antiestrogen drug that is used to treat breast cancer. Evista enhances estrogen function in the bones but competes with estrogen for binding sites in the uterus and the breast. This drug is produced by Eli Lilly and was approved on September 13, 2007. The active ingredient is *raloxifene hydrochloride*.
Gardasil	A vaccine that targets the papillomavirus, the major cause of cervical cancer. The vaccine is produced by Merck & Co. and was approved by the FDA in June 2006.
Gleevec	A protein tyrosine kinase inhibitor that is used to treat patients with Philadelphia-chromosome-positive chronic myeloid leukemia (CML). This drug is produced by Novartis and was approved on April 18, 2003. The active ingredient is *imatinib mesylate*.
Herceptin	A monoclonal antibody that is used to treat breast cancer. Herceptin binds to, and inactivates, the human epidermal growth factor receptor 2 (HER-2). This drug is produced by Genetech and was approved on September 25, 1998. The active ingredient is *trastuzumab*.
Rituxan	A monoclonal antibody that is used to treat leukemia. Rituxan is designed to inactivate a cell-surface glycoprotein that occurs in normal and malignant B lymphocytes. This drug is produced by Genentech and was approved on November 26, 1997. The active ingredient is *rituximab*.

Note: The drug names are U.S. brand names. The active ingredients are shown in italics.

The side effects of this treatment are due primarily to the incompatibility between the patient's tissues and the foreign immune cells. The patient must take immunosuppressants for the rest of his or her life in order to keep the new immune system from attacking the patient's body.

CHEMOTHERAPY

Certain drugs may be used to kill or inhibit the growth of cancer cells. The nature of a drug varies depending on the type of cancer, its location in the body, the effect it has on normal body functions, and the overall health of the patient. In general, drugs used for chemotherapy damage DNA, block the synthesis of DNA and RNA, or damage the mitotic spindle.

Cancer drugs that damage DNA or RNA effectively block replication (DNA synthesis) or transcription (RNA synthesis). In some cases these drugs lead to the production of defective messenger RNA that is incapable of coding for protein. In some cases, these drugs can induce apoptosis when the cell is unable to repair the DNA damage the drug has caused. Other cancer drugs can block DNA and RNA synthesis indirectly by blocking the formation of their essential building blocks, the ribonucleotides and deoxyribonucleotides. Without nucleotides, the cell cannot replicate, cannot repair its DNA, and is incapable of synthesizing new proteins. Some of these drugs are either alkylating agents or nucleotide analogs. An alkylating agent adds a molecule, such as a methyl group, to a nucleotide. These corrupted nucleotides block transcription when they are incorporated into a growing chain of DNA. Scientists create nucleotide analogs by replacing some of the hydrogen atoms with fluorine atoms. Examples of these drugs are Gemzar (gemcitabine), fluorouracil, cisplatin, carboplatin, and Temodar. (See the table on page 119.)

Several drugs have been developed that can damage the mitotic spindle, a collection of microtubules that serve to carry the chromosomes to opposite poles of a dividing cell. Disruption of the spindle is an effective way of blocking cell division. As explained in chapter 10, this structure is a collection of microtubules that serves to carry the chromosomes to opposite poles of a dividing cell. Drugs in this class include Taxol (paclitaxel) and Taxotere (docetaxel).

Breast, prostate, and blood cancers often spread to the bones, which can lead to fractures, bone marrow suppression, spinal cord compression, and hypercalcemia (high blood calcium levels). Bisphosphonates are drugs that stimulate bone repair and have been used for several years to treat osteoporosis (a disease that weakens the bones).

Researchers have shown that bisphosphonates can also slow the progression of bone metastasis and may even block metastasis in newly diagnosed patients with stage I breast cancer. For reasons that are still unclear, breast cancer cells can stimulate osteoclasts, a type of bone cell that is involved in bone remodeling and repair. Osteoclasts dissolve bone in preparation for bone repair and re-building, which is carried out by a second type of bone cell called an osteoblast. Osteoclasts, stimulated by breast cancer cells, in-hibit the osteoblasts and, in turn, stimulate the cancer cells. Thus, bone remodeling shifts toward bone destruction, decreasing bone density, and accounting for the increased incidence of bone frac-tures and high blood calcium levels. Zometa (zoledronic acid) is a bisphosphonate commonly used as a cancer drug. (See the table on page 120.)

Finally, several chemotherapy drugs are available that block cell receptors. Breast cancer may be caused by the lifelong exposure of breast cells to the growth-stimulating effects of the female steroid hormone estrogen. Under normal circumstances, the effects of estro-gen are essential for the growth of breast cells leading to the produc-tion of milk after a woman gives birth. However, if a tumor appears in the breast, a reasonable strategy is to neutralize the stimulatory effects of estrogen in the hope that it will arrest the growth of the cancer. A drug called tamoxifen has been shown to be an estrogen antagonist; that is, it binds to the estrogen receptor, thus blocking the hormone's normal functions. The male counterpart to this strategy involves the use of anti-androgen drugs, specifically to block testosterone receptors to treat prostate cancer. Other drugs that are used to block cell receptors or their associated enzymes are Evista (raloxifene) and Gleevec (imatinib mesylate).

The FDA currently lists several hundred cancer drugs that have been approved for medical therapy since 1949. The following table shows examples of these various drug categories. All of these drugs vary with regard to administration and side effects.

Administration

Chemotherapy may be administered daily, weekly, or monthly but generally occurs in cycles that include long rest periods, giving the body a chance to recover. Normally the drugs are administered intravenously (IV), although some may be taken as a pill or in the case of surface cancers, such as melanoma, applied directly to the skin. Patients requiring many IV treatments are fitted with a catheter, a soft flexible tube that is inserted into a large vein, thus avoiding the necessity of daily injections.

Side Effects

Drugs used in chemotherapy are designed to target cancer cells, but they often damage or kill normal cells as well. Death of normal cells leads to a variety of side effects, some of them quite severe. Cancer drugs target actively dividing cells; consequently, any normal tissue consisting of proliferating cells will also be affected, most notably the bone marrow, digestive tract, testes, ovaries, and hair follicles. Some drugs may also affect post-mitotic cells in the heart, kidney, bladder, lungs, and nervous system. In some cases, these tissues may be permanently damaged. Given the range of tissues affected, it is not surprising that chemotherapy is often associated with a large

CHEMOTHERAPY DRUGS

NAME	DESCRIPTION
Camptosar	This drug blocks DNA synthesis and is used to treat colon cancer. Camptosar is manufactured by Pfizer Inc. and was approved on June 14, 1996. The active ingredient is *irinotecan hydrochloride*.
Carboplatin	A platinum-based drug that blocks DNA synthesis and is used to treat a variety of cancers. Carboplatin is manufactured by Sandoz and was approved on March 18, 2005. The active ingredient is *carboplatin*.
Cisplatin	The first member of a family of platinum-based drugs that block DNA synthesis. More effective than carboplatin but with serious side effects. This drug is made by Novartis and was approved on November 7, 2000. The active ingredient is *cisplatin*.
Gemzar	This drug is a nucleotide analog in which some of the hydrogen atoms of cytosine have been replaced with fluorine, thus producing fluorocytosine. Gemzar is sold by Eli Lilly and was approved on May 15, 1996. The active ingredient is *Gemcitabine hydrochloride*.
Tamoxifen	An antiestrogen drug that is used to treat breast cancer. Tamoxifen competes with estrogen for binding sites in target tissues such as the breast. This drug is produced by Teva and was approved on February 20, 2003. (The original formulation was approved in 1977.) The active ingredient is *tamoxifen citrate*.
Taxol	A natural product obtained from the plant *Taxus baccata* that is used to treat ovarian and bladder cancer. Taxol inhibits cancer growth by blocking cell division. This drug is manufactured by Bristol-Myers-Squibb and was approved on December 29, 1992. The active ingredient is *paclitaxel*.

(continues)

CHEMOTHERAPY DRUGS

(continued)

NAME	DESCRIPTION
Taxotere	A natural product extracted from the yew plant that blocks cell division. This drug, which is used to treat prostate cancer, is produced by Sanofi Aventis and was approved on May 14, 1996. The active ingredient is *docetaxel*.
Temodar	An alkylating agent that is used to treat brain cancer and melanoma. This drug is produced by Schering and was approved on February 27, 2009. (The original formulation was approved in 1999.) The active ingredient is *temozolomide*.
Zometa	A drug that stimulates bone repair and can also block metastasis in some forms of cancer. Zometa is made by Novartis and was approved on August 20, 2001. The active ingredient is *zoledronic acid*.

Note: The drug names are U.S. brand names. The active ingredients are shown in italics.

number of side effects: fatigue, nausea and vomiting, pain, hair loss, anemia, secondary infections, and poor blood clotting.

Fatigue

Feeling tired, with a complete lack of energy, is the most common symptom reported by cancer patients. This is partly due to the stress of hospitalization and the lack of sleep this may entail, but it is mainly the result of low blood counts and poor appetite brought on by the cancer drugs.

Nausea and Vomiting

This side effect is due almost entirely to the death of epithelial cells lining the digestive tract. These are actively dividing cells that are very sensitive to chemotherapy. Anticancer drugs are designed to minimize this side effect, but residual discomfort may be minimized with antinausea treatments.

Pain

Chemotherapy sometimes damages neurons in the peripheral nervous system, leading to burning, numbness, and tingling or shooting pain, usually in the fingers or toes. Some cancer drugs can also cause mouth sores, headaches, muscle pain, and stomach pain associated with nausea and vomiting. These pains are usually no more severe than those accompanying a flu and are treated with common painkillers such as aspirin or Tylenol.

Hair Loss

Hair follicles, like intestinal epithelium, are actively dividing cells that are killed by chemotherapy. The death of these cells is responsible for the loss of hair, not only on the head, but over the entire body. The hair grows back when chemotherapy is discontinued, but sometimes the new hair is a different color or a different texture.

Anemia

Chemotherapy greatly reduces the bone marrow's ability to make red blood cells (RBC); consequently, the amount of oxygen reaching the cells is reduced. A decrease in the RBC count leads to a condition known as anemia, the symptoms of which include shortness of breath, dizziness, and a feeling of being tired and weak. In severe cases, anemia can be treated with a blood transfusion or with a growth factor called erythropoietin that stimulates the formation of red blood cells.

Infection

In addition to reducing production of RBCs, chemotherapy also reduces the production of white blood cells (WBC), the cells of the immune system. Consequently, the patient becomes more susceptible to infections and must take precautions, such as staying away from people who have a cold or flu and avoiding sharp objects that might cut the skin, including sewing needles and razors. Treating the patient with colony-stimulating factor, a type of hormone that promotes the growth and differentiation of white blood cells, offsets the reduction in the WBC count.

Blood Clotting Problems

In addition to RBC and WBC, the bone marrow produces a third kind of blood cell, called platelets, that is needed for the blood to clot properly. In the absence of external cuts, low platelet counts can lead to excessive bruising, red spots under the skin, blood in the urine, bleeding nose and gums, and headaches.

GENE THERAPY

Since cancer is a disease of the genes it can, in theory, be treated by either repairing the defective gene or by introducing a normal copy of the gene into the affected tissue. This procedure, known as gene therapy, was pioneered in the 1990s to treat genetic deficiencies of the immune system. Since that time, more than 600 gene therapy trials have been launched in the United States alone, of which 60 percent are designed to treat various types of cancer.

Introducing a gene into a cell is a complex and often dangerous business that depends on the natural ability of viruses to infect cells. Some RNA viruses, called retroviruses, have the added ability to incorporate their genome into cellular chromosomes. Scientists have developed methods for adding a human gene to the retroviral genome so that when the retrovirus infects a cell and inserts its genome into a chromosome it has in effect delivered and installed the therapeutic gene. To be sure, there are many wrinkles in this procedure, and much work is needed to ensure the virus does not damage the cell or the patient and that the therapeutic gene is expressed at levels sufficient to cure the cancer. (See chapter 10 for a gene therapy primer.)

Most of the gene therapy trials aimed at treating cancer introduce a normal copy of the tumor suppressor gene *P53*. As described in chapter 3, *P53* codes for a protein (P53) that blocks cell division in abnormal cells and can, if necessary, force defective cells to commit suicide. The *P53* gene is abnormal in more than half of all cancers and is thus a prime target for therapy. *P53* therapy clinical trials are currently under way to treat cancers of the ovaries, breast, prostate, head and neck, liver, and bone marrow (leukemia). Other genes, specific for breast cancer (*Brca1* and *Brca2*), melanoma (*Cdkn2,* or cyclin-dependent kinase N2), and colon cancer (*Msh1* and *Msh2*) are also the subjects of gene therapy trials.

Side effects associated with gene therapy are invariably due either to immune attack on the cells that become infected with the vector (the virus carrying the therapeutic gene) or to complications resulting from insertional mutagenesis, whereby the vector damages a cellular gene when it inserts itself into a chromosome. In the former case, the immune response can be so extreme as to lead to multiorgan failure and subsequent death of the patient. In the latter case, insertional mutagenesis can produce additional cancers.

RADIOTHERAPY

The use of ionizing radiation to destroy cancer cells and tumors is known as radiation therapy, X-ray therapy, irradiation, or simply radiotherapy. This therapy relies on high-energy electromagnetic beams or subatomic particles to damage the DNA in cancer cells so that the cell is incapable of dividing and quickly dies. The main goal is to kill the cancer cells while leaving the normal cells intact. This can be achieved in some cases by focusing the beam of radiation on specific parts of the body or, if possible, directly on the cancerous tumor. Thus radiotherapy has the potential for greater precision than some forms of chemotherapy and produces fewer side effects.

Most patients receive external radiotherapy, in which a machine directs the high-energy radiation at the site of the tumor. The most common type of radiation machine is called a linear accelerator.

This machine heats a radioactive substance, such as cobalt-60, causing it to liberate high-energy rays. Accelerators can produce X-rays and gamma rays (from cobalt), as well as protons and neutrons. Internal radiotherapy is also possible, in which a radioactive material is sealed inside a holder which is implanted near or within a tumor. This procedure is sometimes used after a tumor has been removed surgically. The implant is placed in the tumor bed (the area previously occupied by the tumor) to kill any residual cancer cells.

For most types of cancer, radiotherapy is given five days a week for six or seven weeks. The total dose of radiation depends on the size of the tumor, but normally many small doses of daily radiation are preferred to fewer but larger doses in order to minimize damage to surrounding tissue. This strategy is augmented by the recent development of computer-based radiotherapy, which allows precise mapping of the tumor and surrounding tissue so that multiple beams can be shaped to the contour of the treatment area. This type of radiotherapy is used extensively to treat prostate cancer, lung cancer, and certain brain tumors. Radiotherapy is also used to treat cancers of the skin, tongue, breast, uterus, and bone marrow. Side effects are as broad as those described for chemotherapy, although less severe.

STEM CELL THERAPY

Stem cells are progenitor cells, capable of differentiating into many different cell types that reside in various parts of the body. These cells are used to restore bone marrow in patients who have received chemotherapy, or radiotherapy, for a variety of cancers, but are most commonly used to treat leukemia and lymphomas. In the latter case, the patient's cancerous bone marrow or lymph glands are destroyed with radiotherapy and then reconstituted using stem cells.

Stem cell therapy is similar to the use of bone marrow transplants but has three major advantages: First, the cells are easily isolated from peripheral blood or from umbilical cord blood; second, stem cells are less likely to invoke graft-versus-host disease (GVHD), particularly those from umbilical cord blood, thus most patients do not require immunosuppressants; third, because of reduced risk of GVHD, the donor tissue can be allogeneic, and there is no need for tissue matching.

The patient receives the stem cells through a venous catheter placed in a large vein in the neck or chest area. The cells travel to the bone marrow, where they produce new white blood cells, red blood cells, and platelets in a process called engraftment. Reconstitution of the bone marrow takes several weeks, although full recovery of the immune system can take a year or more. The most severe side effect associated with this therapy is the risk of serious infections developing during the period of bone marrow reconstitution. Other side effects, such as nausea, vomiting, and hair loss, are due to the radiotherapy.

SURGERY

Surgical removal of a tumor usually precedes chemotherapy or radiotherapy whenever possible. This is accomplished using traditional scalpel-based surgical procedures as well as more recent techniques such as cryosurgery, laser surgery, and photodynamic laser surgery.

Cryosurgery

Freezing cancer cells or tumors with liquid nitrogen -320 °F (-196 °C) is called cryosurgery. For external tumors of the skin, liquid nitrogen is applied with a very fine spray gun. For internal locations, surgeons use an instrument called a cryoprobe that is placed in contact with the tumor. Ultrasound imaging is sometimes used to monitor the placement of the probe and freezing of the tissue. The treatment generally involves three freeze-thaw cycles to ensure destruction of the cancer cells.

Cryosurgery is used to treat skin, prostate, lung, and cervical cancers. Research is in progress to test the effectiveness of this treatment on other types of cancers, such as cancers of bone, brain, spine, and windpipe. This procedure offers several advantages over other forms of treatment. The procedure is less invasive than traditional surgery, requiring only a small incision in the skin for insertion of the cryoprobe and imaging tube. Treatment is highly localized, with minimal damage to surrounding tissue, and can be repeated many times. The main disadvantage with this procedure is that it is restricted to tumors confined to a small area. In addition, cancer cells that have separated from the main tumor mass will be missed. Consequently, cryosurgery is often used in conjunction with chemotherapy or radiotherapy.

Cryosurgery does have some side effects, but they are much less severe than those associated with other forms of therapy. Used on liver cancers, the procedure will sometimes damage the bile ducts or major blood vessels, leading to hemorrhage (extensive bleeding) or infection. Cryosurgery of the prostate gland can damage the urinary tract and local nerves, leading to sexual impotence and incontinence (lack of control over urine flow), although these side effects are often temporary.

Laser Surgery

Some cancers may be treated with high-intensity light—a laser—that shrinks or destroys localized tumors. This treatment is often required to treat cancers that are resistant to chemotherapy or radiotherapy. Three types of lasers are currently in use: carbon dioxide (CO_2), neodymium aluminum garnet (NAG), and argon lasers. The CO_2 laser, being of medium intensity, is best suited for treating skin cancers and other superficial tumors. The NAG laser is high intensity and can penetrate deeper into tissue than light from other lasers. The light can be carried through optical fibers to organs and tissue deep within the body. The argon laser has the lowest intensity and is used to treat the most superficial skin lesions. It is also used in photodynamic therapy (described below).

CO_2 and NAG lasers are used routinely to treat cancers of the vocal cords, skin, lung, vagina, and colon. The side effects associated with this form of cancer therapy are the same as those for cryosurgery.

Photodynamic Laser Surgery

Treatment using the argon laser, in conjunction with photosensitizing agents, to destroy cancer cells and tumors is called photodynamic therapy. The photosensitizing agent is injected into the bloodstream and absorbed by cells throughout the body. The agents are designed to remain in cancer cells longer than in normal cells. When the treated cancer cells are exposed to the argon laser light, the agent absorbs the light energy, causing it to release oxygen free radicals that kill the cells. The timing of the therapy is important. It must be given after the agent has left normal cells but is still present in cancer cells. In 1998, the FDA approved the use of an agent called porfimer sodium (Photofrin) for the treatment of lung cancer. Several clinical trials are also underway to test the effectiveness of Photofrin on cancers of the bladder, brain, larynx, and oral cavity.

The side effects associated with this therapy can be severe. Photofrin makes the skin and eyes sensitive to light for six weeks or more after treatment. Patients have to avoid sunlight and bright indoor light. Moderate exposure to daylight can result in red, swollen, and blistered skin. Other temporary side effects include coughing, difficulty swallowing, abdominal pain, painful breathing, and shortness of breath. Photodynamic laser surgery was introduced by Dr. Julia Levi, who is professor emeritus in the department of microbiology and immunology at the University of British Columbia.

Clinical Trials

The fight against cancer is waged on three fronts simultaneously: in research laboratories, where scientists are trying to learn more about cancer cells, in the hospitals where patients are treated with the various therapies previously described, and in clinical trials where new procedures or modifications to preexisting methods are tested for their effectiveness. (The design of clinical trials is discussed in chapter 10.) Several hundred cancer-related trials are underway in the United States alone. This chapter will discuss a representative sample of trials that were concluded and published between 2005 and 2009. The cancer drugs used in these trials were discussed in chapter 8.

BLADDER CANCER

In many cases, the only treatment for bladder cancer is to remove the bladder (cystectomy). But recently, a phase II clinical trial sponsored by the National Cancer Institute (NCI) tested a combination of three cancer drugs for their ability to block the spread of this type of cancer. The trial included only patients who were eligible for cystectomy, in the event that the bladder-preserving therapy failed.

In the trial, headed by Dr. James Montie at the University of Michigan, 68 patients with invasive bladder cancer received three cycles of chemotherapy, which included Taxol (paclitaxel) and carboplatin on day one, and Gemzar (gemcitabine) on days one and eight of each 21-day cycle. These drugs are potent blockers of DNA replication and cell division. Taxol blocks mitosis by binding to microtubules. Carboplatin is a DNA alkylating agent that blocks DNA synthesis (replication). Gemzar is a nucleotide analog of cytosine called fluorocytosine. The incorporation of this analog into a growing DNA chain blocks replication. These drugs effectively blocked the spread of the cancer, but the researchers found a greater than anticipated toxicity. Some of the more serious side effects associated with these drugs include fever, difficulty swallowing, shortness of breath, exhaustion, chest pains, and neutropenia (a blood disorder characterized by a loss of neutrophils, a type of white blood cell).

This study, entitled "Phase II Trial of Paclitaxel, Carboplatin, and Gemcitabine in Patients with Locally Advanced Carcinoma of the Bladder" was published in 2008 in the *Journal of Urology*.

BRAIN CANCER

Gliomas, such as anaplastic oligodendroglioma (AO), anaplastic astrocytoma (AA), and glioblastoma multiforme (GBM), are the most common forms of brain cancer. High-grade gliomas are extremely aggressive tumors that are nearly impossible to cure with conventional surgery or radiotherapy. The main obstacle to surgery is tumor infiltration of surrounding brain tissue, and radiotherapy frequently leads to neurotoxicity. Consequently, glioma patients rarely survive for more than two years.

A multicenter team, headed by Dr. Casilda Balmaceda, tested a second-generation alkylating agent Temodar (temozolomide) in a

Phase II trial on high-grade gliomas. This trial enrolled 120 patients with AO, AA, or GBM. An initial oral dose of Temodar was followed by nine consecutive doses every 12 hours. The treatment cycle was repeated every 28 days and the dose was either increased or decreased slightly depending on the presence or absence of serious side effects. This procedure is in contrast to earlier trials that used a once-daily dosing protocol.

The results showed that a twice-daily regimen is more effective than previous regimens. In some cases, the median overall survival was nearly double that for a once-daily treatment regime. The researchers suggest that survival could be increased further by increasing the dose twofold and administering the treatment in four to six cycles. This study, entitled "Multi-Institutional Phase II Study of Temozolomide Administered Twice Daily in the Treatment of Recurrent High-Grade Gliomas" was published in 2008 in the journal *Cancer*.

In another study, Japanese scientists, led by Dr. Shuichi Izumoto, tested biotherapy (or immunotherapy) as a treatment for glioblastoma multiforme. The trial, entitled "Phase II Clinical Trial of Wilms Tumor 1 Peptide Vaccination for Patients with Recurrent Glioblastoma Multiforme," was published in the *Journal of Neurosurgery* in 2008. The usual treatment for gliomas is surgery followed by chemotherapy, which is only moderately effective. In such cases, patient survival is about 14 months on average with a two-year survival rate of 26 percent.

Recent studies have identified a large number of tumor-associated antigens that could be used as targets for cancer vaccination. One of the identified antigens is the product of the Wilms tumor gene, *Wt1*, which is known to be responsible for cancer of the kidneys (first described by Dr. Max Wilms, a German surgeon). Researchers have shown that gliomas, and many other types of cancer, overexpress the Wt1 protein making it a good target for immunotherapy.

Izumoto's team enrolled 21 patients in a trial to test the effectiveness of Wt1 vaccine therapy against recurrent or progressive glioblastoma. The patients were injected with the vaccine once weekly for 12 consecutive weeks, after which the response was evaluated with magnetic resonance imaging (MRI). If an effect was observed after the 12 vaccinations, Wt1 vaccination was continued at one-week intervals until tumor progression was observed. More than half of the patients responded to the therapy: tumor regression in two patients and stable disease in 10 patients. Nine of the patients experienced progressive disease (i.e., the tumors continued to grow). Overall survival of the treated patients was one to two years. This is similar to the survival rate for patients treated with conventional surgery followed by chemotherapy.

While these results may seem to be disappointing, the authors point out that this survival rate was obtained without the serious side effects that always accompany chemotherapy or radiotherapy. Moreover, immunotherapy has tremendous potential and will continue to improve as scientists identify additional antigens. Someday it will be possible to produce a vaccine that is specific for a given cancer. When that happens, the survival rate will increase dramatically.

BREAST CANCER

Breast cancer clinical trials most commonly study the effects of tamoxifen, Taxol (paclitaxel), Evista (raloxifene), Avastin (bevacizumab), and Zometa (zoledronic acid), either individually or in various combinations.

An Italian research group, headed by Dr. Maurizio Belfiglio, conducted one of the most comprehensive studies, which evaluated the effectiveness of tamoxifen after 12 years of follow-up. This Phase III study focused on postmenopausal women with breast carcinoma, aged 50 to 70 years. A total of 1,901 women were randomly assigned to two groups, one of which received treatment for two years and the other for five years. Treatment consisted of a single daily dose (20 mg) of tamoxifen. The results showed that survival between the two treatment groups began to diverge after nine years, with the five-year treatment group showing a 25 percent improvement in overall survival. This study, entitled "Twelve-Year Mortality Results of a Randomized Trial of two versus five Years of Adjuvant Tamoxifen for Postmenopausal Early-Stage Breast Carcinoma Patients," underscored the importance of a five-year treatment schedule and a lengthy follow-up.

In 2009, a research team in Vienna, headed by Dr. Michael Gnant, showed that the effectiveness of Tamoxifen could be increased by adding Zometa (zoledronic acid) to the treatment schedule. A group of 1,803 patients were randomly assigned to two groups, one of which received tamoxifen (20 mg per day) and the other received Tamoxifen with Zometa (four mg given intravenously every six months) for three years. After a follow-up of one year, the results showed disease-free survival rates of 92.8 percent in the Tamoxifen group and 94 percent in the combined treatment group. This trial, entitled "Endocrine Therapy Plus Zoledronic Acid in Premenopausal Breast Cancer," was published in the *New England Journal of Medicine.*

Another trial, conducted by an American team and headed by Dr. Kathy Miller, tested Taxol (paclitaxel) alone and in combination with the monoclonal antibody Avastin (bevacizumab). A total of 722 patients were enrolled in this Phase III trial, half of whom received Taxol and the other half a combination of Taxol and Avastin. The combined drugs nearly doubled the progression-free survival as compared to Taxol alone (11.8 versus 5.9 months). The overall survival rate, however, was similar in the two groups (26.7 versus 25.2 months). This trial, entitled "Paclitaxel Plus Bevacizumab versus Paclitaxel Alone for Metastatic Breast Cancer" was published in the *New England Journal of Medicine* in 2007.

In 2006, an American research team, headed by Dr. Victor Vogel, showed that Evista (raloxifene) is just as effective as tamoxifen in reducing the risk of invasive breast cancer while producing fewer side effects. A 2008 follow-up study, conducted by Dr. Deborah Grady and her team at the University of California, San Francisco, confirmed the effectiveness of Evista but found that it increased the risk of cardiovascular disease. This study, entitled "Reduced Incidence of Invasive Breast Cancer with Raloxifene among Women at Increased Coronary Risk," was published in the *Journal of the National Cancer Institute.*

COLON CANCER

Studies in the early 2000s showed that the daily use of aspirin or certain vitamins (E and C) is associated with a lower risk of developing colorectal adenomas and colon cancer. (Adenomas are abnormal growths, or polyps, that precede the development of most colorectal cancers.) Later studies, however, have not confirmed these results.

In a trial conducted by Dr. Nancy Cook and her team at the Harvard Medical School, nearly 40,000 women were given aspirin (100 mg on alternate days) or a placebo and followed up for 10 years. The study found that the treatment did not lower the risk of colon, breast, or other site-specific cancers. The trial, entitled "Low-Dose Aspirin in the Primary Prevention of Cancer" was published in the *Journal of the American Medical Association (JAMA).* Similar results were obtained in 2008 by a British team, led by Dr. John Burn, on patients known to be genetically susceptible to colon cancer. This study, entitled "Effect of Aspirin or Resistant Starch on Colorectal Neoplasia in the Lynch Syndrome" was published in the *New England Journal of Medicine.*

In 2009, a team at Harvard University, led by Dr. J. Michael Gaziano, conducted a trial to test the effects of vitamins E and C on cancer in men. More than 14,000 male physicians were enrolled in the study, with half receiving 400 IU of vitamin E and 500 mg of vitamin C every other day, while the other half received placebos. After eight years, the results showed that the vitamins had no effect on the incidence of colon cancer, prostate cancer, lung cancer, or other site-specific cancers in middle-aged and older men. This study, entitled "Vitamins E and C in the Prevention of Prostate and Total Cancer in Men" was published in *JAMA*.

An international team, headed by Dr. Eric Van Cutsem, tested a combination of biotherapy and chemotherapy for metastatic colon cancer. In this trial, 599 patients received Erbitux (cetuximab) plus Camptosar (irinotecan) and flurouracil, a drug closely related to Gemzar (gemcitabine). Erbitux is a biotherapeutic drug, whereas camptosar and fluorouracil are chemotherapeutic. An additional 599 patients received chemotherapy alone. Although the combination therapy was more effective at slowing the progression of the disease, surprisingly, there was no difference between the two treatment groups with respect to overall survival.

A breast cancer trial (the Miller trial) discussed above found a similar short-term benefit but no difference in overall survival. A tumor develops from a single cancer cell, but because of the genetic instability and high mutation rate of cancer cells it will eventually consist of many genetic variants. Thus, the results of the Van Cutsem and Miller trials may be due to a shift in the genetic composition of the tumor that was initiated by the therapy. The drugs kill most of the cells in the tumor, but a few genetic variants, which happen to be resistant to the treatment, survive to form additional and apparently fatal tumors.

The Van Cutsem trial, entitled "Cetuximab and Chemotherapy as Initial Treatment for Metastatic Colorectal Cancer" was published in the *New England Journal of Medicine* in 2009.

LEUKEMIA

Leukemia is one of the most treatable forms of cancer. Indeed, complete cures have been possible for some childhood and adult forms of this disease. The most successful therapies involve transplants of bone marrow, hematopoietic stem cells (HSC), or umbilical cord blood, which is another source of stem cells. Prior to the treatment, the patient's cancerous bone marrow is destroyed with full body radiation or with chemotherapy (a process known as myeloablation). Several clinical trials have reported more than a 50 percent cure rate with these therapies.

One such trial, conducted by Dr. Franco Locatelli and his team in Pavia, Italy, tested the effectiveness of HSC transplants on a form of leukemia that affects children as young as two months of age. The HSCs were isolated from bone marrow, peripheral blood, and cord blood. The trial enrolled 100 children (67 boys and 33 girls), ranging in age from about two months to 14 years. The children received chemotherapy, consisting of three alkylating agents, to destroy their cancerous bone marrow before the final therapy was administered. Previous studies had shown that chemotherapy was an effective and safe pretreatment that avoided radiation-induced growth retardation, neurological complications, and secondary malignancies.

The results of this trial were very encouraging. After a five-year follow-up, it was determined that the HSC transplants had cured more than half of the patients. Moreover, they found that reconstituting the patients' bone marrow with stem cells greatly reduced the incidence of graft versus host disease (GVHD). This study, entitled "Hematopoietic Stem Cell Transplantation (HSCT) in Children with Juvenile Myelomonocytic Leukemia" was published in the journal *Blood* in 2005.

In 2009, Dr. Yoshiko Atsuta led a trial in Japan that compared cord blood and bone marrow transplants in adults with acute lymphoblastic leukemia (ALL) and acute myeloid leukemia (AML). This study enrolled 484 patients with AML and 336 patients with AML. All of the patients were at least 16 years of age and myeloablation was carried out with chemotherapy. After a two-year follow-up, the study showed that overall survival was greater among the AML patients who received bone marrow transplants (60 percent versus 43 percent). Overall survival among the ALL patients was about 50 percent for both types of transplants.

These results are important because they show that in some cases bone marrow transplants are more effective than stem cells. The authors suggested that the reason for this is that a stem cell transplant can take longer to reestablish a functional bone marrow. AML is a very aggressive cancer, which leaves the patient in an especially weakened condition. In such cases, any delay in the reconstitution of a healthy bone marrow can be fatal. This study, entitled "Disease-Specific Analyses of Unrelated Cord Blood Transplantation Compared with Unrelated Bone Marrow Transplantation in Adult Patients with Acute Leukemia" was published in the journal Blood.

LUNG CANCER

Non–small cell lung cancer (NSCLC) accounts for about 80 percent of all lung cancer cases. The average five-year survival rate is about 50 percent for patients whose NSCLC is found early and treated with surgery before it has spread to other organs. In advanced-stage disease, chemotherapy offers modest improvements in median survival, although overall survival is poor.

Taxotere (docetaxel), a drug that inhibits mitosis, is the current standard treatment for NSCLC that recurs after chemotherapy. In previous studies, docetaxel improved survival compared with other chemotherapy drugs but was found to cause severe side effects, such as high fever and infections. Other studies have suggested that the experimental drug pemetrexed might be an effective alternative to docetaxel. Pemetrexed is an enzyme inhibitor that interferes with the production of DNA and RNA nucleotides. In the early 2000s, several studies showed that this drug produced response rates of 16 to 23 percent, median survival of seven to nine months and one-year survival rates of 25 to 32 percent. In studies that combined premextred with cisplatin, the response rates were higher (39 to 45 percent) with a one-year survival rate of 50 percent, but serious side effects occurred, including neutropenia.

In 2009, Dr. Robert Pirker and his team tested a combination of biotherapy, using Erbitux (cetuximab), and chemotherapy, using cisplatin, in the hope of finding an effective treatment with less severe side effects. In a Phase III trial, 1,125 patients were randomly assigned to chemotherapy plus Erbitux or chemotherapy alone. The results showed that the combination of Erbitux and cisplatin was more effective than chemotherapy alone (median survival of 11 months versus 10 months). Moreover, the main side effect was an acnelike rash that appeared in 10 percent of the patients. This study, entitled "Cetuximab Plus Chemotherapy in Patients with Advanced non–small-cell lung cancer," was published in the *Lancet*.

Lung cancer often metastasizes to the bones. When a tumor spreads to the vertebrae, the spinal cord can be compressed and can cause some patients to lose mobility or bladder control. Researchers wondered whether surgery to remove the tumor in addition to radiation would benefit patients by alleviating the pressure and stabilizing the spine. Spinal cord compression occurs in 10 to 20 percent of all cancer patients but is most common for lung, prostate, and breast cancers.

A randomized Phase III study of 101 patients compared the advantages of surgery combined with radiation as opposed to radiation alone in relieving spinal cord compression. In this NCI-funded study, as much tumor as possible was removed from the spinal columns of 50 patients, who were then treated with radiation. Fifty-one patients received radiation only. Patients who received surgery in addition to radiation for their spinal compression showed a marked improvement in their ability to walk as compared to patients receiving radiation only. Surgically treated patients also maintained continence for a much longer period. Sixteen patients in each group entered the study unable to walk. Nine patients treated with surgery and radiation regained the ability to walk (56 percent), compared to only three receiving radiation alone (19 percent). The study, entitled "Direct Decompressive Surgical Resection in the Treatment of Spinal Cord Compression Caused by Metastatic Cancer: A Randomized Trial" was published in the *Lancet*.

PANCREATIC CANCER

Cancer of the pancreas is the most deadly cancer of all, with fewer than 4 percent of patients surviving for more than five years. The best chance for long-term survival is complete surgical removal (resection) of the tumor. But even with resection, patients are faced with the likelihood of recurrence. To improve the long-term prognosis, physicians treat these patients with postoperative (adjuvant) chemotherapy and radiation therapy.

In one study, led by Dr. Helmut Oettle, 368 patients with resection of pancreatic cancer were divided into two groups: one group received six cycles of Gemzar (gemcitabine) on days one, eight, and 15 every four weeks for six months, and the second was simply observed for the duration of the trial. After a follow-up of four years, 74 percent of the treatment group and 92 percent of the control group developed recurrent disease (the cancer returned). Disease-free survival after five years was 16.5 percent in the treated group and 5.5 percent in the control group. Thus, even though the treatment had an effect, the rate of recurrent disease was unacceptably high. This study, entitled "Adjuvant Chemotherapy with Gemcitabine versus Observation in Patients Undergoing Curative-Intent Resection of Pancreatic Cancer" was published in *JAMA* in 2007.

More recent studies are throwing everything (resection, radiotherapy, chemotherapy, and biotherapy) at this very aggressive form of cancer. In a Phase II trial headed by Dr. Jordan Berlin at NCI, patients with completely resected pancreatic cancer are being treated with adjuvant chemotherapy and radiation therapy plus additional treatment with either Avastin (bevacizumab) or Erbitux (cetuximab). These two compounds are monoclonal antibodies that target different proteins thought to be important for tumor growth. Bevacizumab blocks the activity of vascular endothelial growth factor

(VEGF), a protein that is necessary for the formation of new blood vessels. Cetuximab blocks the activity of the epidermal growth factor receptor (EGFR), a receptor that promotes cell growth and proliferation. This trial was launched in February 2006 with an enrollment of 126 patients and is expected to run until 2010.

PROSTATE CANCER

Tumors can evade the immune system as long as their surface antigens are close to normal. T cells, when confronted with an ambiguous tumor, will usually err on the conservative side and will fail to destroy the cancer. The decision to leave an ambiguous tumor alone is mediated by a T cell surface protein called Cytotoxic T Lymphocyte Antigen 4 (CTLA4). Dr. Lawrence Fong and his team reasoned that if they could inhibit CTLA4 it might force the T cells to destroy such tumors.

This hypothesis was tested in a trial that enrolled 14 patients. Each subject received an antibody that blocks CTLA4 activity, plus a cancer vaccine made up of a small segment of a protein found on the surface of melanoma cells. The hope was that the vaccine would stimulate the immune system to attack the cancer cells. In previous clinical trials, this type of vaccine alone did not cause melanoma tumors to shrink. The researchers speculated that CTLA4s inhibition of T cell activity might have been responsible for the lack of an effective immune response. Blocking CTLA4 did indeed improve the response to treatment. In two of the patients in the study, all tumors, which included significant metastases in the lung and brain, disappeared completely. A partial response, defined as a 30 to 100 percent decrease in tumor size, was seen in one additional patient. In another two patients, some tumors decreased in size but other tumors continued to grow. Six patients, including all of those whose tumors regressed, experienced significant autoimmune effects in normal tissues in response to the treatment. That is, there were signs that the immune system was attacking not only tumors but normal tissue as well. This is a potentially lethal side effect as it can lead to multiorgan failure. The researchers found, however, that treatment with steroids could eliminate the symptoms of auto-immunity that occurred during the course of the trial. Other side effects of this treatment included skin rashes, inflammation of the colon, and hepatitis. With special treatment, all of these symptoms were resolved, but critics maintain that blocking CTLA4 activity can be more dangerous than the cancer being treated.

This study, entitled "Potentiating Endogenous Antitumor Immunity to Prostate Cancer through Combination Immunotherapy with CTLA4 Blockade," was published in *Cancer Research* in 2009.

Medical personnel have long encouraged men to get regular checkups, including a blood test for prostate specific antigen (PSA), which, if positive, suggests the presence of prostate cancer. The rationale for such screening, as for many cancers, is that early detection will simplify treatment and reduce the number of fatalities.

This assumption was tested by a large American screening trial, in which 38,343 men were offered annual PSA testing for six years. The control group, consisting of 38,350 men, received usual care, which included some screening on a casual basis. After seven years of follow-up, the incidence of prostate cancer was low and the rate of death was about the same in both groups (50 deaths in the screening group and 44 deaths in the control group). This study, entitled "Mortality Results from a Randomized Prostate-Cancer Screening Trial" was published in the *New England Journal of Medicine* in 2009.

SKIN CANCER

Scientists at NCI have recently discovered a way to increase the cancer-fighting capabilities of T lymphocytes. Clinical trials involving an immunotherapy known as adoptive cell transfer successfully treated metastatic melanoma in some patients. In those trials, tumor-infiltrating T lymphocytes (TILs) were harvested from the patient's tumors, grown in tissue culture in order to increase their numbers, and then injected back into the patient. These T cells, by virtue of the fact that they had already encountered the tumor, were self-programmed to target an antigen called Mart-1, which is found on the surface of all melanoma cells. Thus, expanding their population in culture and then injecting back into the patient greatly increases their ability to destroy the cancer cells.

Unfortunately, TILs cannot be isolated from most patients suffering from melanoma. In an attempt to make this strategy effective for patients, scientists at NCI, led by Dr. Stephen Rosenberg, decided to convert ordinary T cells into TILs. This was accomplished by inserting the gene for the Mart-1 receptor into T cells isolated from a patient using gene therapy. These cells were then grown in culture to increase their numbers before injecting them back into the patient. Thus, the patient's T cells were genetically engineered to recognize and attack cancer cells. The Mart-1 receptor, known as a tumor cell receptor (TCR), makes it possible for the T cell to bind to and destroy the cancer cell. This procedure was tested on 17 patients, several of whom experienced cancer regression (i.e., the tumors were destroyed). One month after treatment, 14 of the patients still had 9 percent to 56 percent of their genetically engineered T cells. There were no toxic side effects in any of the patients.

These results, published in the journal *Science* in 2006, represent the first time gene therapy has been used to successfully treat a cancer. Rosenberg's team is now trying to improve the effectiveness of this therapy by developing TCRs that bind more effectively to the cancer cells. They have also isolated TCRs that recognize common cancers other than melanoma.

CONCLUDING REMARKS

The battle against cancer has been long and difficult. The clinical trials discussed above are a clear testament to this fact. With the exception of leukemia, attempts to treat this disease have been largely ineffectual. To be sure, some of the treatments show an effect, but the increased survival among the treated patients is usually measured in weeks or months, rather than years.

Cancer cells are not only a hardy bunch, but a tumor consists of many genetic variants and as a group is capable of resisting a wide range of therapeutic agents. Resection, followed by aggressive radiotherapy and/or chemotherapy, will often drive the cancer into complete remission, but then to everyone's dismay it reappears stronger than ever. By that time, the patient is in such a weakened state that another round of therapy is out of the question, or the recurrent disease has metastasized throughout the body where it is beyond control. These failures serve to highlight the need for more specific therapies that kill all of the cancer without serious side effects. Radiotherapy and chemotherapy can give a patient a little more time, but because these therapies kill cells indiscriminately they often do more harm than good.

The situation would be bleak indeed were it not for stem cell therapy, gene therapy, and biotherapy. These therapies are the wave of the future and will eventually provide real cures for every type of cancer. Biotherapy, or immunotherapy, is likely to become the most effective form of cancer therapy. Owing to the lack of specific targets, current biotherapy trials have met with limited success. The targets for biotherapy are cell-surface antigens that are specific to different kinds of cancer cells. For now, only a few of these antigens have been identified, but that is likely to change in the near future as scientists refine their understanding of the cell membrane and the molecular nature of carcinogenesis.

10

Resource Center

Cancer research depends on an understanding of the cell and the experimental procedures, known as biotechnology, that are used to explore cell structure and function. This chapter discusses the basics of cell biology and biotechnology. Additional discussions are included that cover the following relevant topics: gene therapy, methods for matching tissues, the human genome project, the design of clinical trials, and gene and protein nomenclature.

CELL BIOLOGY

A cell is a microscopic life-form made from a variety of nature's building blocks. The smallest of these building blocks are sub-atomic particles known as quarks and leptons that form protons, neutrons, and electrons, which in turn form atoms. Scientists have identified more than 200 atoms, each of which represents a fundamental element of nature; carbon, oxygen, and nitrogen are

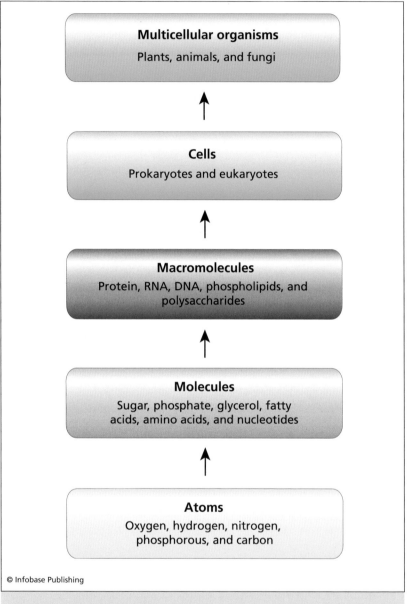

Nature's building blocks. Particles known as quarks and leptons, created in the heat of the big bang, formed the first atoms, which combined to form molecules in the oceans of the young Earth. Heat and electrical storms promoted the formation of macromolecules, providing the building blocks for cells, which in turn went on to form multicellular organisms.

common examples. Atoms, in their turn, can associate with each other to form another kind of building block known as a molecule. Sugar, for example, is a molecule constructed from carbon, oxygen, and hydrogen, while ordinary table salt is a molecule consisting of just two elements: sodium and chloride. Molecules can link up with each other to form yet another kind of building block known as a macromolecule. Macromolecules, present in the atmosphere of the young Earth, gave rise to cells, which in turn went on to form multicellular organisms; in forming those organisms, cells became a new kind of building block.

The Origin of Life

Molecules essential for life are thought to have formed spontaneously in the oceans of the primordial Earth about 4 billion years ago. Under the influence of a hot stormy environment, the molecules combined to produce macromolecules, which in turn formed microscopic bubbles that were bounded by a sturdy macromolecular membrane analogous to the skin on a grape. It took about half a billion years for the prebiotic bubbles to evolve into the first cells, known as prokaryotes, and another 1 billion years for those cells to evolve into the eukaryotes. Prokaryotes, also known as bacteria, are small cells (about five micrometers in diameter) that have a relatively simple structure and a genome consisting of about 4,000 genes. Eukaryotes are much larger (about 30 micrometers in diameter), with a complex internal structure and a very large genome, often exceeding 20,000 genes. These genes are kept in a special organelle called the nucleus (eukaryote means "true nucleus"). Prokaryotes are all single-cell organisms, although some can form short chains or temporary fruiting bodies. Eukaryotes, on the other hand, gave rise to all of the multicellular plants and animals that now inhabit the Earth.

A Typical Eukaryote

Eukaryotes assume a variety of shapes that are variations on the simple spheres from which they originated. Viewed from the side,

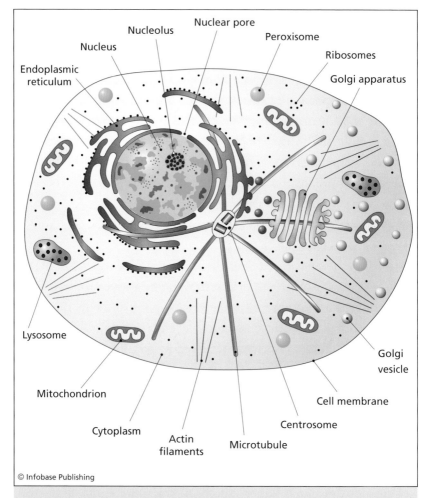

The eukaryote cell. The structural components shown here are present in organisms as diverse as protozoans, plants, and animals. The nucleus contains the DNA genome and an assembly plant for ribosomal subunits (the nucleolus). The endoplasmic reticulum (ER) and the Golgi work together to modify proteins, most of which are destined for the cell membrane. These proteins travel from the ER to the Golgi and from the Golgi to their final destination in transport vesicles (red and yellow spheres). Mitochondria provide the cell with energy in the form of ATP. Ribosomes, some of which are attached to the ER, synthesize proteins. Lysosomes and peroxisomes recycle cellular material. The microtubules and centrosome form the spindle apparatus for moving chromosomes to the daughter cells during cell division. Actin and other protein filaments form a weblike cytoskeleton.

they often have a galactic profile, with a central bulge (the nucleus) tapering to a thin disclike shape at the perimeter. The internal structure is complex, being dominated by a large number of organelles.

The functional organization of a eukaryote is analogous to a carpentry shop, which is usually divided into two main areas: The shop floor where the machinery, building materials, and finishing rooms are kept and the shop office where the work is coordinated and where the blueprints are stored for everything the shop makes. Carpentry shops keep a blueprint on file for every item that is made. When the shop receives an order, perhaps for a chair, someone in the office makes a copy of the chair's blueprint and delivers it to the carpenters on the shop floor. In this way, the master copy is kept out of harm's way, safely stored in the filing cabinet. The carpenters, using the blueprint copy and the materials and tools at hand, build the chair, and then they send it into a special room where it is painted. After the chair is painted, it is taken to another room where it is polished and then packaged for delivery. The energy for all of this activity comes through the electrical wires, which are connected to a power generator somewhere in the local vicinity. The shop communicates with other shops and its customers by using the telephone, e-mail, or postal service.

In the cell, the shop floor is called the cytoplasm and the shop office is the nucleus. Eukaryotes make a large number of proteins and keep a blueprint for each one, only in this case the blueprints are not pictures on pieces of paper but molecules of deoxyribonucleic acid (DNA) that are kept in the nucleus. A cellular blueprint is called a gene, and a typical cell has thousands of them. A human cell, for example, has 30,000 genes, all of which are kept on 46 separate DNA molecules known as chromosomes (23 from each parent). When the cell decides to make a protein it begins by making a ribonucleic acid (RNA) copy of the protein's gene. This blueprint copy, known as messenger RNA, is made in the nucleus and delivered to the cell's carpenters in the cytoplasm. These carpenters are enzymes that control and regulate all of the cell's chemical reactions. Some of the enzymes are part of a complex protein-synthesizing machine known as a ribosome. Cytoplasmic enzymes and the ribosomes synthesize proteins using mRNA as the template, after which many of the proteins are sent to a compartment known as the endoplasmic reticulum (ER), where they are glycosylated or "painted" with sugar molecules. From there they are shipped to another compartment called the Golgi apparatus where the glycosylation is refined before the finished products, now looking like molecular trees, are loaded into transport bubbles and shipped to their final destination.

The shape of the cell is maintained by an internal cytoskeleton comprised of actin and intermediate filaments. Mitochondria, once free-living prokaryotes, provide the cell with energy in the form of adenosine triphosphate (ATP). The production of ATP is carried out by an assembly of metal-containing proteins, called the electron transport chain, located in the mitochondrion inner membrane. Lysosomes and peroxisomes process and recycle cellular material and molecules. The cell communicates with other cells and the outside world through a forest of glycoproteins, known as the glycocalyx, that covers the cell surface. Producing and maintaining the glycocalyx is the principal function of the ER and Golgi apparatus and a major priority for all eukaryotes.

Cells are biochemical entities that synthesize many thousands of molecules. Studying these chemicals and the biochemistry of the cell would be extremely difficult were it not for the fact that most of the chemical variation is based on six types of molecules that are assembled into just five types of macromolecules. The six basic molecules are amino acids, phosphate, glycerol, sugars, fatty acids, and nucleotides. The five macromolecules are proteins, DNA, RNA, phospholipids, and sugar polymers called polysaccharides.

Molecules of the Cell

Amino acids have a simple core structure consisting of an amino group, a carboxyl group, and a variable R group attached to a carbon atom. There are 20 different kinds of amino acids, each with a unique R group. The simplest and most ancient amino acid is

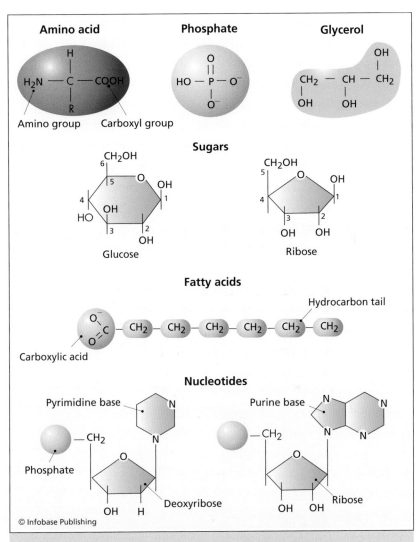

Molecules of the cell. Amino acids are the building blocks for proteins. Phosphate is an important component of many other molecules and is added to proteins to modify their behavior. Glycerol is an alcohol that is an important ingredient in cell membranes and fat. Sugars, like glucose, are a primary energy source for most cells and also have many structural functions. Fatty acids are involved in the production of cell membranes and storage of fat. Nucleotides are the building blocks for DNA and RNA. Note that the sugar carbon atoms are numbered. P: Phosphate, C: Carbon, H: Hydrogen, O: Oxygen, N: Nitrogen, R: Variable molecular group glycine, with an R group that consists only of hydrogen. The chemistry of the various amino acids varies considerably: Some carry a positive electric charge while others are negatively charged or electrically neutral, some are water soluble (hydrophilic) while others are hydrophobic.

Phosphates are extremely important molecules that are used in the construction or modification of many other molecules. They are also used to store chemical-bond energy in the form of adenosine triphosphate (ATP). The production of phosphate-to-phosphate chemical bonds for use as an energy source is an ancient cellular process, dating back at least 2 billion years.

Glycerol is a simple three-carbon alcohol that is an important component of cell membranes and fat reservoirs. This molecule may have stabilized the membranes of prebiotic bubbles. Interestingly, it is often used today as an ingredient in a solution for making long-lasting soap bubbles.

Sugars are versatile molecules, belonging to a general class of compounds known as carbohydrates, that serve a structural role as well as providing energy for the cell. Glucose, a six-carbon sugar, is the primary energy source for most cells, and the principal sugar used to glycosylate the proteins and lipids that form the outer coat of all cells. Plants have exploited the structural potential of sugars in their production of cellulose; wood, bark, grasses, and reeds are all polymers of glucose and other monosaccharides. Ribose, a five-carbon sugar, is a component of nucleic acids as well as the cell's main energy depot, ATP. The numbering convention for sugar carbon atoms is shown in figure 37 on page 149. Ribose carbons are numbered as 1' (1 prime), 2', and so on. Consequently, references to nucleic acids, which include ribose, often refer to the 3' or 5' carbon.

Fatty acids consist of a carboxyl group (the hydrated form is called carboxylic acid) linked to a hydrophobic hydrocarbon tail. These molecules are used in the construction of cell membranes and fat. The hydrophobic nature of fatty acids is critically important to the normal function of the cell membrane since it prevents the passive entry of water and water-soluble molecules.

Nucleotides are building blocks for DNA and RNA. These molecules consist of three components: a phosphate, a ribose sugar, and a nitrogenous (nitrogen-containing) ring compound that behaves as a base in solution (a base is a substance that can accept a proton in solution). Nucleotide bases appear in two forms: A single-ring nitrogenous base, called a pyrimidine, and a double-ringed base, called a purine. There are two kinds of purines (adenine and guanine) and three pyrimidines (uracil, cytosine, and thymine). Uracil is specific to RNA, substituting for thymine. In addition, RNA nucleotides contain ribose, whereas DNA nucleotides contain deoxyribose (hence the origin of their names). Ribose has a hydroxyl (OH) group attached to both the 2′ and 3′ carbons, whereas deoxyribose is missing the 2′ hydroxyl group.

Macromolecules of the Cell

The six basic molecules are used by all cells to construct five essential macromolecules: proteins, RNA, DNA, phospholipids, and polysaccharides. Macromolecules have primary, secondary, and tertiary structural levels. The primary structural level refers to the chain that is formed by linking the building blocks together. The secondary structure involves the bending of the linear chain to form a three-dimensional object. Tertiary structural elements involve the formation of chemical bonds between some of the building blocks in the chain to stabilize the secondary structure. A quaternary structure can also occur when two identical molecules interact to form a dimer or double molecule.

Proteins are long chains or polymers of amino acids. The primary structure is held together by peptide bonds that link the carboxyl end of one amino acid to the amino end of a second amino acid. Thus, once constructed, every protein has an amino end and a carboxyl end. An average protein consists of about 400

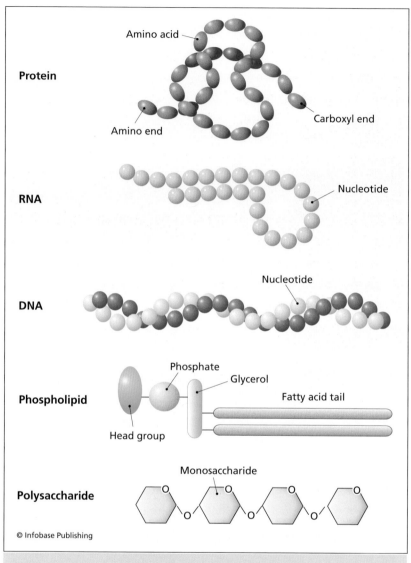

Protein

Amino acid

Amino end

Carboxyl end

RNA

Nucleotide

DNA

Nucleotide

Phospholipid

Phosphate

Glycerol

Fatty acid tail

Head group

Polysaccharide

Monosaccharide

© Infobase Publishing

Macromolecules of the cell. Protein is made from amino acids linked together to form a long chain that can fold up into a three-dimensional structure. RNA and DNA are long chains of nucleotides. RNA is generally single-stranded but can form localized double-stranded regions. DNA is a double-stranded helix, with one strand coiling around the other. A phospholipid is composed of a hydrophilic head-group, a phosphate, a glycerol molecule, and two hydrophobic fatty acid tails. Polysaccharides are sugar polymers.

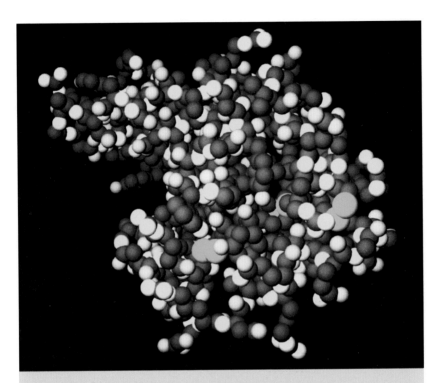

Computer generated model of lysozyme. This enzyme is found in tears and mucus and protects against bacterial infection by literally dissolving the bacteria. *(Kenneth Eward/BioGrafx/Photo Researchers, Inc.)*

amino acids. There are 21 naturally occurring amino acids; with this number the cell can produce an almost infinite variety of proteins. Evolution and natural selection, however, have weeded out most of these, so that eukaryote cells function well with 10,000 to 30,000 different proteins. In addition, this select group of proteins has been conserved over the past 2 billion years (i.e., most of the proteins found in yeast can also be found, in modified form, in humans and other higher organisms). The secondary structure of a protein depends on the amino acid sequence and can be quite complicated, often producing three-dimensional structures possessing multiple functions.

RNA is a polymer of the ribonucleotides adenine, uracil, cytosine, and guanine. RNA is generally single-stranded, but it can form localized double-stranded regions by a process known as

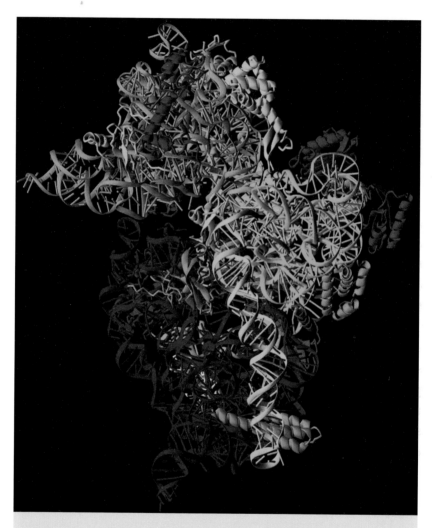

Molecule model of the 30S ribosomal subunit. This consists of protein (corkscrew structures) and RNA (coiled ladders). The overall shape of the molecule is determined by the RNA, which is also responsible for the catalytic function of the ribosome. *(V. Ramakrishnan, MRC Laboratory of Molecular Biology, Cambridge)*

complementary base pairing, whereby adenine forms a bond with uracil and cytosine pairs with guanine. RNA is involved in the synthesis of proteins and is a structural and enzymatic component of ribosomes.

DNA is a double-stranded nucleic acid. This macromolecule encodes cellular genes and is constructed from adenine, thymine, cytosine, and guanine deoxyribonucleotides. The two DNA strands coil around each other like strands in a piece of rope, creating a double helix. The two strands are complementary throughout the length of the molecule: adenine pairs with thymine, and cytosine pairs with guanine. Thus, if the sequence of one strand is known to be ATCGTC, the sequence of the other strand must be TAGCAG.

Phospholipids are the main component in cell membranes. These macromolecules are composed of a polar head group (usually an alcohol), a phosphate, glycerol, and two hydrophobic fatty acid tails. Fat that is stored in the body as an energy reserve has a structure similar to a phospholipid, being composed of three fatty acid chains attached to a molecule of glycerol. The third fatty acid takes the place of the phosphate and head group of a phospholipid.

Polysaccharides are sugar polymers consisting of two or more monosaccharides. Disaccharides (two monosaccharides) and oligosaccharides (about three to 12 monosaccharides), are attached to proteins and lipids destined for the cell surface or the extracellular matrix. Polysaccharides, such as glycogen and starch, may contain several hundred monosaccharides and are stored in cells as an energy reserve.

Basic Cellular Functions

There are six basic cellular functions: DNA replication, DNA maintenance, gene expression, power generation, cell division, and cell communication. DNA replication usually occurs in conjunction with cell division, but there are exceptions known as polyploidization (see the glossary). Gene expression refers to the process whereby the information stored in a gene is used to synthesize RNA or protein. The production of power is accomplished by extracting energy from food molecules and then storing that energy in a form that is readily available to the cell. Cells communicate with their environment and with other cells. The communication hardware consists of a variety of special macromolecules that are embedded in the cell membrane.

DNA Replication

Replication is made possible by the complementarity of the two DNA strands. Since adenine (A) always pairs with thymine (T), and guanine (G) always pairs with cytosine (C), replication enzymes are able to duplicate the molecule by treating each of the original strands as templates for the new strands. For example, if a portion of the template strand reads ATCGTTGC, the new strand will be TAGCAACG.

DNA replication requires the coordinated effort of a team of enzymes, led by DNA helicase and primase. The helicase separates the two DNA strands at the astonishing rate of 1,000 nucleotides every second. This enzyme gets its name from the fact that it unwinds the DNA helix as it separates the two strands. The enzyme that is directly responsible for reading the template strand and for synthesizing the new daughter strand is called DNA polymerase. This enzyme also has an editorial function; it checks the preceding nucleotide to make sure it is correct before it adds a nucleotide to the growing chain. The editor function of this enzyme introduces an interesting problem. How can the polymerase add the very first nucleotide, when it has to check a preceding nucleotide before adding a new one? A special enzyme, called primase, which is attached to the helicase, solves this problem. Primase synthesizes short pieces of RNA that form a DNA-RNA double-stranded region. The RNA becomes a temporary part of the daughter strand, thus priming the DNA polymerase by providing the crucial first nucleotide in the new strand. Once the chromosome is duplicated, DNA repair enzymes, discussed below, remove the RNA primers and replace them with DNA nucleotides.

DNA Maintenance

Every day, in a typical human cell, thousands of nucleotides are being damaged by spontaneous chemical events, environmental pollutants, and radiation. In many cases, it takes only a single defective nucleotide within the coding region of a gene to produce an inactive, mutant protein. The most common forms of DNA damage are depurination and deamination. Depurination is the loss of a purine base (guanine or adenine) resulting in a gap in the DNA sequence, referred to as a "missing tooth." Deamination converts cytosine to uracil, a base that is normally found only in RNA.

About 5,000 purines are lost from each human cell every day, and over the same time period 100 cytosines are deaminated per cell. Depurination and deamination produce a great deal of damage and, in either case, the daughter strand ends up with a missing nucleotide and possibly a mutated gene, as the DNA replication machinery simply bypasses the uracil or the missing tooth. If left unrepaired, the mutated genes will be passed on to all daughter cells, with catastrophic consequences for the organism as a whole.

DNA damage caused by depurination is repaired by special nuclear proteins that detect the missing tooth, excise about 10 nucleotides on either side of the damage, and using the complementary strand as a guide reconstruct the strand correctly. Deamination is dealt with by a special group of DNA repair enzymes known as base-flippers. These enzymes inspect the DNA one nucleotide at a time. After binding to a nucleotide, a base-flipper breaks the hydrogen bonds holding the nucleotide to its complementary partner. It then performs the maneuver for which it gets its name. Holding on to the nucleotide, it rotates the base a full 180 degrees, inspects it carefully, and, if it detects any damage, cuts the base out and discards it. In this case, the base-flipper leaves the final repair to the missing-tooth crew that detects and repairs the gap as described previously. If the nucleotide is normal, the base-flipper rotates it back into place and reseals the hydrogen bonds. Scientists have estimated that these maintenance crews inspect and repair the entire genome of a typical human cell in less than 24 hours.

Gene Expression

Genes encode proteins and several kinds of RNA. Extracting the coded information from DNA requires two sequential processes known as transcription and translation. A gene is said to be expressed when either or both of these processes have been completed. Transcription, catalyzed by the enzyme RNA polymerase, copies one strand of the DNA into a complementary strand of mRNA, which is sent to the cytoplasm where it joins with a ribosome. Translation is a process that is orchestrated by the ribosomes. These particles synthesize proteins using mRNA and the genetic code as guides. The ribosome can synthesize any protein specified by the mRNA and the mRNA can be translated many times before it is recycled. Some RNAs, such as ribosomal RNA and transfer RNA, are never translated. Ribosomal RNA (rRNA) is a structural and enzymatic component of ribosomes. Transfer RNA (tRNA), though separate from the ribosome, is part of the translation machinery.

The genetic code provides a way for the translation machinery to interpret the sequence information stored in the DNA molecule and represented by mRNA. DNA is a linear sequence of four different kinds of nucleotides, so the simplest code could be one in which each nucleotide specifies a different amino acid; that is, adenine coding for the amino acid glycine, cytosine for lysine, and so on. The earliest cells may have used this coding system, but it is limited to the construction of proteins consisting of only four different kinds of amino acids. Eventually, a more elaborate code evolved in which a combination of three out of the four possible DNA nucleotides, called codons, specifies a single amino acid. With this scheme, it is possible to have a unique code for each of the 20 naturally occurring amino acids. For example, the codon AGC specifies the amino acid serine, whereas TGC specifies the amino acid cysteine. Thus, a gene may be viewed as a long continuous sequence of codons. However, not all codons specify an amino acid. The sequence TGA signals the end of the gene, and a special codon, ATG, signals the start site, in addition to specifying the amino acid methionine. Consequently, all proteins begin with this amino acid, although it is sometimes removed once construction of the protein is complete. As mentioned above, an average protein may consist of 300 to 400 amino acids; since the codon consists of three nucleotides for each amino acid, a typical gene may be 900 to 1,200 nucleotides long.

Power Generation

Dietary fats, sugars, and proteins, not targeted for growth, storage, or repairs, are converted to ATP by the mitochondria. This process requires a number of metal-binding proteins, called the respiratory chain (also known as the electron transport chain), and a special ion channel-enzyme called ATP synthase. The respiratory chain consists of three major components: NADH dehydrogenase, cytochrome b, and cytochrome oxidase. All of these components are protein complexes with an iron (NADH dehydrogenase, cytochrome b) or a copper core (cytochrome oxidase), and, together with the ATP synthase, are located in the inner membrane of the mitochondria.

The respiratory chain is analogous to an electric cable that transports electricity from a hydroelectric dam to our homes, where it is used to turn on lights or to run our stereos. The human body, like that of all animals, generates electricity by processing food molecules through a metabolic pathway called the Krebs cycle, also located within the mitochondria. The electrons (electricity) so generated are transferred to hydrogen ions, which quickly bind to a special nucleotide called nicotinamide adenine dinucleotide (NAD). Binding of the hydrogen ion to NAD is noted by abbreviating the resulting molecule as NADH. The electrons begin their journey down the respiratory chain when NADH binds to NADH dehydrogenase, the first component in the chain. This enzyme does just what its name implies: it removes the hydrogen from NADH, releasing the stored electrons, which are conducted through the chain by the iron and copper as though they were traveling along an electric wire. As the electrons travel from one end of the chain to the other they energize the synthesis of ATP, which is released from the mitochondria for use by the cell. All electrical circuits must have a ground, that is, the electrons need someplace to go once they have completed the circuit. In the case of the respiratory chain, the ground is oxygen. After passing through cytochrome oxidase, the last component in the chain, the electrons are picked up by oxygen, which combines with hydrogen ions to form water.

The Cell Cycle

Free-living single cells divide as a way of reproducing their kind. Among plants and animals, cells divide as the organism grows from a seed or an embryo into a mature individual. This form of cell division in which the parent cell divides into two identical daughter cells is called mitosis. A second form of cell division known as meiosis is intended for sexual reproduction and occurs exclusively in gonads.

Cell division is part of a grander process known as the cell cycle, which consists of two phases: interphase and M phase (meiosis or mitosis). Interphase is divided into three subphases called Gap 1 (G_1), S phase (a period of DNA synthesis), and Gap 2 (G_2). The conclusion of interphase, and with it the termination of G_2, occurs with division of the cell and a return to G_1. Cells may leave the cycle by entering a special phase called G_0. Some cells, such as post-mitotic neurons in an animal's brain, remain in G_0 for the life of the organism. For most cells, the completion of the cycle, known as the generation time, can take 30 to 60 minutes.

Cells grow continuously during interphase while preparing for the next round of division. Two notable events are the duplication of the spindle (the centrosome and associated microtubules), a structure

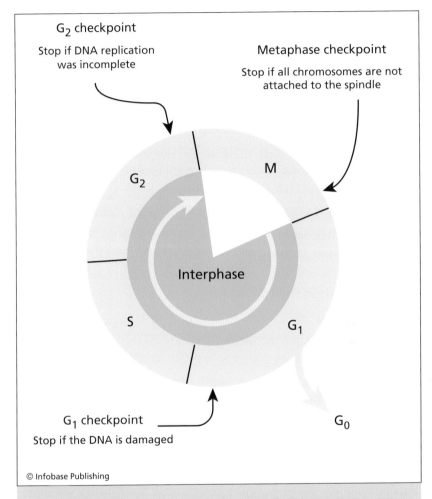

© Infobase Publishing

The cell cycle. Many cells spend their time cycling between interphase and M phase (cell division by mitosis or meiosis). Interphase is divided into three subphases: Gap 1(G1), S phase (DNA synthesis), and Gap 2 (G2). Cells may exit the cycle by entering G0. The cell cycle is equipped with three checkpoints to ensure the daughter cells are identical and that there is no genetic damage. The yellow arrow indicates the direction of the cycle.

that is crucial for the movement of the chromosomes during cell division, and the appearance of an enzyme called maturation promoting factor (MPF) at the end of G_2. MPF phosphorylates histones, proteins that bind to the DNA, and when phosphorylated compact (or condense) the chromosomes in preparation for cell division. MPF is also responsible for the breakdown of the nuclear membrane. When cell division is complete, MPF disappears, allowing the chromosomes to decondense and the nuclear envelope to reform. Completion of a normal cell cycle always involves the division of a cell into two daughter cells, either meiotically or mitotically.

Cell division is such a complex process that many things can and do go wrong. Cell cycle monitors, consisting of a team of enzymes, check to make sure that everything is going well each time a cell divides. If it is not, those monitors stop the cell from dividing until the problem is corrected. If the damage cannot be repaired, a cell remains stuck in midstream for the remainder of its life. If this happens to a cell in an animal's body, it is forced to commit suicide, in a process called apoptosis, by other cells in the immediate neighborhood or by the immune system.

The cell cycle includes three checkpoints: the first is a DNA-damage checkpoint that occurs in G_1. The monitors check for damage that may have occurred as a result of the last cell cycle or were caused by something in the environment, such as UV radiation or toxic chemicals. If damage is detected, DNA synthesis is blocked until it can be repaired. The second checkpoint occurs in G_2, where the monitors make sure errors were not introduced when the chromosomes were duplicated during S-phase. The G_1 and G_2 checkpoints are sometimes referred to collectively as DNA damage checkpoints. The third and final checkpoint occurs in M-phase to ensure that all of the chromosomes are properly attached to the spindle. This checkpoint is intended to prevent gross abnormalities in the daughter cells with regard to chromosome number. If a chromosome fails to attach to the spindle, one daughter cell will end up with too many chromosomes, while the other will have too few.

Mitosis

Mitosis is divided into four stages known as prophase, metaphase, anaphase, and telophase. The behavior and movement of the chromosomes characterize each stage. At prophase, DNA replication has already occurred and the nuclear membrane begins to break down. Condensation of the duplicated chromosomes initiates the phase (i.e., the very long, thin chromosomes are folded up to produce short thick chromosomes that are easy to move and maneuver). Under the microscope, the chromosomes become visible as X-shaped structures, which are the two duplicated chromosomes, often called sister chromatids. A special region of each chromosome, called a centromere, holds the chromatids together. Proteins bind to the centromere to form a structure called the kinetochore. The centrosome is duplicated, and the two migrate to opposite ends of the cell.

During metaphase, the chromosomes are sorted out and aligned between the two centrosomes. By this time, the nuclear membrane has completely broken down. The two centrosomes and the microtubules fanning out between them form the mitotic spindle. The area in between the spindles where the chromosomes are aligned is known as the metaphase plate. Some of the microtubules make contact with the kinetochores, while others overlap, with motor proteins situated in between.

Anaphase begins when the duplicated chromosomes move to opposite poles of the cell. The first step is the release of an enzyme that breaks the bonds holding the kinetochores together, thus allowing the sister chromatids to separate from each other while remaining bound to their respective microtubules. Motor proteins, using energy supplied by ATP, move along the microtubule dragging the chromosomes to opposite ends of the cell.

During telophase, the daughter chromosomes arrive at the spindle poles and decondense to form the relaxed chromosomes characteristic of interphase nuclei. The nuclear envelope begins forming around the chromosomes, marking the end of mitosis. By the end of telophase, individual chromosomes are no longer distinguishable and are referred to as chromatin. While the nuclear membrane reforms, a contractile ring, made of the proteins myosin and actin, begins pinching the parental cell in two. This stage, separate from mitosis, is called cytokinesis and leads to the formation of two daughter cells, each with one nucleus.

Meiosis

Many eukaryotes reproduce sexually through the fusion of gametes (eggs and sperm). If gametes were produced mitotically, a catastrophic growth in the number of chromosomes would occur each time a sperm fertilized an egg. Meiosis is a special form of cell division that prevents this from happening by producing haploid gametes, each possessing half as many chromosomes as the diploid cell. When haploid gametes fuse, they produce an embryo with the correct number of chromosomes.

Unlike mitosis, which produces two identical daughter cells, meiosis produces four genetically unique daughter cells that have half the number of chromosomes found in the parent cell. This is possible because meiosis consists of two rounds of cell division, called meiosis I and meiosis II, with only one round of DNA synthesis. Microbiologists discovered meiosis almost 100 years ago by comparing the number of chromosomes in somatic cells and germ cells. The roundworm, for example, was found to have four chromosomes in its somatic cells, but only two in its gametes. Many other studies also compared the amount of DNA in nuclei from somatic cells and gonads (ovaries or testes), always with the same result: The amount of DNA in somatic cells is at least double the amount in fully mature gametes (they are produced in the gonads).

Meiotic divisions are divided into the four mitotic stages discussed above. Indeed, meiosis II is virtually identical to a mitotic division. Meiosis I resembles mitosis, but close examination shows two important differences: gene swapping occurs between homologous chromosomes in prophase, producing recombinant chromosomes, and the distribution of maternal and paternal chromosomes to different daughter cells. At the end of meiosis I, one of the daughter cells contains a mixture of normal and recombinant maternal chromosomes and the other contains normal and recombinant paternal chromosomes. During meiosis II, the duplicated chromosomes are distributed to different daughter cells, yielding four genetically unique cells: paternal, paternal recombinant, maternal, and maternal recombinant. Mixing genetic material in this way is unique to meiosis, and it is one of the reasons sexual reproduction has been such a powerful evolutionary force.

Cell Communication

A forest of glycoproteins and glycolipids covers the surface of every cell like trees on the surface of the Earth. The cell's forest is called the glycocalyx, and many of its trees function like sensory antennae. Cells use these antennae to communicate with their environment and with other cells. In multicellular organisms, the glycocalyx also plays an important role in holding cells together. In this case, the antennae of adjacent cells are connected to each other through the formation of chemical bonds.

The sensory antennae, also known as receptors, are linked to a variety of secondary molecules that serve to relay messages to the interior of the cell. These molecules, some of which are called second messengers, may activate machinery in the cytoplasm, or they may enter the nucleus to activate gene expression. The signals that a cell receives are of many different kinds, but generally fall into one of five categories: 1) proliferation, which stimulates the cell to grow and divide; 2) activation, which is a request for the cell to synthesize and release specific molecules; 3) deactivation, which serves as a brake for a previous activation signal; 4) navigation, which helps direct the cell to a specific location. (This is very important for free-living cells hunting for food and for immune system cells that are hunting for invading microorganisms.); 5) termination, which is a signal that orders the cell to commit suicide. This death signal occurs during embryonic development (e.g., the loss of webbing between the fingers and toes) and during an infection. In some cases, the only way the immune system can deal with an invading pathogenic microbe is to order some of the infected cells to commit suicide. This process is known as apoptosis.

BIOTECHNOLOGY

Biotechnology (also known as recombinant DNA technology) consists of several procedures that are used to study the structure and function of genes and their products. Central to this technology is the ability to clone specific pieces of DNA and to construct libraries of these DNA fragments that represent the genetic repertoire of an entire organism or a specific cell type. With these libraries at hand, scientists have been able to study the cell and whole organisms in unprecedented detail. The information so gained has revolutionized biology as well as many other disciplines, including medical science, pharmacology, psychiatry, and anthropology, to name but a few.

DNA Cloning

In 1973, scientists discovered that restriction enzymes (enzymes that can cut DNA at specific sites), DNA ligase (an enzyme that can join two pieces of DNA together), and bacterial plasmids could be used to clone DNA molecules. Plasmids are small (about 3,000 base pairs) circular minichromosomes that occur naturally in bacteria and are often exchanged between cells by passive diffusion. A bacterium is said to be transfected when it acquires a new plasmid. For bacteria, the main advantage to swapping plasmids is that they often carry antibiotic resistance genes, so that a cell sensitive to ampicillin can become resistant simply by acquiring the right plasmid. For scientists, plasmid-swapping provided an ideal method for amplifying or cloning a specific piece of DNA.

The first cloning experiment used a plasmid from the bacterium *Escherichia coli* that was cut with the restriction enzyme *Eco*RI. The

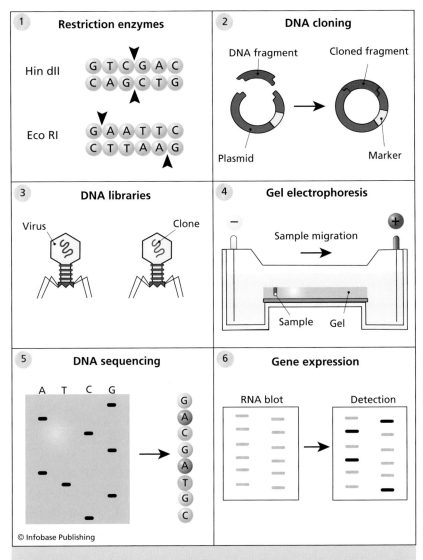

1 Restriction enzymes

Hin dll G T C G A C
         C A G C T G

Eco RI   G A A T T C
         C T T A A G

2 DNA cloning

DNA fragment   Cloned fragment

Plasmid   Marker

3 DNA libraries

Virus   Clone

4 Gel electrophoresis

−   +

Sample migration

Sample   Gel

5 DNA sequencing

A T C G

G
A
C
G
A
T
G
C

© Infobase Publishing

6 Gene expression

RNA blot   Detection

Biotechnology. This technology consists of six basic steps: 1) digestion of DNA with restriction enzymes in order to isolate specific DNA fragments; 2) cloning of restriction fragments in circular bacterial minichromosomes to increase their numbers; 3) storing the fragments for further study in viral-based DNA libraries; 4) isolation and purification of DNA fragments from gene libraries using gel electrophoresis; 5) sequencing cloned DNA fragments; 6) determining the expression profile of selected DNA clones using RNA blots and radioactive detection procedures.

plasmid had a single *Eco*RI site so the restriction enzyme simply opened the circular molecule. Foreign DNA, cut with the same restriction enzyme, was incubated with the plasmid. Because the plasmid and foreign DNA were both cut with *Eco*RI, the DNA could insert itself into the plasmid to form a hybrid, or recombinant plasmid, after which DNA ligase sealed the two together. The reaction mixture was added to a small volume of *E. coli* so that some of the cells could take up the recombinant plasmid before being transferred to a nutrient broth containing streptomycin. Only those cells carrying the recombinant plasmid, which contained an anti-streptomycin gene, could grow in the presence of this antibiotic. Each time the cells divided, the plasmid DNA was duplicated along with the main chromosome. After the cells had grown overnight, the foreign DNA had been amplified billions of times and was easily isolated for sequencing or expression studies. In this procedure, the plasmid is known as a cloning vector because it serves to transfer the foreign DNA into a cell.

DNA Libraries

The basic cloning procedure described above not only provides a way to amplify a specific piece of DNA but can also be used to construct DNA libraries. In this case, however, the cloning vector is a bacterio-phage called lambda. The lambda genome is double-stranded DNA of about 40,000 base pairs (bp), much of which can be replaced by foreign DNA without sacrificing the ability of the virus to infect bacteria. This is the great advantage of lambda over a plasmid. Lambda can accommodate very long pieces of DNA, often long enough to contain an entire gene, whereas a plasmid cannot accommodate foreign DNA that is larger than 2,000 base pairs. Moreover, bacterio-phage has the natural ability to infect bacteria, so that the efficiency of transfection is 100 times greater than it is for plasmids.

The construction of a DNA library begins with the isolation of genomic DNA and its digestion with a restriction enzyme to produce fragments of 1,000 to 10,000 bp. These fragments are ligated into lambda genomes, which are subjected to a packaging reaction to produce mature viral particles, most of which carry a different piece of the genomic DNA. This collection of viruses is called a genomic library and is used to study the structure and organization of specific genes. Clones from a library such as this contain the coding sequences, in addition to noncoding sequences such as introns, intervening sequences, promoters, and enhancers. An alternative form of a DNA library can be constructed by isolating messenger RNA (mRNA) from a specific cell type. This RNA is converted to the complimentary DNA (cDNA) using an RNA-dependent DNA polymerase called reverse transcriptase. The cDNA is ligated to lambda genomes and packaged as for the genomic library. This collection of recombinant viruses is known as a cDNA library and contains genes that were being expressed by the cells when the mRNA was extracted. It does not include introns or controlling elements as these are lost during transcription and the processing that occurs in the cell to make mature mRNA. Thus a cDNA library is intended for the purpose of studying gene expression and the structure of the coding region only.

Labeling Cloned DNA

Many of the procedures used in biotechnology were inspired by the events that occur during DNA replication (described above). This includes the labeling of cloned DNA for use as probes in expression studies, DNA sequencing, and PCR (described below). DNA replication involves duplicating one of the strands (the parent, or template strand) by linking nucleotides in an order specified by the template and depends on a large number of enzymes, the most important of which is DNA polymerase. This enzyme, guided by the template strand, constructs a daughter strand by linking nucleotides together. One such nucleotide is deoxyadenine triphosphate (dATP). Deoxyribonucleotides have a single hydroxyl group located at the 3′ carbon of the sugar group while the triphosphate is attached to the 5′ carbon.

The procedure for labeling DNA probes, developed in 1983, introduces radioactive nucleotides into a DNA molecule. This method supplies DNA polymerase with a single-stranded DNA template, a primer, and the four nucleotides, in a buffered solution to induce in vitro replication. The daughter strand, which becomes the labeled probe, is made radioactive by including a ^{32}P-labeled nucleotide in the reaction mix. The radioactive nucleotide is usually deoxycytosine triphosphate (dCTP) or dATP. The ^{32}P is always part of the α (alpha) phosphate (the phosphate closest to the 5′ carbon), as this is the one used by the polymerase to form the phosphodiester bond between nucleotides. Nucleotides can also be labeled with a fluorescent dye molecule.

Single-stranded DNA hexamers (six bases long) are used as primers and are produced in such a way that they contain all possible permutations of four bases taken six at a time. Randomizing the base sequence for the primers ensures that there will be at least one primer site in a template that is only 50 bp long. Templates used in labeling reactions such as this are generally 100 to 800 bp long. This strategy of labeling DNA is known as random primer labeling.

Gel Electrophoresis

This procedure is used to separate DNA and RNA fragments by size in a slab of agarose (highly refined agar) or polyacrylamide subjected to an electric field. Nucleic acids carry a negative charge and thus will migrate toward a positively charged electrode. The gel acts as a sieving medium that impedes the movement of the molecules. Thus, the rate at which the fragments migrate is a function of their size; small fragments migrate more rapidly than large fragments. The gel, containing the samples, is run submerged in a special pH-regulated solution, or buffer. Agarose gels are run horizontal as shown in the figure. But DNA sequencing gels, made of polyacrylamide, are much bigger and are run in a vertical tank.

DNA Sequencing

A sequencing reaction developed by the British biochemist Dr. Fred Sanger in 1976 is a technique that takes its inspiration from the natural process of DNA replication. DNA polymerase requires a primer with a free 3′ hydroxyl group. The polymerase adds the first nucleotide to this group, and all subsequent bases are added to the 3′ hydroxyl of the previous base. Sequencing by the Sanger method is usually performed with the DNA cloned into a special sequencing plasmid. This simplifies the choice of the primers since their sequence can be derived from the known plasmid sequence. Once the primer binds to the primer site the cloned DNA may be replicated.

Sanger's innovation involved the synthesis of chain-terminating nucleotide analogues lacking the 3′ hydroxyl group. These analogues, also known as dideoxynucleotides (ddATP, ddCTP, ddGTP, and ddTTP), terminate the growth of the daughter strand at the point of insertion, and this can be used to determine the distance of each base on the daughter strand from the primer. These distances can be visualized by separating the Sanger reaction products on a polyacrylamide gel and then exposing the gel to X-ray film to produce an autoradiogram. The DNA sequence is read directly from this film beginning with the smallest fragment at the bottom of the gel (the nucleotide closest to the primer), and ending with the largest fragment at the top. A hypothetical autoradiogram and the derived DNA sequence are shown in panel 5 of the figure on page 167. The smallest fragment in this example is the C nucleotide at the bottom of lane 3. The next nucleotide in the sequence is the G nucleotide in lane 4, then the T nucleotide in lane 2, and so on to the top of the gel.

Automated versions of the Sanger sequencing reaction use fluorescent-labeled dideoxynucleotides, each with a different color, so the sequence of the template can be recorded by a computer as the reaction mix passes a sensitive photocell. Machines such as this were used to sequence the human genome—a job that cost many millions of dollars and took years to complete. Recent advances in DNA-sequencing technology will make it possible to sequence the human genome in less than a week at a cost of $1,000.

Gene Expression

The production of a genomic or cDNA library, followed by the sequencing of isolated clones, is a very powerful method for characterizing genes and the genomes from which they came. But the icing on the cake is the ability to determine the expression profile for a gene (i.e., to determine which cells express the gene and exactly when the gene is turned on and off). Typical experiments may wish to determine the expression of specific genes in normal versus cancerous tissue or tissues obtained from groups of different ages. There are essentially three methods for doing this: RNA blotting, fluorescent in situ hybridization (FISH), and the polymerase chain reaction.

RNA Blotting

This procedure consists of the following steps:

1. Extract mRNA from the cells or tissue of interest.
2. Fractionate (separate by size) the mRNA sample using gel electrophoresis.
3. Transfer the fractionated sample to a nylon membrane (the blotting step).
4. Incubate the membrane with a gene fragment (usually a cDNA clone) that has been labeled with a radioisotope.
5. Expose the membrane to X-ray film to visualize the signal.

The RNA is transferred from the gel to a nylon membrane using a vacuum apparatus or a simple dish containing a transfer buffer topped by a large stack of ordinary paper towels and a weight. The paper towels pull the transfer buffer through the gel, eluting the RNA from the gel and trapping it on the membrane. The location of specific mRNAs can be determined by hybridizing the membrane to a radiolabeled cDNA or genomic clone. The hybridization procedure involves placing the membrane in a buffer solution containing a labeled probe. During a long incubation period the probe binds to the target sequence immobilized on the membrane. A-T and G-C base pairing (also known as hybridization) mediate the binding between the probe and target. The double stranded molecule that is formed is a hybrid, being formed between the RNA target, on the membrane, and the DNA probe.

Fluorescent in Situ Hybridization (FISH)

Studying gene expression does not always depend on RNA blots and membrane hybridization. In the 1980s, scientists found that cDNA probes could be hybridized to DNA or RNA in situ, that is, while located within cells or tissue sections fixed on a microscope slide. In this case, the probe is labeled with a fluorescent dye molecule, rather than a radioactive isotope. The samples are then examined and photographed under a fluorescent microscope. FISH is an extremely powerful variation on RNA blotting. This procedure gives precise information regarding the identity of a cell that expresses a specific gene, information that usually cannot be obtained with membrane hybridization. Organs and tissues are generally composed of many different kinds of cells, which cannot be separated from each other using standard biochemical extraction procedures. Histological sections, however, show clearly the various cell types, and when subjected to FISH analysis provide clear information as to which cells express specific genes. FISH is also used in clinical laboratories for the diagnosis of genetic abnormalities.

Polymerase Chain Reaction (PCR)

PCR is simply repetitive DNA replication over a limited, primer-defined region of a suitable template. It provides a way of amplifying a short segment of DNA without going through the cloning procedures described above. The region defined by the primers is amplified to such an extent that it can be easily isolated for further study. The reaction exploits the fact that a DNA duplex, in a low salt buffer, will melt (i.e., separate into two single strands) at 167°F (75°C), but will re-anneal (rehybridize) at 98.6°F (37°C).

The reaction is initiated by melting the template, in the presence of primers and polymerase in a suitable buffer, cooling quickly to 98.6°F (37°C), and allowing sufficient time for the polymerase to replicate both strands of the template. The temperature is then increased to 167°F (75°C) to melt the newly formed duplexes and then cooled to 98.6°F (37°C). At the lower temperature more primer will anneal to initiate another round of replication. The heating-cooling cycle is repeated 20 to 30 times, after which the reaction products are fractionated on an agarose gel, and the region containing the amplified fragment is cut out of the gel and purified for further study. The DNA polymerase used in these reactions is isolated from thermophilic bacteria that can withstand temperatures of 158°F (70°C) to 176°F (80°C). PCR applications are nearly limitless. It is used to amplify DNA from samples containing, at times, no more than a few cells. It is being used in the development of ultrafast DNA sequencers identification of tissue samples in criminal investigations, amplification of ancient DNA obtained from fossils, and the identification of genes that are turned on or off during embryonic development or during cellular transformation (cancer formation).

GENE THERAPY

An illness is often due to invading microbes that destroy or damage cells and organs in our body. Cholera, smallpox, measles, diphtheria, AIDS, and the common cold are all examples of infectious diseases.

For some, a physician may prescribe a drug that will remove the microbe from the body, thus curing the disease. Unfortunately, not all diseases can be cured this way. Sometimes, there are no microbes to fight, no drugs to apply. Instead, doctors are faced with a far more difficult problem, for this type of disease is an ailment that damages a gene. Gene therapy attempts to cure these diseases by replacing, or supplementing, the damaged gene.

When a gene is damaged, it usually is caused by a point mutation, a change that affects a single nucleotide. Sickle-cell anemia, a disease affecting red blood cells, was the first genetic disorder of this kind to be described. The mutation occurs in a gene that codes for the β (beta) chain of hemoglobin, converting the codon GAG to GTG, which substitutes the amino acid valine at position six, for glutamic acid. This single amino-acid substitution is enough to cripple the hemoglobin molecule, making it impossible for it to carry enough oxygen to meet the demands of a normal adult. Scientists have identified several thousand genetic disorders that are known to be responsible for diseases such as breast cancer, colon cancer, hemophilia, Alzheimer's disease, and Parkinson's disease.

Gene therapy is made possible by recombinant DNA technology (biotechnology). Central to this technology is the use of viruses to clone specific pieces of DNA. That is, the DNA is inserted into a viral chromosome and is amplified as the virus multiplies. Viruses are parasites that specialize in infecting bacterial and animal cells. Consequently, scientists realized that a therapeutic gene could be inserted into a patient's cells by first introducing it into a virus and then letting the virus carry it into the affected cells. In this context, the virus is referred to as gene therapy delivery vehicle or vector (in recombinant technology it is referred to as a cloning vector).

Commonly used viruses are the retrovirus and the adenovirus. A retrovirus gets its name from the fact that it has an RNA genome that is copied into DNA after it infects a cell. Coronaviruses (which cause the common cold) and the AIDS virus are common

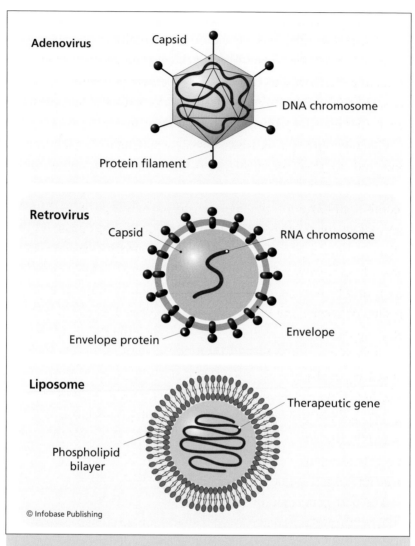

Vectors used in gene therapy. Adenoviruses have a DNA genome, contained in a crystalline protein capsid, and normally infect cells of the upper respiratory tract, causing colds and flulike symptoms. The protein filaments are used to infect cells. Retroviruses have an RNA genome that is converted to DNA when a cell is infected. The capsid is enclosed in a phospholipid envelope, studded with proteins that are used to infect cells. The AIDS virus is a common example of a retrovirus. Artificial vectors have also been used, consisting of a phospholipid bilayer enclosing the therapeutic gene.

examples of retroviruses. The adenovirus (from "adenoid," a gland from which the virus was first isolated) normally infects the upper respiratory tract causing colds and flulike symptoms. This virus, unlike the retrovirus, has a DNA genome. Artificial vectors, called liposomes, have also been used which consist of a phospholipid vesicle (bubble), containing the therapeutic gene.

Gene therapy vectors are prepared by cutting the viral chromosome and the therapeutic gene with the same restriction enzyme, after which the two are joined together with a DNA ligase. This recombinant chromosome is packaged into viral particles to form the final vector. The vector may be introduced into cultured cells, suffering from a genetic defect, and then returned to the patient from whom they were derived (ex vivo delivery). Alternatively, the vector may be injected directly into the patient's circulatory system (in vivo delivery). The ex vivo procedure is used when the genetic defect appears in white blood cells, or stem cells that may be harvested from the patient and grown in culture. The in vivo procedure is used when the genetic defect appears in an organ, such as the liver, brain, or pancreas. This is the most common form of gene therapy, but it is also potentially hazardous because the vector, being free in the circulatory system, may infect a wide range of cells, thus activating an immune response that could lead to widespread tissue and organ damage.

The first gene therapy trial, conducted in 1990, used ex vivo delivery. This trial cured a young patient named Ashi deSilva of an immune deficiency (adenosine deaminase deficiency) that affects white blood cells. Other trials since then have either been ineffective or devastating failures. Such a case occurred in 1999, when Jesse Gelsinger, an 18-year-old patient suffering from a liver disease, died while participating in a gene therapy trial. His death was caused by multiorgan failure brought on by the viral vector. In 2002, two children being treated for another form of immune deficiency developed vector-induced leukemia (cancer of the white blood cells). Subsequent studies, concluded in 2009, appear to have resolved these

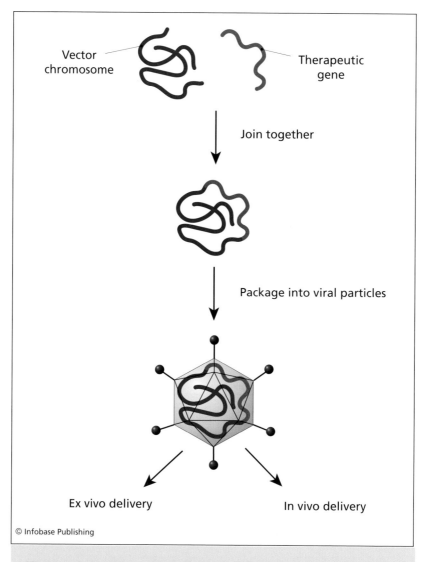

Vector chromosome

Therapeutic gene

Join together

Package into viral particles

Ex vivo delivery

In vivo delivery

© Infobase Publishing

Vector preparation and delivery. A viral chromosome and a therapeutic gene are cut with the same restriction enzyme, and the two are joined together, after which the recombinant chromosome is packaged into viral particles to form the vector. The vector may be introduced into cultured cells and then returned to the patient from whom they were derived (ex vivo delivery), or the vector may be injected directly into the patient's circulatory system (in vivo delivery).

problems. Gene therapy holds great promise as a medical therapy. In the United States alone, there are currently more than 600 trials in progress to treat a variety of genetic disorders.

MATCHING TISSUES

A molecular forest, called the glycocalyx, covers the surface of every cell and has a central role in the process of matching tissues for transplant operations. The glycocalyx consists of a diverse population of treelike glycoproteins and glycolipids that have "trunks" made of protein, or lipid, and "leaves" made of sugar. These molecular trees are embedded in the cell membrane much like the trees of Earth are rooted in the soil. A panoramic view of the glycocalyx, consisting of different kinds of glycoproteins and glycolipids, enhances the impression of a forested, though surrealistic, landscape.

The exact composition of the glycocalyx varies with each individual, much in the way a forest on Earth, located at the equator, is different from one located in the Northern Hemisphere. The human immune system uses the spatial arrangement of the exposed sugar groups to decide whether a cell is foreign or not. Thus the glycocalyx is like a cell's fingerprint, and if that fingerprint does not pass the recognition test the cell is destroyed or is forced to commit suicide. Immunologists refer to the glycoproteins and glycolipids in the glycocalyx as cell-surface antigens. The term *antigen* derives from the fact that cell-surface glycoproteins, on a foreign cell, can generate a response from the immune system that leads to the production of antibodies, capable of binding to, and destroying, the foreign cell.

An extremely important pair of cell-surface glycolipids are known as the A and B antigens. These glycolipids occur on the surface of red blood cells and form the ABO blood group system that determines each individual's basic blood type. The A and B antigens are derived from a third antigen, called H, that all individuals possess. Blood type A is produced by the *A* gene, which codes for a glycosyl transferase that adds an N-acetylgalactosamine to the H antigen. Blood type B is produced by a different transferase that places a galactose molecule on the H antigen. Some individuals have both A and B transferases and thus are said to have blood type AB. Individuals with blood type O have neither transferase. In North America, blood types A and O dominate, with A occurring in 41 percent of the population and O in 45 percent. Blood types B and AB are rare, with B occurring at a frequency of 10 percent and AB at only 4 percent.

An individual with blood type A will form antibodies against the B antigen and therefore cannot receive blood from a type B individual but can receive blood from type O individuals. Similarly, a type B individual cannot receive blood from someone with blood type A but can receive it from someone type O. Individuals with blood type AB can receive blood from individuals with blood types A, B, or O, and therefore such individuals are called universal recipients. On the other hand, people with blood type O can only receive type O blood since they will form antibodies against both A and B antigens. While individuals with type AB blood are universal recipients, individuals with type O blood are called universal donors, because their blood may be given to anyone without fear of invoking an immune response.

The importance of blood type with respect to organ transplantation is best illustrated by the recent case of Jesica Santillan, a 17-year-old girl who required a heart-lung transplant to correct a congenital lung defect that also damaged her heart. On February 7, 2003, physicians at Duke University Hospital in Durham, North Carolina, replaced Jesica's heart and lungs without checking the blood type of the donor. Jesica was blood type O, but the donor was type A. Jesica's immune system rejected the mismatched organs, and she lapsed into a deep coma soon after the operation was completed. In a desperate attempt to correct the mistake, Jesica's surgeons replaced the mismatched heart and lungs with organs obtained from a type O donor, but it was too late. Jesica had already suffered severe and irreparable brain damage, and on February 22, 2003, she died.

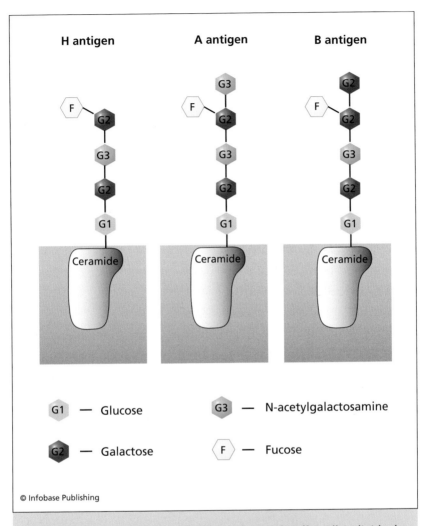

H antigen   A antigen   B antigen

G1 — Glucose   G3 — N-acetylgalactosamine

G2 — Galactose   F — Fucose

© Infobase Publishing

ABO antigens on the surface of red blood cells. All individuals have the H antigen. In addition, 41 percent of North Americans have the A antigen, 10 percent have B, 4 percent have both A and B, and 45 percent have neither. The latter group is said to be type O.

The A and B antigens, as critically important as they are to the success of transplant surgery, are only two of many thousands of cell-surface antigens that play a role in the rejection of foreign tissue. A second major group of antigens, called the human leukocyte antigens (HLA), may in fact number in the millions. These antigens are glycoproteins that cover the surface of virtually every cell in the body. They are called leukocyte antigens simply because that was the cell from which they were originally identified. When faced with this level of complexity, transplant surgeons have had to content themselves with matching only five or six of the most common HLA antigens between the recipient and donor. This, of course, leaves many mismatched antigens, but it seems that some antigens elicit a much stronger immune response than others, an effect that is likely quantitative in nature. That is, a million copies of antigen X will catch the attention of the immune system much more effectively than would 10 copies of antigen Y. By matching the dominant antigens, surgeons hope to avoid what is called the hyper-acute immune response that leads to the immediate destruction of the transplanted organ and death of the patient. It was a hyper-acute response, brought on by a mismatch of dominant antigens, that killed Jesica Santillan. Matching dominant antigens does not mean the transplanted organ is compatible but only that the patient has a good chance of surviving the first year. Beyond that, the immune system begins a slow chronic attack on the remaining mismatched antigens, leading to eventual failure of most transplanted organs. The slow chronic attack is responsible for the poor five- and 10-year survival of transplant patients.

THE HUMAN GENOME PROJECT

Sequencing the entire human genome is an idea that grew over a period of 20 years, beginning in the early 1980s. At that time, the Sanger sequencing method was but a few years old and had only been used to sequence viral or mitochondrial genomes. Indeed, one of the first genomes to be sequenced was that of bacteriophage G4, a virus that infects the bacterium *Escherichia coli (E. coli)*. The G4 genome consists of 5,577 nucleotide pairs (or base pairs, abbreviated bp) and was sequenced in Sanger's laboratory in 1979. By 1982, the Sanger protocol was used by others to sequence the genome of the animal virus SV40 (5,224 bp), the human mitochondrion (16,569 bp), and bacteriophage lambda (48,502 bp). Besides providing invaluable data, these projects demonstrated the feasibility of sequencing very large genomes.

The possibility of sequencing the entire human genome was first discussed at scientific meetings organized by the U.S. Department of Energy (DOE) between 1984 and 1986. A committee appointed by the U.S. National Research Council endorsed the idea in 1988 but recommended a broader program to include the sequencing of the genes of humans, bacteria, yeast, worms, flies, and mice. They also called for the establishment of research programs devoted to the ethical, legal, and social issues raised by human genome research. The program was formally launched in late 1990 as a consortium consisting of coordinated sequencing projects in the United States, Britain, France, Germany, Japan, and China. At about the same time, the Human Genome Organization (HUGO) was founded to provide a forum for international coordination of genomic research.

By 1995, the consortium had established a strategy, called hierarchical shotgun sequencing, which they applied to the human genome as well as to the other organisms mentioned. With this strategy, genomic DNA is cut into one-megabase (Mb) fragments (i.e., each fragment consists of 1 million bases) that are cloned into bacterial artificial chromosomes (BACs) to form a library of DNA fragments. The BAC fragments are partially characterized, then organized into an overlapping assembly called a contig. Clones are selected from the contigs for shotgun sequencing. That is, each shotgun clone is digested into small 1,000 bp fragments, sequenced, and then assembled into the final sequence with the aid of computers. Organizing the initial BAC fragments into contigs greatly simplifies the final assembly stage.

Sequencing of the human genome was divided into two stages. The first stage, completed in 2001, was a rough draft that covered about 80 percent of the genome with an estimated size of more than 3 billion bases (also expressed as 3 gigabases, or 3 Gb). The final draft, completed in April 2003, covers the entire genome and refines the data for areas of the genome that were difficult to sequence. It also filled in many gaps that occurred in the rough draft. The final draft of the human genome gives us a great deal of information that may be divided into three categories: gene content, gene origins, and gene organization.

Gene Content

Analysis of the final draft has shown that the human genome consists of 3.2 Gb of DNA, encoding about 30,000 genes (estimates range between 25,000 to 32,000). Functions are known for only half of these genes. With an average size of 3,000 bases, the genes occupy only about 2 percent of the DNA, a result that was both unexpected and baffling. The human genome appears to be much larger than it needs to be. The vast regions of noncoding DNA, known as intervening sequences, have been the subject of much study and speculation. Some researchers believe that these regions do nothing at all and have taken to calling them junk DNA. More creative minds have suggested that the intervening sequences are involved in the control of gene expression, the maintenance of chromosome structure, and the protection of genes from insertional mutagenesis.

The estimated number of genes in the human genome is another surprising result. Some scientists, noting the complexity of our brains and physiology, had predicted it would be closer to 100,000 genes. By comparison, the fruit fly has 13,338 genes and the simple roundworm, *Caenorhabditis elegans (C. elegans),* has 18,266. These numbers seemed absurd, because they were so close to that of humans. But on reflection, the genome data suggests that human complexity, as compared to the fruit fly or the worm, is not due to the absolute number of genes but involves the complexity of

THE GENOMES OF SOME ANIMALS, PLANTS, AND MICROBES

ORGANISM	GENOME SIZE (BP)	NUMBER OF GENES
Human	3.2 billion	30,000
Mouse	2.6 billion	25,000
Mustard weed	100 million	25,000
Corn	2.5 billion	50,000
Roundworm	97 million	18,266
Fruit fly	137 million	13,338
Yeast	12.1 million	6,000
Bacterium	4.6 million	3,200
Human immuno-deficiency virus	9,700	9

the proteins that are encoded by those genes. In general, human proteins tend to be much more complex than those of lower organisms. Data from the final draft and other sources also provides a detailed overview of the functional profile of human cellular proteins.

Gene origins

Fully one-half of human genes originated as transposable elements, also known as jumping genes (described below). Equally surprising is the fact that 220 of our genes were obtained by horizontal transfer from bacteria, rather than by ancestral, or vertical, inheritance. In other words, humans have obtained genes directly from bacteria, probably mediated by viral infections in a kind of natural gene therapy or gene swapping. Researchers know this to be the case because while these genes occur in bacteria, they are not present in yeast, fruit flies, or any other eukaryotes that have been tested.

The function of most of the horizontally transferred genes is unclear, although a few may code for basic metabolic enzymes. A notable exception is the *MAO* gene that codes for an enzyme called monoamine oxidase (MAO). (Note that by convention, gene names are written in upper or lowercase italic, while the proteins are uppercase roman letters.) Monoamines are neurotransmitters, such as dopamine, norepinephrine, and serotonin, which are needed for neural signaling in the human central nervous system. Monoamine oxidase plays a crucial role in the turnover of these neurotransmitters. How *MAO*, obtained from bacteria, could have developed such an important role in human physiology is a great mystery.

Gene Organization

In prokaryotes (bacteria), genes are simply arranged in tandem along a single chromosome, with little if any DNA separating one gene from the other. Each gene is transcribed into messenger RNA, which is translated into protein. Indeed, in prokaryotes, which have no nucleus, translation often begins even before transcription is complete. In eukaryotes, as one might expect, gene organization is more complex. Data from the genome project shows clearly that eukaryote genes are split into subunits, called exons, and that each exon is separated by a length of DNA called an intron. A gene, consisting of introns and exons, is separated from other genes by the intervening sequences. Eukaryote genes are transcribed into a primary RNA molecule that includes exon and intron sequences. The primary transcript never leaves the nucleus and is never translated into protein. Nuclear enzymes remove the introns from the primary transcript, after which the exons are joined together to form the mature mRNA. Thus, only the exons carry the necessary code to produce a protein.

UNDERSTANDING CLINICAL TRIALS

Clinical trials are conducted in four phases and are always preceded by experiments conducted on animals such as mice, rats, or monkeys. The format for preclinical research is informal. It is conducted in a variety of research labs around the world and the results are published in scientific journals. Formal approval from a governmental regulatory body is not required.

Phase I Clinical Trial

Pending the outcome of the preclinical research, investigators may apply for permission to try the experiments on human subjects. Applications in the United States are made to the Food and Drug Administration (FDA), the National Institutes of Health (NIH), and the Recombinant DNA Advisory Committee (RAC). RAC was set up by NIH to monitor any research, including clinical trials, dealing with cloning, recombinant DNA, or gene therapy. Phase I trials are conducted on a small number of adult volunteers, usually between two and 20, who have given informed consent. That is, the investigators explain the procedure, the possible outcomes, and, especially, the dangers associated with the procedure before the subjects sign a consent form. The purpose of the Phase I trial is to determine the overall effect the treatment has on humans. A treatment that works well in monkeys or mice may not work at all on humans. Similarly, a treatment that appears safe in lab animals may be toxic, even deadly, when given to humans. Since most clinical trials are testing a new drug of some kind, the first priority is to determine a safe dosage for humans. Consequently, subjects in the Phase I trial are given a range of doses, all of which, even the high dose, are less than the highest dose given to the animals. If the results from the Phase I trial are promising, the investigators may apply for permission to proceed to Phase II.

Phase II Clinical Trial

Having established the general protocol, or procedure, the investigators now try to replicate the encouraging results from Phase I, but with a much larger number of subjects (100 to 300). Only with a large number of subjects is it possible to prove the treatment has an effect. In addition, dangerous side effects may have been missed in Phase I because of a small sample size. The results from Phase II will determine how safe the procedure is and whether it works or not. If the statistics show the treatment is effective, and toxicity is low, the investigators may apply for permission to proceed to Phase III.

Phase III Clinical Trial

Based on Phase II results, the procedure may look very promising, but, before it can be used as a routine treatment, it must be tested on thousands of patients at a variety of research centers. This is the expensive part of bringing a new drug or therapy to market, costing millions, sometimes billions, of dollars. It is for this reason that Phase III clinical trials invariably have the financial backing of large pharmaceutical or biotechnology companies. If the results of the Phase II trial are confirmed in Phase III, the FDA will approve the use of the drug for routine treatment. The use of the drug or treatment now passes into an informal Phase IV trial.

Phase IV Clinical Trial

Even though the treatment has gained formal approval, its performance is monitored for very long-term effects, sometimes stretching on for 10 to 20 years. In this way, the FDA retains the power to recall the drug long after it has become a part of standard medical procedure. It can happen that in the long term, the drug costs more than an alternative, in which case, health insurance providers may refuse to cover the cost of the treatment.

GENE AND PROTEIN NOMENCLATURE

Scientists who were, in effect, probing around in the dark have discovered many genes and their encoded proteins. Once discovered, the new genes or proteins had to be named. Usually the name is nothing more than a lab book code or an acronym suggested by the system under study at the time. Sometimes it turns out, after further study, that the function observed in the original study is a minor aspect of the gene's role in the cell. It is for this reason that gene and protein names sometimes seem absurd and poorly chosen.

In 2003, an International Committee on Standardized Genetic Nomenclature agreed to unify the rules and guidelines for gene and protein names for the mouse and rat. Similar committees have attempted to standardize gene-naming conventions for human, frog, zebrafish, and yeast genes. In general, the gene name is expected to be brief and to begin with a lowercase letter unless it is a person's name. The gene symbols are acronyms taken from the gene name, and are expected to be three to five characters long, not more than 10. The symbols must be written with roman letters and Arabic numbers. The same symbol is used for orthologs (i.e., the same gene) among different species, such as human, mouse, or rat. Thus the gene sonic hedgehog is symbolized as *Shh* and the gene myelocytomatosis is symbolized as *Myc*.

Unfortunately, the various committees were unable to agree on a common presentation for the gene and protein symbols. A human gene symbol, for example, is italicized, uppercase letters, and the protein is uppercase and not italicized. A frog gene symbol is lowercase and the protein is uppercase, while neither is italicized. Thus the *Myc* gene and its protein, for example, are written as *MYC* and MYC in humans, myc and MYC in frogs, and *Myc* and Myc in mice and rats. The latter convention, *Myc* and Myc, is used throughout the New Biology set, regardless of the species.

WEIGHTS AND MEASURES

The following table presents some common weights, measures, and conversions that appear in this book and other volumes of the New Biology set.

QUANTITY	EQUIVALENT
length	1 meter (m) = 100 centimeters (cm) = 1.094 yards = 39.37 inches 1 kilometer (km) = 1,000 m = 0.62 miles 1 foot = 30.48 cm 1 inch = 1/12 foot = 2.54 cm 1 cm = 0.394 inch = 10^{-2} (or 0.01) m 1 millimeter (mm) = 10^{-3} m 1 micrometer (μm) = 10^{-6} m 1 nanometer (nm) = 10^{-9} m 1 Ångström (Å) = 10^{-10} m
mass	1 gram (g) = 0.0035 ounce 1 pound = 16 ounces = 453.6 grams 1 kilogram (kg) = 2.2 pounds (lb) 1 milligram (mg) = 10^{-3} g 1 microgram (μg) = 10^{-6} g
volume	1 liter (l) = 1.06 quarts (US) = 0.264 gallon (US) 1 quart (US) = 32 fluid ounces = 0.95 liter 1 milliliter (ml) = 10^{-3} liter = 1 cubic centimeter (cc)
temperature	°C = 5/9 (°F - 32) °F = (9/5 × °C) + 32
energy	calorie = the amount of heat needed to raise the temperature of 1 gram of water by 1°C. kilocalorie = 1,000 calories. Used to describe the energy content of foods.

 **Glossary**

acetyl   A chemical group derived from acetic acid. Important in energy metabolism and for the modification of proteins.

acetyl-CoA   A water-soluble molecule, coenzyme A (CoA) that carries acetyl groups in cells.

acetylcholine   A neurotransmitter released at axonal terminals by cholinergic neurons. Found in the central and peripheral nervous system, and is released at the vertebrate neuromuscular junction.

acid   A substance that releases protons when dissolved in water. Carries a net negative charge.

actin filament   A protein filament formed by the polymerization of globular actin molecules. Forms the cytoskeleton of all eucaryotes and part of the contractile apparatus of skeletal muscle.

action potential   A self-propagating electrical impulse that occurs in the membranes of neurons, muscles, photoreceptors, and hair cells of the inner ear.

active transport   Movement of molecules across the cell membrane, utilizing the energy stored in ATP.

adenylate cyclase   A membrane-bound enzyme that catalyzes the conversion of ATP to cyclic AMP. An important component of cell signaling pathways.

adherens junction   A cell junction in which the cytoplasmic face of the membrane is attached to actin filaments

adipocyte   A fat cell.

adrenaline (epinephrine)   A hormone released by chromaffin cells in the adrenal gland. Prepares an animal for extreme activity, increases the heart rate and blood sugar levels.

adult stem cells   Stem cells isolated from adult tissues, such as bone marrow or epithelium.

aerobic   Refers to a process that either requires oxygen or occurs in its presence.

agar   A polysaccaride isolated from sea weed that forms a gel when boiled in water and cooled to room temperature. Used by microbiologists as a solid culture medium for the isolation and growth of bacteria and fungi.

agarose   A purified form of agar that is used to fractionate (separate by size) biomolecules.

allele   An alternate form of a gene. Diploid organisms have two alleles for each gene, located at the same locus (position) on homologous chromosomes.

alpha helix   A common folding pattern of proteins in which a linear sequence of amino acids twists into a right-handed helix stabilized by hydrogen bonds.

allogeneic transplant   A cell, tissue, or organ transplant from an unrelated individual.

amino acid   An organic molecule containing amino and carboxyl groups that is a building block of protein.

aminoacyl-tRNA synthetase   An enzyme that attaches the correct amino acid to a tRNA.

amino terminus   The end of a protein or polypeptide chain that carries a free amino group.

aminoacyl tRNA   An amino acid linked by its carboxyl group to a hydroxyl group on tRNA.

amphipathic   Having both hydrophilic and hydrophobic regions, as in a phospholipid.

anabolism   A collection of metabolic reactions in a cell whereby large molecules are made from smaller ones.

anaerobic   A cellular metabolism that does not depend on molecular oxygen.

anaphase   A mitotic stage in which the two sets of chromosomes move away from each other towards opposite spindle poles.

anchoring junction   A cell junction that attaches cells to each other.

angiogenesis   Sprouting of new blood vessels from preexisting ones.

angstrom   A unit of length, equal to 10^{-10} meter or 0.1 nanometer (nM), that is used to measure molecules and atoms.

anterior   A position close to or at the head end of the body.

antibiotic   A substance made by bacteria, fungi, and plants that is toxic to microorganisms. Common examples are penicillin and streptomycin.

antibody   A protein made by B cells of the immune system in response to invading microbes.

anticodon   A sequence of three nucleotides in tRNA that is complementary to a messenger RNA codon.

antigen   A molecule that stimulates an immune response, leading to the formation of antibodies.

antigen-presenting cell   A cell of the immune system, such as a monocyte, that presents pieces of an invading microbe (the antigen) to lymphocytes.

antiparallel   The relative orientation of the two strands in a DNA double helix; the polarity of one strand is oriented in the opposite direction to the other.

antiporter   A membrane carrier protein that transports two different molecules across a membrane in opposite directions.

apoptosis   Regulated or programmed form of cell death that may be activated by the cell itself or by the immune system to force cells to commit suicide when they become infected with a virus or bacterium.

archaea   The archaea are prokaryotes that are physically similar to bacteria (both lack a nucleus and internal organelles), but they have retained a primitive biochemistry and physiology that would have been commonplace 2 billion years ago.

asexual reproduction   The process of forming new individuals without gametes or the fertilization of an egg by a sperm. Individuals produced this way are identical to the parent and referred to as a clone.

aster   The star-shaped arrangement of microtubules that is characteristic of a mitotic or meiotic spindle.

ATP (adenosine triphosphate)   A nucleoside consisting of adenine, ribose, and three phosphate groups that is the main carrier of chemical energy in the cell.

ATP synthase A protein located in the inner membrane of the mitochondrion that catalyzes the formation of ATP from ADP and inorganic phosphate using the energy supplied by the electron transport chain.

ATPase Any enzyme that catalyzes a biochemical reaction by extracting the necessary energy from ATP.

autogeneic transplant A patient receives a transplant of his or her own tissue.

autologous Refers to tissues or cells derived from the patient's own body.

autosome Any chromosome other than a sex chromosome.

autoradiograph (autoradiogram) X-ray film that has been exposed to x-rays or to a source of radioactivity. Used to visualize internal structures of the body and radioactive signals from sequencing gels and DNA or RNA blots.

axon A long extension of a neuron's cell body that transmits an electrical signal to other neurons.

axonal transport The transport of organelles, such as Golgi vesicles, along an axon to the axonal terminus. Transport also flows from the terminus to the cell body.

B cell (B lymphocyte) A white blood cell that makes antibodies and is part of the adaptive immune response.

bacteria One of the most ancient forms of cellular life (the other is the archaea). Bacteria are procaryotes and some are known to cause disease.

bacterial artificial chromosome (BAC) A cloning vector that accommodates DNA inserts of up to 1 million base pairs.

bacteriophage A virus that infects bacteria. Bacteriophages were used to prove that DNA is the cell's genetic material and are now used as cloning vectors.

base A substance that can accept a proton in solution. The purines and pyrimidines in DNA and RNA are organic bases and are often referred to simply as bases.

base pair Two nucleotides in RNA or DNA that are held together by hydrogen bonds. Adenine bound to thymine or guanine bound to cytosine are examples of base pairs.

benign   Tumors that grow to a limited size, and do not spread to other parts of the body.

beta sheet   Common structural motif in proteins in which different strands of the protein run alongside each other and are held together by hydrogen bonds.

biopsy   The removal of cells or tissues for examination under a microscope. When only a sample of tissue is removed, the procedure is called an incisional biopsy or core biopsy. When an entire lump or suspicious area is removed, the procedure is called an excisional biopsy. When a sample of tissue or fluid is removed with a needle, the procedure is called a needle biopsy or fine-needle aspiration.

biosphere   The world of living organisms

biotechnology   A set of procedures that are used to study and manipulate genes and their products.

blastomere   A cell formed by the cleavage of a fertilized egg. Blastomeres are the totipotent cells of the early embryo.

blotting   A technique for transferring DNA (Southern blotting), RNA (northern blotting), or proteins (western blotting) from an agarose or polyacrylamide gel to a nylon membrane.

BRCA1 (breast cancer gene 1)   A gene on chromosome 17 that may be involved in regulating the cell cycle. A person who inherits an altered version of the BRCA1 gene has a higher risk of getting breast, ovarian, or prostate cancer.

BRCA2 (breast cancer gene 2)   A gene on chromosome 13 that, when mutated, increases the risk of getting breast, ovarian, or prostate cancer.

budding yeast   The common name for the baker's yeast *Saccharomyces cerevisiae,* a popular experimental organism that reproduces by budding off a parental cell.

buffer   A pH-regulated solution with a known electrolyte (salt) content. Used in the isolation, manipulation, and storage of biomolecules and medicinal products.

cadherin   Belongs to a family of proteins that mediates cell-cell adhesion in animal tissues.

calorie   A unit of heat. One calorie is the amount of heat needed to raise the temperature of 1 gram of water by 1°C. Kilocalories (1000 calories) are used to describe the energy content of foods.

capsid   The protein coat of a virus, formed by autoassembly of one or more proteins into a geometrically symmetrical structure.

carbohydrate   A general class of compounds that includes sugars, containing carbon, hydrogen, and oxygen.

carboxyl group   A carbon atom attached to an oxygen and a hydroxyl group.

carboxyl terminus   The end of a protein containing a carboxyl group.

carcinogen   A compound or form of radiation that can cause cancer.

carcinogenesis   The formation of a cancer.

carcinoma   Cancer of the epithelium, representing the majority of human cancers.

cardiac muscle   Muscle of the heart. Composed of myocytes that are linked together in a communication network based on free passage of small molecules through gap junctions.

caspase   A protease involved in the initiation of apoptosis.

catabolism   Enzyme regulated breakdown of large molecules for the extraction of chemical-bond energy. Intermediate products are called catabolites.

catalyst   A substance that lowers the activation energy of a reaction.

CD28   Cell-surface protein located in T cell membranes, necessary for the activation of T cells by foreign antigens.

cDNA (complementary DNA)   DNA that is synthesized from mRNA, thus containing the complementary sequence. cDNA contains coding sequence, but not the regulatory sequences that are present in the genome. Labeled probes are made from cDNA for the study of gene expression.

cell adhesion molecule (CAM)   A cell surface protein that is used to connect cells to each other.

cell body   The main part of a cell containing the nucleus, Golgi complex, and endoplasmic reticulum. Used in reference to neurons that have long processes (dendrites and axons) extending some distance from the nucleus and cytoplasmic machinery.

cell coat   (see **glycocalyx**)

cell fate   The final differentiated state that a pluripotent embryonic cell is expected to attain.

cell-cycle control system   A team of regulatory proteins that governs progression through the cell cycle.

cell-division-cycle gene (*cdc* gene)   A gene that controls a specific step in the cell cycle.

cell-medicated immune response   Activation of specific cells to launch an immune response against an invading microbe.

cell nuclear transfer   Animal cloning technique whereby a somatic cell nucleus is transferred to an enucleated oocyte. Synonymous with somatic cell nuclear transfer.

celsius   A measure of temperature. This scale is defined such that 0°C is the temperature at which water freezes, and 100°C is the temperature at which water boils.

central nervous system (CNS)   That part of a nervous system that analyzes signals from the body and the environment. In animals, the CNS includes the brain and spinal cord.

centriole   A cylindrical array of microtubules that is found at the center of a centrosome in animal cells.

centromere   A region of a mitotic chromosome that holds sister chromatids together. Microtubules of the spindle fiber connect to an area of the centromere called the kinetochore.

centrosome   Organizes the mitotic spindle and the spindle poles. In most animal cells it contains a pair of centrioles.

chiasma (plural **chiasmata**)   An X-shaped connection between homologous chromosomes that occurs during meiosis I, representing a site of crossing-over, or genetic exchange between the two chromosomes.

chromatid   A duplicate chromosome that is still connected to the original at the centromere. The identical pair are called sister chromatids.

chromatin   A complex of DNA and proteins (histones and nonhistones) that forms each chromosome, and is found in the nucleus of all eucaryotes. Decondensed and thread-like during interphase.

chromatin condensation   Compaction of different regions of interphase chromosomes that is mediated by the histones.

chromosome   One long molecule of DNA that contains the organism's genes. In procaryotes the chromosome is circular and naked;

in eucaryotes it is linear and complexed with histone and nonhistone proteins.

chromosome condensation Compaction of entire chromosomes in preparation for cell division.

clinical breast exam An exam of the breast performed by a physician to check for lumps or other changes.

cnidoblast A stinging cell found in the Cnidarians (jellyfish).

cyclic adenosine monophosphate (cAMP) A second messenger in a cell-signaling pathway that is produced from ATP by the enzyme adenylate cyclase.

cyclin A protein that activates protein kinases (cyclin-dependent protein kinases, or Cdk) that control progression from one stage of the cell cycle to another.

cytochemistry The study of the intracelluar distribution of chemicals.

cytochrome Colored, iron-containing protein that is part of the electron transport chain.

cytotoxic T-cell A T-lymphocyte that kills infected body cells.

dendrite An extension of a nerve cell that receives signals from other neurons.

dexrazoxane A drug used to protect the heart from the toxic effects of anthracycline drugs such as doxorubicin. It belongs to the family of drugs called chemoprotective agents.

dideoxynucleotide A nucleotide lacking the 2′ and 3′ hydroxyl groups.

dideoxy sequencing A method for sequencing DNA that employs dideoxyribose nucleotides. Also known as the Sanger sequencing method, after Fred Sanger, a chemist who invented the procedure in 1976.

diploid A genetic term meaning two sets of homologous chromosomes, one set from the mother and the other from the father. Thus, diploid organisms have two versions (alleles) of each gene in the genome.

DNA (deoxyribonucleic acid) A long polymer formed by linking four different kinds of nucleotides together like beads on a string. The sequence of nucleotides is used to encode an organism's genes.

DNA helicase An enzyme that separates and unwinds the two DNA strands in preparation for replication or transcription.

DNA library   A collection of DNA fragments that are cloned into plasmids or viral genomes.

DNA ligase   An enzyme that joins two DNA strands together to make a continuous DNA molecule.

DNA microarray   A technique for studying the simultaneous expression of a very large number of genes.

DNA polymerase   An enzyme that synthesizes DNA using one strand as a template.

DNA primase   An enzyme that synthesizes a short strand of RNA that serves as a primer for DNA replication.

dorsal   The backside of an animal. Also refers to the upper surface of anatomical structures, such as arms or wings.

dorsalventral   The body axis running from the backside to the frontside or the upperside to the underside of a structure.

double helix   The three-dimensional structure of DNA in which the two strands twist around each other to form a spiral.

doxorubicin   An anticancer drug that belongs to a family of antitumor antibiotics.

Drosophila melanogaster   Small species of fly, commonly called a fruit fly that is used as an experimental organism in genetics, embryology, and gerontology.

ductal carcinoma in situ (DCIS)   Abnormal cells that involve only the lining of a breast duct. The cells have not spread outside the duct to other tissues in the breast. Also called intraductal carcinoma.

dynein   A motor protein that is involved in chromosome movements during cell division.

dysplasia   Disordered growth of cells in a tissue or organ, often leading to the development of cancer.

ectoderm   An embryonic tissue that is the precursor of the epidermis and the nervous system.

electrochemical gradient   A differential concentration of an ion or molecule across the cell membrane that serves as a source of potential energy and may polarize the cell electrically.

electron microscope   A microscope that uses electrons to produce a high resolution image of the cell.

electrophoresis   The movement of a molecule, such as protein, DNA or RNA, through an electric field. In practice, the molecules migrate through a slab of agarose or polyacrylamide that is immersed in a special solution and subjected to an electric field.

elution　To remove one substance from another by washing it out with a buffer or solvent.

embryogenesis　The development of an embryo from a fertilized egg.

embryonic stem cell (ES cell)　A pluripotent cell derived from the inner cell mass (the cells that give rise to the embryo instead of the placenta) of a mammalian embryo.

endocrine cell　A cell that is specialized for the production and release of hormones. Such cells make up hormone-producing tissue such as the pituitary gland or gonads.

endocytosis　Cellular uptake of material from the environment by invagination of the cell membrane to form a vesicle called an endosome. The endosome's contents are made available to the cell after it fuses with a lysosome.

endoderm　An embryonic tissue layer that gives rise to the gut.

endoplasmic reticulum (ER)　Membrane-bounded chambers that are used to modify newly synthesized proteins with the addition of sugar molecules (glycosylation). When finished, the glycosylated proteins are sent to the Golgi apparatus in exocytotic vesicles.

enhancer　A DNA regulatory sequence that provides a binding site for transcription factors capable of increasing the rate of transcription for a specific gene. Often located thousands of base pairs away from the gene it regulates.

enveloped virus　A virus, containing a capsid that is surrounded by a lipid bilayer originally obtained from the membrane of a previously infected cell.

enzyme　A protein or RNA that catalyzes a specific chemical reaction.

epidermis　The epithelial layer, or skin, that covers the outer surface of the body.

ER marker sequence　The amino terminal sequence that directs proteins to enter the endoplasmic reticulum (ER). This sequence is removed once the protein enters the ER.

erythrocyte　A red blood cell that contains the oxygen-carrying pigment hemoglobin, used to deliver oxygen to cells in the body.

***Escherichia coli* (E. coli)**   Rod shape, gram negative, bacterium that inhabits the intestinal tract of most animals and is used as an experimental organism by geneticists and biomedical researchers.

eukaryote (eucaryote)   A cell containing a nucleus and many membrane-bounded organelles. All lifeforms, except bacteria and viruses, are composed of eucaryote cells.

euchromatin   Lightly staining portion of interphase chromatin, in contrast to the darkly staining heterochromatin (condensed chromatin). Euchromatin contains most, if not all, of the active genes.

exocytosis   The process by which molecules are secreted from a cell. Molecules to be secreted are located in Golgi-derived vesicles that fuse with the inner surface of the cell membrane, depositing the contents into the intercellular space.

exon   Coding region of a eucaryote gene that is represented in messenger RNA, and thus directs the synthesis of a specific protein.

expression studies   Examination of the type and quantity of mRNA or protein that is produced by cells, tissues, or organs.

fat   A lipid material, consisting of triglycerides (fatty acids bound to glycerol), that is stored adipocytes as an energy reserve.

fatty acid   A compound that has a carboxylic acid attached to a long hydrocarbon chain. A major source of cellular energy and a component of phospholipids.

fertilization   The fusion of haploid male and female gametes to form a diploid zygote.

fibroblast   The cell type that, by secreting an extracellular matrix, gives rise to the connective tissue of the body.

Filopodium   A finger-like projection of a cell's cytoplasmic membrane, commonly observed in amoeba and embryonic nerve cells.

filter hybridization   The detection of specific DNA or RNA molecules, fixed on a nylon filter (or membrane), by incubating the filter with a labelled probe that hybridizes to the target sequence. Also known as membrane hybridization.

fixative   A chemical that is used to preserve cells and tissues. Common examples are formaldehyde, methanol, and acetic acid.

flagellum (plural flagella)   Whip-like structure found in procaryotes and eucaryotes that are used to propel cells through water.

fluorescein   Fluorescent dye that produces a green light when illuminated with ultraviolet or blue light.

fluorescent dye   A dye that absorbs UV or blue light, and emits light of a longer wavelength, usually as green or red light.

fluorescent in situ hybridization (FISH)   A procedure for detecting the expression of a specific gene in tissue sections or smears through the use of DNA probes labelled with a fluorescent dye.

fluorescent microscope   A microscope that is equipped with special filters, and a beam splitter, for the examination of tissues and cells stained with a fluorescent dye.

follicle cell   Cells that surround, and help feed, a developing oocyte.

G_0   G "zero" refers to a phase of the cell cycle. State of withdrawal from the cycle as the cell enters a resting or quiescent stage. Occurs in differentiated body cells, as well as developing oocytes.

G_1   Gap 1 refers to the phase of the cell cycle that occurs just after mitosis, and before the next round of DNA synthesis.

G_2   The Gap 2 phase of the cell cycle follows DNA replication and precedes mitosis.

gap junction   A communication channel in the membranes of adjacent cells that allows free passage of ions and small molecules.

gel electrophoresis   A procedure that is used to separate biomolecules by forcing them to migrate through a gel matrix (agarose or polyacrylamide) subjected to an electric field.

gene   A region of the DNA that specifies a specific protein or RNA molecule that is handed down from one generation to the next. This region includes both the coding, noncoding, and regulatory sequences.

gene regulatory protein   Any protein that binds to DNA and thereby affects the expression of a specific gene.

gene repressor protein   A protein that binds to DNA and blocks transcription of a specific gene.

gene therapy   A method for treating disease whereby a defective gene, causing the disease, is either repaired, replaced, or supplemented with a functional copy.

genetic code   A set of rules that assigns a specific DNA or RNA triplet, consisting of a three base sequence, to a specific amino acid.

genome   All of the genes that belong to a cell or an organism.

genomic library   A collection of DNA fragments, obtained by digesting genomic DNA with a restriction enzyme, that are cloned into plasmid or viral vectors.

genomics   The study of DNA sequences and their role in the function and structure of an organism.

genotype   The genetic composition of a cell or organism.

germ cell   Cells that develop into gametes, either sperm or oocytes.

glucose   Six-carbon monosaccharide (sugar) that is the principle source of energy for many cells and organisms. Stored as glycogen in animal cells and as starch in plants. Wood is an elaborate polymer of glucose and other sugars.

glycerol   A three carbon alcohol that is an important component of phospholipids.

glycocalyx   A molecular "forest," consisting of glycosylated proteins and lipids, that covers the surface of every cell. The glycoproteins and glycolipids, carried to the cell membrane by Golgi-derived vesicles, have many functions including the formation of ion channels, cell-signaling receptors, and transporters.

glycogen   A polymer of glucose, used to store energy in an animal cell.

glycolysis   The degradation of glucose with production of ATP.

glycoprotein   Any protein that has a chain of glucose molecules (oligosaccharide) attached to some of the amino acid residues.

glycosylation   The process of adding one or more sugar molecules to proteins or lipids.

glycosyl transferase   An enzyme in the Golgi complex that adds glucose to proteins.

Golgi complex (Golgi apparatus)   Membrane-bounded organelle in eucaryote cells that receives glycoproteins from the ER, which are modified and sorted before being sent to their final destination. The Golgi complex is also the source of glycolipids that are destined for the cell membrane. The glycoproteins and glycolipids leave the Golgi by exocytosis. This organelle is named after the Italian histologist, Camillo Golgi, who discovered it in 1898.

Gram stain   A bacterial stain that detects different species of bacteria based on the composition of their cell wall. Bacteria that retain the Gram stain are colored blue (Gram positive), whereas those that do not are colored orange (Gram negative).

granulocyte   A type of white blood cell that includes the neutrophils, basophils, and eosinophils.

growth factor   A small protein (polypeptide) that can stimulate cells to grow and proliferate.

haploid   Having only one set of chromosomes. A condition that is typical in gametes, such as sperm and eggs.

HeLa cell   A tumor-derived cell line, originally isolated from a cancer patient in 1951. Currently used by many laboratories to study the cell biology of cancer and carcinogenesis.

helix-loop-helix   A structural motif common to a group of gene regulatory proteins.

helper T cell   A type of T lymphocyte that helps stimulate B cells to make antibodies directed against a specific microbe or antigen.

hemoglobin   An iron-containing protein complex, located in red blood cells, that picks up oxygen in the lungs and carries it to other tissues and cells of the body.

hemopoiesis   Production of blood cells, occurring primarily in the bone marrow.

hematopoietic   Refers to cells, derived from the bone marrow, that give rise to red and white blood cells.

hematopoietic stem cell transplantation (HSCT)   The use of stem cells isolated from the bone marrow to treat leukemia and lymphoma.

hepatocyte   A liver cell.

heterochromatin   A region of a chromosome that is highly condensed and transcriptionally inactive.

histochemistry   The study of chemical differentiation of tissues.

histology   The study of tissues.

histone   Small nuclear proteins, rich in the amino acids arginine and lysine, that form the nucleosome in eucaryote nuclei, a bead-like structure that is a major component of chromatin.

HIV   The human immunodeficiency virus that is responsible for AIDS.

homolog   One of two or more genes that have a similar sequence, and are descended from a common ancestor gene.

homologous   Organs or molecules that are similar in structure because they have descended from a common ancestor. Used primarily in reference to DNA and protein sequences.

homologous chromosomes   Two copies of the same chromosome, one inherited from the mother, and the other from the father.

hormone   A signaling molecule, produced and secreted by endocrine glands. Usually released into general circulation for coordination of an animal's physiology.

housekeeping gene   A gene that codes for a protein that is needed by all cells, irregardless of the cell's specialization. Genes encoding enzymes involved in glycolysis and Krebs cycle are common examples.

hybridization   A term used in molecular biology (recombinant DNA technology), meaning the formation of a double stranded nucleic acid through complementary base-pairing. A property that is exploited in filter hybridization, a procedure that is used to screen gene libraries, and to study gene structure and expression.

hydrolysis   The breaking of a covalent chemical bond with the subsequent addition of a molecule of water.

hydrophilic   A polar compound that mixes readily with water.

hydrophobic   A non-polar molecule that dissolves in fat and lipid solutions, but not in water.

hydroxyl group (-OH)   Chemical group consisting of oxygen and hydrogen that is a prominent part of alcohol.

image analysis   A computerized method for extracting information from digitized microscopic images of cells or cell organelles.

immunofluorescence   Detection of a specific cellular protein with the aid of a fluorescent dye that is coupled to an antibody.

immunoglobulin (Ig)   An antibody made by B cells as part of the adaptive immune response.

incontinence   Inability to control the flow of urine from the bladder (urinary incontinence) or the escape of stool from the rectum (fecal incontinence).

insertional mutagenesis   Damage suffered by a gene when a virus or a jumping gene inserts itself into a chromosome.

***in situ* hybridization**   A method for studying gene expression, whereby a labeled cDNA or RNA probe hybridizes to a specific mRNA in intact cells or tissues. The procedure is usually carried out on tissue sections or smears of individual cells.

in vitro   Refers to cells growing in culture, or a biochemical reaction occurring in a test tube (Latin for "in glass").

in vivo A biochemical reaction, or a process, occurring in living cells or a living organism (Latin for "in life").

insulin Polypeptide hormone secreted by β (beta) cells in the vertebrate pancreas. Production of this hormone is regulated directly by the amount of glucose that is in the blood.

interleukin A small protein hormone, secreted by lymphocytes, to activate and coordinate the adaptive immune response.

interphase The period between each cell division, which includes the G_1, S, and G_2 phases of the cell cycle.

intron A section of a eucaryotic gene that is non-coding. It is transcribed, but does not appear in the mature mRNA.

ion channel A transmembrane channel that allows ions to diffuse across the membrane, down their electrochemical gradient.

ion An atom that has gained or lost electrons, thus acquiring a charge. Common examples are Na^+ and Ca^{++} ions.

ischemia An inadequate supply of blood to a part of the body, caused by degenerative vascular disease.

Jak-STAT signaling pathway One of several cell signaling pathways that activates gene expression. The pathway is activated through cell surface receptors and cytoplasmic Janus kinases (Jaks), and signal transducers and activators of transcription (STATs).

karyotype A pictorial catalog of a cell's chromosomes, showing their number, size, shape, and overall banding pattern.

keratin Proteins produced by specialized epithelial cells called keratinocytes. Keratin is found in hair, fingernails, and feathers.

kilometer 1,000 meters, which is equal to 0.621 miles.

kinesin A motor protein that uses energy obtained from the hydrolysis of ATP to move along a microtubule.

kinetochore A complex of proteins that forms around the centromere of mitotic or meiotic chromosomes, providing an attachment site for microtubules. The other end of each microtubule is attached to a chromosome.

Krebs cycle (citric acid cycle) The central metabolic pathway in all eucaryotes and aerobic procaryotes. Discovered by the German chemist, Hans Krebs, in 1937. The cycle oxidizes acetyl groups derived from food molecules. The end products are CO_2, H_2O, and high-energy electrons, which pass via NADH and FADH2 to the respiratory chain. In eucaryotes, Krebs cycle is located in the mitochondria.

labeling reaction The addition of a radioactive atom or fluorescent dye to DNA or RNA for use as a probe in filter hybridization.

lagging strand One of the two newly synthesized DNA strands at a replication fork. The lagging strand is synthesized discontinuously, and therefore, its completion lags behind the second, or leading, strand.

lambda bacteriophage A viral parasite that infects bacteria. Widely used as a DNA cloning vector.

leading strand One of the two newly synthesized DNA strands at a replication fork. The leading strand is made by continuous synthesis in the 5′ to 3′ direction.

leucine zipper A structural motif of DNA binding proteins, in which two identical proteins are joined together at regularly-spaced leucine residues, much like a zipper, to form a dimer.

leukemia Cancer of white blood cells.

lipid bilayer Two, closely aligned, sheets of phospholipids that forms the core structure of all cell membranes. The two layers are aligned such that the hydrophobic tails are interior, while the hydrophilic head groups are exterior on both surfaces.

liposome An artificial lipid bilayer vesicle used in membrane studies and as an artificial gene therapy vector.

locus A term from genetics that refers to the position of a gene along a chromosome. Different alleles of the same gene occupy the same locus.

long-term potentiation (LTP) A physical remodeling of synaptic junctions that receive continuous stimulation.

Lumen A cavity completely surrounded by epithelial cells.

lymphocyte A type of white blood cell that is involved in the adaptive immune response. There are two kinds of lymphocytes: T lympho-cytes and B lymphocytes. T lymphocytes (T cells) mature in the thy-mus, and attack invading microbes directly. B lymphocytes (B cells) mature in the bone marrow, and make antibodies that are designed to immobilize or destroy specific microbes or antigens.

lysis The rupture of the cell membrane followed by death of the cell.

lysosome   Membrane-bounded organelle of eucaryotes that contains powerful digestive enzymes.

M phase   The period of the cell cycle (mitosis or meiosis) when the chromosomes separate and migrate to the opposite poles of the spindle.

macromolecule   A very large molecule that is built from smaller molecular subunits. Common examples are DNA, proteins, and polysaccharides.

magnetic resonance imaging (MRI)   A procedure in which radio waves and a powerful magnet linked to a computer are used to create detailed pictures of areas inside the body. These pictures can show the difference between normal and diseased tissue. MRI makes better images of organs and soft tissue than other scanning techniques, such as CT or x-ray. MRI is especially useful for imaging the brain, spine, the soft tissue of joints, and the inside of bones. Also called nuclear magnetic resonance imaging.

major histocompatibility complex   Vertebrate genes that code for a large family of cell-surface glycoproteins that bind foreign antigens and present them to T cells to induce an immune response.

malignant   Refers to the functional status of a cancer cell that grows aggressively and is able to metastasize, or colonize, other areas of the body.

mammography   The use of x-rays to create a picture of the breast.

MAP-kinase (mitogen-activated protein kinase)   A protein kinase that is part of a cell proliferation-inducing signaling pathway.

M-cyclin   A eucaryote enzyme that regulates mitosis.

meiosis   A special form of cell division by which haploid gametes are produced. This is accomplished with two rounds of cell division, but only one round of DNA replication.

melanocyte   A skin cell that produces the pigment melanin.

membrane   The lipid bilayer, and the associated glycocalyx, that surrounds and encloses all cells.

membrane channel   A protein complex that forms a pore or channel through the membrane for the free passage of ions and small molecules.

membrane potential   A build-up of charged ions on one side of the cell membrane establishes an electrochemical gradient that is measured in millivolts (mV). An important characteristic of neurons as it provides the electrical current, when ion channels open, that enable these cells to communicate with each other.

mesoderm An embryonic germ layer that gives rise to muscle, connective tissue, bones, and many internal organs.

messenger RNA (mRNA) An RNA transcribed from a gene that is used as the gene template by the ribosomes, and other components of the translation machinery, to synthesize a protein.

metabolism The sum total of the chemical processes that occur in living cells.

metaphase The stage of mitosis at which the chromosomes are attached to the spindle but have not begun to move apart.

metaphase plate Refers to the imaginary plane established by the chromosomes as they line up at right angles to the spindle poles.

metaplasia A change in the pattern of cellular behavior that often precedes the development of cancer.

metastasis Spread of cancer cells from the site of the original tumor to other parts of the body.

methyl group (-CH$_3$) Hydrophobic chemical group derived from methane. Occurs at the end of a fatty acid.

meter Basic unit in the metric system. Equal to 39.4 inches or 1.09 yards.

micrograph Photograph taken through a light, or electron, microscope.

micrometer (µm or micron) Equal to 10^{-6} meters.

microtubule A fine cylindrical tube made of the protein tubulin, forming a major component of the eucaryote cytoskeleton.

millimeter (mm) Equal to 10^{-3} meters.

mitochondrion (plural mitochondria) Eucaryote organelle, formerly free-living, that produces most of the cell's ATP

mitogen A hormone or signaling molecule that stimulates cells to grow and divide.

mitosis Division of a eucaryotic nucleus. From the Greek *mitos,* meaning a thread, in reference to the threadlike appearance of interphase chromosomes.

mitotic chromosome Highly condensed duplicated chromosomes held together by the centromere. Each member of the pair is referred to as a sister chromatid.

mitotic spindle   Array of microtubules, fanning out from the polar centrioles, and connecting to each of the chromosomes.

molecule   Two or more atoms linked together by covalent bonds.

monoclonal antibody   An antibody produced from a B-cell derived clonal line. Since all of the cells are clones of the original B cell, the antibodies produced are identical.

monocyte   A type of white blood cell that is involved in the immune response.

motif   An element of structure or pattern that may be a recurring domain in a variety of proteins.

multipass transmembrane protein   A membrane protein that passes back and forth across the lipid bilayer.

multipotency   The property by which an undifferentiated animal cell can give rise to many of the body's cell types.

mutant   A genetic variation within a population.

mutation   A heritable change in the nucleotide sequence of a chromosome.

myelin sheath   Insulation applied to the axons of neurons. The sheath is produced by oligodendrocytes in the central nervous system, and by Schwann cells in the peripheral nervous system.

myeloid cell   White blood cells other than lymphocytes.

myoblast   Muscle precursor cell. Many myoblasts fuse into a syncytium, containing many nuclei, to form a single muscle cell.

myocyte   A muscle cell.

NAD (nicotine adenine dinucleotide)   Accepts a hydride ion (H^-), produced by the Krebs cycle, forming NADH, the main carrier of electrons for oxidative phosphorylation.

NADH dehydrogenase   Removes electrons from NADH and passes them down the electron transport chain.

nanometer (nm)   Equal to 10^{-9} meters or 10^{-3} microns.

National Institutes of Health (NIH)   A biomedical research center located in the United States. NIH consists of over 25 research institutes, including the National Institute of Aging (NIA) and the National Cancer Institute (NCI). All of the institutes are funded by the federal government.

natural killer cell (NK cell)   A lymphocyte that kills virus-infected cells in the body. They also kill foreign cells associated with a tissue or organ transplant.

neuromuscular junction   A special form of synapse between a motor neuron and a skeletal muscle cell.

neuron   A cell specially adapted for communication that forms the nervous system of all animals.

neuromodulator   A chemical released by neurons at a synapse that modifies the behavior of the targeted neuron(s).

neurotransmitter   A chemical released by neurons at a synapse that activates the targeted neuron.

non-small cell lung cancer   A group of lung cancers that includes squamous cell carcinoma, adenocarcinoma, and large cell carcinoma. The small cells are endocrine cells.

northern blotting   A technique for the study of gene expression. Messenger RNA (mRNA) is fractionated on an agarose gel and then transferred to a piece of nylon filter paper (or membrane). A specific mRNA is detected by hybridization with a labeled DNA or RNA probe. The original blotting technique invented by E. M. Southern inspired the name. Also known as RNA blotting.

nuclear envelope   The double membrane (two lipid bilayers) enclosing the cell nucleus.

nuclear localization signal (NLS)   A short amino acid sequence located on proteins that are destined for the cell nucleus, after they are translated in the cytoplasm.

nuclei acid   DNA or RNA, a macromolecule consisting of a chain of nucleotides.

nucleolar organizer   Region of a chromosome containing a cluster of ribosomal RNA genes that gives rise to the nucleolus.

nucleolus   A structure in the nucleus where ribosomal RNA is transcribed and ribosomal subunits are assembled.

nucleoside   A purine or pyrimidine linked to a ribose or deoxyribose sugar.

nucleosome   A bead-like structure, consisting of histone proteins.

nucleotide   A nucleoside containing one or more phosphate groups linked to the 5′ carbon of the ribose sugar. DNA and RNA are nucleotide polymers.

nucleus   Eucaryote cell organelle that contains the DNA genome on one or more chromosomes.

oligodendrocyte   A myelinating glia cell of the vertebrate central nervous system.

oligomer A short polymer, usually consisting of amino acids (oligopeptides), sugars (oligosaccharides), or nucleotides (oligonucleotides). Taken from the Greek word, *oligos,* meaning few or little.

oligo labeling A method for incorporating labeled nucleotides into a short piece of DNA or RNA. Also known as the random-primer labeling method.

oncogene A mutant form of a normal cellular gene, known as a proto-oncogene, that can transform a cell to a cancerous phenotype.

oocyte A female gamete or egg cell.

operator A region of a procaryote chromosome that controls the expression of adjacent genes.

operon Two or more procaryote genes that are transcribed into a single mRNA.

organelle A membrane bounded structure, occurring in eucaryote cells, that has a specialized function. Examples are the nucleus, Golgi complex, and endoplasmic reticulum.

osmosis The movement of solvent across a semi-permeable membrane that separates a solution with a high concentration of solutes from one with a low concentration of solutes. The membrane must be permeable to the solvent, but not to the solutes. In the context of cellular osmosis, the solvent is always water, the solutes are ions and molecules, and the membrane is the cell membrane.

osteoblast Cells that form bones.

ovulation Rupture of a mature follicle with subsequent release of a mature oocyte from the ovary.

oxidative phosphorylation Generation of high energy electrons from food molecules that are used to power the synthesis of ATP from ADP and inorganic phosphate. The electrons are eventually transferred to oxygen, to complete the process. Occurs in bacteria and mitochondria.

p53 A tumor suppressor gene that is mutated in about half of all human cancers. The normal function of the *p53* protein is to block passage through the cell cycle when DNA damage is detected.

parthenogenesis A natural form of animal cloning whereby an individual is produced without the formation of haploid gametes and the fertilization of an egg.

pathogen An organism that causes disease.

PCR (polymerase chain reaction) A method for amplifying specific regions of DNA by temperature cycling a reaction mixture containing the template, a heat-stable DNA polymerase, and replication primers.

peptide bond The chemical bond that links amino acids together to form a protein.

pH Measures the acidity of a solution as a negative logarithmic function (p) of H^+ concentration (H). Thus, a pH of 2.0 (10^{-2} molar H^+) is acidic, whereas a pH of 8.0 (10^{-8} molar H^+) is basic.

phagocyte A cell that engulfs other cells or debris by phagocytosis.

phagocytosis A process whereby cells engulf other cells or organic material by endocytosis. A common practice among protozoans, and cells of the vertebrate immune system. (From the Greek *phagein*, to eat)

phenotype Physical characteristics of a cell or organism.

phospholipid The kind of lipid molecule used to construct cell membranes. Composed of a hydrophilic head-group, phosphate, glycerol, and two hydrophobic fatty acid tails.

phosphorylation A chemical reaction in which a phosphate is covalently bonded to another molecule.

phosphokinase An enzyme that adds phosphate to proteins.

photoreceptor A molecule or cell that responds to light.

photosynthesis A biochemical process in which plants, algae, and certain bacteria use energy obtained from sunlight to synthesize macromolecules from CO_2 and H_2O.

phylogeny The evolutionary history of a group of organisms, usually represented diagrammatically as a phylogenetic tree.

pinocytosis A form of endocytosis whereby fluid is brought into the cell from the environment.

pixel One element in a data array that represents an image or photograph.

placebo An inactive substance that looks the same, and is administered in the same way, as a drug in a clinical trial.

plasmid A minichromosome, often carrying antibiotic-resistant genes, that occurs naturally among procaryotes. Used extensively as a DNA cloning vector.

platelet A cell fragment, derived from megakaryocytes and lacking a nucleus, that is present in the bloodstream, and is involved in blood coagulation.

ploidy   The total number of chromosomes (n) that a cell has. Ploidy is also measured as the amount of DNA (C) in a given cell, relative to a haploid nucleus of the same organism. Most organisms are diploid, having two sets of chromosomes, one from each parent, but there is great variation among plants and animals. The silk gland of the moth *Bombyx mori*, for example, has cells that are extremely polyploid, reaching values of 100,000C, flowers are often highly polyploid, and vertebrate hepatocytes may be 16C.

pluripotency   The property by which an undifferentiated animal cell can give rise to most of the body's cell types.

poikilotherm   An animal incapable of regulating its body temperature independent of the external environment. It is for this reason that such animals are restricted to warm tropical climates.

point mutation   A change in DNA, particularly in a region containing a gene, that alters a single nucleotide.

Polarization   A term used to describe the re-establishment of a sodium ion gradient across the membrane of a neuron. Polarization followed by depolarization is the fundamental mechanism by which neurons communicate with each other.

polyploid   Possessing more than two sets of homologous chromosomes.

polyploidization   DNA replication in the absence of cell division. Provides many copies of particular genes and thus occurs in cells that highly active metabolically (see ploidy).

polyacrylamide   A tough polymer gel that is used to fractionate DNA and protein samples.

portal system   A system of liver vessels that carries liver enzymes directly to the digestive tract.

post-mitotic   Refers to a cell that has lost the ability to divide.

probe   Usually a fragment of a cloned DNA molecule that is labeled with a radioisotope or fluorescent dye, and used to detect specific DNA or RNA molecules on Southern or Northern blots.

progenitor cell   A cell that has developed from a stem cell, but can still give rise to a limited variety of cell types.

proliferation   A process whereby cells grow and divide.

promoter   A DNA sequence to which RNA polymerase binds to initiate gene transcription.

prophase The first stage of mitosis. The chromosomes are duplicated and are beginning to condense, but are attached to the spindle.

protein A major constituent of cells and organisms. Proteins, made by linking amino acids together, are used for structural purposes, and regulate many biochemical reactions in their alternative role as enzymes. Proteins range in size from just a few amino acids to over 200.

protein glycosylation The addition of sugar molecules to a protein.

proto-oncogene A normal gene that can be converted to a cancer-causing gene (oncogene) by a point mutation or through inappropriate expression.

protozoa Free living, single-cell eucaryotes that feed on bacteria and other microorganisms. Common examples are *Paramecium* and *Amoeba*. Parasitic forms are also known that inhabit the digestive and urogenital tract of many animals, including humans.

P-site The binding site on the ribosome for the growing protein (or peptide) chain.

purine A nitrogen-containing compound that is found in RNA and DNA. Two examples are adenine and guanine.

pyrimidine A nitrogen-containing compound found in RNA and DNA. Examples are cytosine, thymine, and uracil (RNA only).

radioactive isotope An atom with an unstable nucleus that emits radiation as it decays.

random primer labeling A method for incorporating labeled nucleotides into a short piece of DNA or RNA.

randomized clinical trial A study in which the participants are assigned by chance to separate groups that compare different treatments; neither the researchers nor the participants can choose which group. Using chance to assign people to groups means that the groups will be similar and that the treatments they receive can be compared objectively. At the time of the trial, it is not known which treatment is best.

reagent A chemical solution designed for a specific biochemical or histochemical procedure.

recombinant DNA A DNA molecule that has been formed by joining two or more fragments from different sources.

refractive index A measure of the ability of a substance to bend a beam of light expressed in reference to air which has, by definition, a refractive index of 1.0.

regulatory sequence   A DNA sequence to which proteins bind that regulate the assembly of the transcriptional machinery.

replication bubble   Local dissociation of the DNA double helix in preparation for replication. Each bubble contains two replication forks.

replication fork   The Y-shape region of a replicating chromosome. Associated with replication bubbles.

replication origin (origin of replication, ORI)   The location at which DNA replication begins.

respiratory chain (electron transport chain)   A collection of iron- and copper-containing proteins, located in the inner mitochondrion membrane, that utilize the energy of electrons traveling down the chain to synthesize ATP.

restriction map   The size and number of DNA fragments obtained after digesting with one or more restriction enzymes.

restriction enzyme   An enzyme that cuts DNA at specific sites.

retrovirus   A virus that converts its RNA genome to DNA once it has infected a cell.

reverse transcriptase   An RNA-dependent DNA polymerase. This enzyme synthesizes DNA by using RNA as a template, the reverse of the usual flow of genetic information from DNA to RNA.

ribosomal RNA (rRNA)   RNA that is part of the ribosome, and serves both a structural and functional role, possibly by catalyzing some of the steps involved in protein synthesis.

ribosome   A complex of protein and RNA that catalyzes the synthesis of proteins.

rough endoplasmic reticulum (rough ER)   Endoplasmic reticulum that has ribosomes bound to its outer surface.

Saccharomyces   Genus of budding yeast that are frequently used in the study of eucaryote cell biology.

sarcoma   Cancer of connective tissue.

Schwann cell   Glia cell that produces myelin in the peripheral nervous system.

screening   Checking for disease when there are no symptoms.

senescence   (from the Latin word *senex,* meaning "old man" or "old age") Physical and biochemical changes that occur in cells and organisms with age.

signal transduction   A process by which a signal is relayed to the interior of a cell where it elicits a response at the cytoplasmic or nuclear level.

smooth muscle cell   Muscles lining the intestinal tract and arteries. Lacks the striations typical of cardiac and skeletal muscle, giving it a smooth appearance when viewed under a microscope.

somatic cell   Any cell in a plant or animal except those that produce gametes (germ cells or germ cell precursors).

somatic cell nuclear transfer   Animal cloning technique whereby a somatic cell nucleus is transferred to an enucleated oocyte. Synonymous with cell nuclear transfer or replacement.

Southern transfer   The transfer of DNA fragments from an agarose gel to a piece of nylon filter paper. Specific fragments are identified by hybridizing the filter to a labeled probe. Invented by the Scottish scientist, E. M. Southern, in 1975. Also known as DNA blotting.

stem cell   Pluripotent progenitor cell, found in embryos and various parts of the body, that can differentiate into a wide variety of cell types.

steroid   A hydrophobic molecule with a characteristic four-ringed structure. Sex hormones, such as estrogen and testosterone, are steroids.

structural gene   A gene that codes for a protein or an RNA. Distinguished from regions of the DNA that are involved in regulating gene expression, but are noncoding.

synapse   A neural communication junction between an axon and a dendrite. Signal transmission occurs when neurotransmitters, released into the junction by the axon of one neuron, stimulate receptors on the dendrite of a second neuron.

syncytium   A large multi-nucleated cell. Skeletal muscle cells are syncytiums produced by the fusion of many myoblasts.

syngeneic transplants   A patient receives tissue or an organ from an identical twin.

tamoxifen   A drug that is used to treat breast cancer. Tamoxifen blocks the effects of the hormone estrogen in the body. It belongs to the family of drugs called antiestrogens.

T cell (T lymphocyte)   A white blood cell involved in activating and coordinating the immune response.

telomere   The end of a chromosome. Replaced by the enzyme telomerase with each round of cell division to prevent shortening of the chromosomes.

telophase   The final stage of mitosis in which the chromosomes decondense and the nuclear envelope reforms.

template   A single strand of DNA or RNA whose sequence serves as a guide for the synthesis of a complementary, or daughter, strand.

therapeutic cloning   The cloning of a human embryo for the purpose of harvesting the inner cell mass (embryonic stem cells).

topoisomerase   An enzyme that makes reversible cuts in DNA to relieve strain or to undo knots.

totipotency   The property by which an undifferentiated animal cell can give rise to all of the body's cell types. The fertilized egg and blastomeres from an early embryo are the only cells possessing this ability.

trans Golgi network   The membrane surfaces where glycoproteins and glycolipids exit the Golgi complex in transport vesicles.

transcription   The copying of a DNA sequence into RNA, catalyzed by RNA polymerase.

transcription factor   A general term referring to a wide assortment of proteins needed to initiate or regulate transcription.

transfection   Introduction of a foreign gene into a eukaryote or prokaryote cell.

transfer RNA (tRNA)   A collection of small RNA molecules that transfer an amino acid to a growing polypeptide chain on a ribosome. There is a separate tRNA for amino acid.

transgenic organism   A plant or animal that has been transfected with a foreign gene.

translation   A ribosome-catalyzed process whereby the nucleotide sequence of a mRNA is used as a template to direct the synthesis of a protein.

transposable element (transposon)   A segment of DNA that can move from one region of a genome to another.

ultrasound (ultrasonography)   A procedure in which high-energy sound waves (ultrasound) are bounced off internal tissues or organs producing echoes that are used to form a picture of body tissues (a sonogram).

umbilical cord blood stem cells   Stem cells, produced by a human fetus and the placenta, that are found in the blood that passes from the placenta to the fetus.

vector   A virus or plasmid used to carry a DNA fragment into a bacterial cell (for cloning) or into a eukaryote to produce a transgenic organism.

vesicle   A membrane-bounded bubble found in eucaryote cells. Vesicles carry material from the ER to the Golgi and from the Golgi to the cell membrane.

virus   A particle containing an RNA or DNA genome surrounded by a protein coat. Viruses are cellular parasites that cause many diseases.

western blotting   The transfer of protein from a polyacrylamide gel to a piece of nylon filter paper. Specific proteins are detected with labeled antibodies. The name was inspired by the original blotting technique invented by the Scottish scientist E. M. Southern in 1975. Also known as protein blotting.

xenogeneic transplants (xenograft)   A patient receives tissue or an organ from an animal of a different species.

yeast   Common term for unicellular eucaryotes that are used to brew beer and make bread. Bakers yeast, *Saccharomyces cerevisiae,* are also widely used in studies on cell biology.

zygote   A diploid cell produced by the fusion of a sperm and egg.

Further Resources

BOOKS

Alberts, Bruce, Dennis Bray, Karen Hopkins, and Alexander Johnson. *Essential Cell Biology.* Second ed. New York: Garland Publishing, 2003. A basic introduction to cellular structure and function that is suitable for high school students.

Alberts, Bruce, Alexander Johnson, Julian Lewis, Martin Raff, Keith Roberts, and Peter Walter. *Molecular Biology of the Cell.* Fifth ed. New York: Garland Publishing, 2008. Advanced coverage of cell biology that is suitable for senior high school students and undergraduates.

Arking, Robert. *Biology of Aging: Observations and Principles.* Third ed. New York: Oxford University Press, 2006. A general introduction to gerontology.

Beers, Mark H., and Robert Berkow, eds. *The Merck Manual of Geriatrics.* Third ed. Rahway, N.J., Merck Research Laboratories, 2000. Available online. URL: http://www.merck.com/mkgr/mmg/home.jsp. Accessed October 7, 2009. A handy reference text covering all aspects of health care for the elderly.

Boyles, Peter, and Bernard Levin, eds. *The World Cancer Report 2008.* Lyon, France: The International Agency for Research on Cancer, 2008. Available online. URL: http://www.iarc.fr/. Accessed January 1, 2009. The definitive source for cancer data from around the world.

Ganong, William. *Review of Medical Physiology.* Twenty-second ed. New York: McGraw-Hill, 2005. A well-written overview of human physiology, beginning with basic properties of cells and tissues.

de Grey, Aubrey, and Michael Rae. *Ending Aging: The Rejuvenation Breakthroughs That Could Reverse Human Aging in Our Lifetime.* New York: St. Martin's Griffin, 2008. A comprehensive coverage of human aging aimed at the general public, high school students, and undergraduates.

Krause, W. J. *Krause's Essential Human Histology for Medical Students.* Boca Raton, Fla.: Universal Publishers, 2005. This book goes well with histology videos provided free on Google video.

Panno, Joseph. *Aging: Modern Theories and Therapies.* Rev. ed. New York: Facts On File, 2010. Explains why and how people age and why the incidence of cancer increases as people get older.

———. *Animal Cloning: The Science of Nuclear Transfer.* Rev. ed. New York: Facts On File, 2010. Medical applications of cloning technology are discussed including therapeutic cloning.

———. *The Cell: Nature's First Life-form.* Rev. ed. New York: Facts On File, 2010. Everything you need to know about the cell without having to read a 1,000-page textbook.

———. *Gene Therapy: Treatments and Cures for Genetic Diseases.* Rev. ed. New York: Facts On File, 2010. Discusses not only the great potential of this therapy but also its dangers and many failures.

———. *Stem Cell Research: Medical Applications and Ethical Controversies.* Rev. ed. New York: Facts On File, 2010. All about a special type of cell, the stem cell, and its use in medical therapies.

JOURNALS AND MAGAZINES

Andriole, Gerald, et al. "Mortality Results from a Randomized Prostate-Cancer Screening Trial." *New England Journal of*

Medicine 360 (March 18, 2009): 1,310–1,319. Screening for prostate cancer does not reduce the death rate for this disease.

Atsuta, Yoshiko, et al. "Disease-Specific Analyses of Unrelated Cord Blood Transplantation Compared with Unrelated Bone Marrow Transplantation in Adult Patients with Acute Leukemia." *Blood* 113 (2009): 1,631–1,638. This study showed that in some cases a bone transplant is more effective than a stem cell transplant.

Balmaceda, Casilda, et al. "Multi-Institutional Phase II Study of Temozolomide Administered Twice Daily in the Treatment of Recurrent High-Grade Gliomas." *Cancer* 112 (March 1, 2008): 1,139–1,146. This trial found a more effective treatment protocol for certain forms of brain cancer.

Belfiglio, M., et al. "Twelve-Year Mortality Results of a Randomized Trial of two Versus five Years of Adjuvant Tamoxifen for Postmenopausal Early-Stage Breast Carcinoma Patients." *American Cancer Society.* Published online October 24, 2005 in *Wiley Interscience* (DOI 10.1002/cncr.21474). This trial established the importance of a five-year treatment schedule combined with a very long followup.

Burn, John, et al. "Effect of Aspirin or Resistant Starch on Colorectal Neoplasia in the Lynch Syndrome." *New England Journal of Medicine* 359 (December 11, 2008): 2,567–2,578. Aspirin does not reduce the risk of colon cancer in a population especially susceptible to this disease.

Chanock, Stephen, and David Hunter. "Genomics: When the Smoke Clears . . ." *Nature* 452 (2008): 537–538. The authors describe research that has identified a gene that, when mutated, can cause lung cancer.

Church, George. "Genomes for All." *Scientific American* 294 (January 2006): 46–54. This article discusses fast and cheap DNA sequencers that could make it possible for everyone to have their genome sequenced, giving new meaning to personalized medicine.

Cook, Nancy, et al. "Low-Dose Aspirin in the Primary Prevention of Cancer." *JAMA* 294 (2005): 47–55. Aspirin does not reduce the risk of colon cancer.

Collins, Francis, Michael Morgan, and Aristides Patrinos. "The Human Genome Project: Lessons from Large-Scale Biology." *Science* 300 (2003): 286–290. Provides an overview of the many organizational problems that had to be overcome in order to complete the project.

Ding, Li, et al. "Somatic Mutations Affect Key Pathways in Lung Adenocarcinoma." *Nature* 455 (October 23, 2008): 1,069–1,075. This group sequenced 623 genes isolated from 188 human lung tumors and found 26 genes that were mutated and likely involved in carcinogenesis.

Fong, Lawrence, et al. "Potentiating Endogenous Antitumor Immunity to Prostate Cancer through Combination Immunotherapy with CTLA4 Blockade." *Cancer Research* 69 (January 15, 2009): 609–615. This study, with partial success, treated prostate cancer by augmenting the antitumor activity of T lymphocytes.

Gaziano, J. Michael, et al. "Vitamins E and C in the Prevention of Prostate and Total Cancer in Men." *JAMA* 301 (January 7, 2009): 52–62. The vitamins had no effect on the occurrence of various cancers in middle-aged and older men.

Gnant, Michael, et al. "Endocrine Therapy Plus Zoledronic Acid in Premenopausal Breast Cancer." *New England Journal of Medicine* 360 (February 12, 2009): 679–691. This clinical trial showed that tamoxifen is a more effective treatment when combined with zoledronic acid.

Grady, Deborah, et al. "Reduced Incidence of Invasive Breast Cancer with Raloxifene among Women at Increased Coronary Risk." *Journal of the National Cancer Institute* 100 (2008): 854–861. Evista (raloxifene) reduces the risk of breast cancer but not the risk of cardiovascular disease.

Izumoto, S., et al. "Phase II Clinical Trial of Wilms Tumor 1 Peptide Vaccination for Patients with Recurrent Glioblastoma Multiforme." *Journal of Neurosurgery* 108 (2008): 963–971. This trial demonstrated the effectiveness and potential of cancer biotherapy.

Ley, Timothy, et al. "DNA Sequencing of a Cytogenetically Normal Acute Myeloid Leukemia Genome." *Nature* 456 (November 6, 2008): 66–72. Available online. URL: http://www.nature.com/nature/journal/v456/n7218/abs/nature07485.html. Accessed June 9, 2009. Researchers sequenced the genome of a patient suffering from leukemia and found 10 mutated genes, eight of which were new mutations that were present in all tumor cells.

Locatelli, Franco, et al. "Hematopoietic Stem Cell Transplantation (HSCT) in Children with Juvenile Myelomonocytic Leukemia." *Blood* 105 (2005): 410–419. An Italian team cures over half of the enrolled patients with a stem cell–based therapy for childhood leukemia.

Miller, Kathy, et al. "Paclitaxel Plus Bevacizumab versus Paclitaxel Alone for Metastatic Breast Cancer." *New England Journal of Medicine* 357 (2007): 2,666–2,676. A combination of Taxol (paclitaxel) and Avastin (bevacizumide) gave very promising initial results, but they did not improve the overall survival of the treated patients.

Morgan, Richard, et al. "Cancer Regression in Patients after Transfer of Genetically Engineered Lymphocytes." *Science* 314 (October 6, 2006): 126–129. Steven Rosenberg's team at NCI treats melanoma with gene therapy.

Oettle, Helmut, et al. "Adjuvant Chemotherapy with Gemcitabine versus Observation in Patients Undergoing Curative-Intent Resection of Pancreatic Cancer." *JAMA* 297 (2007): 267–277. This study showed a modest benefit for patients with pancreatic cancer.

Passeron, Thierry, et al. "Upregulation of SOX9 Inhibits the Growth of Human and Mouse Melanomas and Restores Their Sensitivity to Retinoic Acid." *Journal of Clinical Investigation* 119 (April 2009): 954–963. The growth of melanomas was inhibited and their sensitivity to chemotherapy was restored when scientists increased the expression of a transcription factor called Sox9.

Patchell, Roy, et al. "Direct Decompressive Surgical Resection in the Treatment of Spinal Cord Compression Caused by Metastatic Cancer: A Randomised Trial." *Lancet* 366 (August 20, 2005): 643–648. Dramatic results obtained to correct spinal compression caused by metastatic cancer.

Pirker, Robert, et al. "Cetuximab Plus Chemotherapy in Patients with Advanced Non–Small Cell Lung Cancer." *Lancet* 373 (May 2, 2009): 1,525–1,531. A combination of biotherapy and chemotherapy proved more effective at treating lung cancer than chemotherapy alone.

Smith, David, et al. "Phase II Trial of Paclitaxel, Carboplatin and Gemcitabine in Patients with Locally Advanced Carcinoma of the Bladder." *Journal of Urology* 180 (2008): 2,384–2,388. This trial, headed by James Montie, inhibited the growth of bladder cancer but with toxic side effects.

Stratton, Michael, et al. "The Cancer Genome." *Nature* 458 (April 9, 2009): 719–724. In this review article, the authors discuss sequencing the genomes of cancer patients in the hope of identifying all mutations that are involved in carcinogenesis.

Tavera-Mendoza, Luz, and John White. "Cell Defenses and the Sunshine Vitamin." *Scientific American* 297 (November 2007): 62–72. A comprehensive overview of vitamin D and its role in human physiology and susceptibility to disease.

Van Cutsem, Eric, et al. "Cetuximab and Chemotherapy as Initial Treatment for Metastatic Colorectal Cancer." *New England Journal of Medicine* 360 (April 2, 2009): 1,408–1,417. A combination of biotherapy (cetuximab) and chemotherapy is more effective in the short term than chemotherapy alone.

Vogel, Victor, et al. "Effects of Tamoxifen versus Raloxifene on the Risk of Developing Invasive Breast Cancer and Other Disease Outcomes." *Journal of the American Medical Association* 295 (June 21, 2006): 2,727–2,741. Evista (raloxifene) is just as effective as tamoxifen, but with fewer side effects.

INTERNET ARTICLES

American Institute of Physics. "Madam Curie and the Science of Radioactivity." Available online. URL: http://www.aip.org/history/curie/radinst3.htm. Accessed June 3, 2009. This article discusses the life of Marie Curie and the dangers of working with radioactive materials.

Campbell, Shannon. "Cancer Report Yields Three Clear Prevention Guidelines." American Institute for Cancer Research (November 13, 2007). Available online. URL: http://www.aicr.org/site/News2?abbr=pr_&page=NewsArticle&id=12968. Accessed June 3, 2009. Recent research has shown that weight management, diet, and physical activity reduce the risk of developing cancer.

International Agency for Research on Cancer (IARC). "Vitamin D and Cancer." IARC Working Group Reports, vol. 5, International Agency for Research on Cancer, Lyon, 2008. Available online. URL: http://www.iarc.fr/en/publications/pdfs-online/wrk/wrk5/index.php/. Accessed June 3, 2009. As discussed in this report, vitamin D supplements can reduce the incidence of certain cancers.

———. *World Cancer Report 2008.* Available online. URL: http://www.iarc.fr/en/publications/pdfs-online/wcr/index.php. Accessed June 3, 2009. The report is available as a free download.

Luo, Ji, and Stephen Elledge. "Cancer: Deconstructing Oncogenesis." *Nature* 453 (2008): 995–996. Available online. URL: http://www.nature.com/nature/journal/v453/n7198/full/453995a.html. Accessed June 3, 2009. A news article that discusses the search for gene mutations that are responsible for cancer formation.

National Institutes of Health. "Stem Cell Information." Available online. URL: http://stemcells.nih.gov/index.asp. Accessed June 3, 2009. Covers both the scientific and political aspects of stem cell research.

Nelson, Mya. "AICR Study: Walnuts Slow Growth of Breast Cancer Tumors." American Institute for Cancer Research (September 29, 2008). Available online. URL: http://www.aicr.org/site/News2?abbr=pr_&page=NewsArticle&id=14000&news_iv_ctrl=1102. Accessed June 3, 2009. Consumption of walnuts for 35 days reduced the size of breast tumors in mice by half.

Yabroff, Robin, William Davis, Elizabeth Lamont, Angela Fahey, Marie Topor, Martin Brown, and Joan Warren. "Patient Time Costs Associated with Cancer Care." *Journal of the National Cancer Institute* 99 (2007): 14–23. Available online. URL: http://jnci.oxfordjournals.org/cgi/content/abstract/99/1/14. Accessed June 3, 2009. This paper, available as a free download, estimates the costs of caring for American cancer patients who are 65 or older.

WEB SITES

American Institute for Cancer Research. Available online. URL: http://www.aicr.org/site/PageServer?pagename=res_home. Accessed June 3, 2009. This site provides extensive coverage of cancer research, with special attention paid to the role of diet and exercise in reducing the risk of developing cancer.

Department of Energy Human Genome Project (United States). Available online. URL: http://genomics.energy.gov. Accessed June 3, 2009. Covers every aspect of the human genome project with extensive color illustrations.

Genetic Science Learning Center at the University of Utah. Available online. URL: http://learn.genetics.utah.edu/. Accessed June 3, 2009. An excellent resource for beginning students. This site contains information and illustrations covering basic cell biology, human genetics, animal cloning, stem cells, and other new biology topics.

Google Video. Available online. URL: http://video.google.com/
videosearch?q=histology+tissue&emb=0&aq=3&oq=histology#.
Accessed June 3, 2009. This site contains many videos covering
human histology and cell biology.

Institute of Molecular Biotechnology, Jena, Germany. Available
online. URL: http://www.imb-jena.de/IMAGE.html. Accessed
June 3, 2009. Image library of biological macromolecules.

International Agency for Research on Cancer. Available online.
URL: http://www.iarc.fr. Accessed June 3, 2009. This agency is
the research arm of the World Health Organization.

International Cancer Genome Consortium. Available online. URL:
http://www.icgc.org/home. Accessed June 8, 2009. The goal
of this consortium is to sequence the genomes of 50 different
kinds of cancer in order to identify all cancer-causing somatic
mutations.

National Cancer Institute. Available online. URL: http://www.
cancer.gov/. Accessed June 3, 2009. A very comprehensive site,
established by the National Institutes of Health, that covers
basic cancer information and links to clinical trials.

National Center for Biotechnology Information (NCBI). Available
online. URL: http://www.ncbi.nlm.nih.gov. Accessed June 3,
2009. This site, established by the National Institutes of Health,
is an excellent resource for anyone interested in biology. The
NCBI provides access to GenBank (DNA sequences), literature
databases (Medline and others), molecular databases, and topics
dealing with genomic biology. With the literature database, for
example, anyone can access Medline's 11 million biomedical
journal citations to research biomedical questions. Many of
these links provide free access to full-length research papers.

National Health Museum Resource Center. Washington, D.C.
Available online. URL: http://www.accessexcellence.org/RC/.
Accessed June 3, 2009. Covers many areas of biological research,
supplemented with extensive graphics and animations.

National Human Genome Research Institute. Available online. URL: http://www.genome.gov/. Accessed June 3, 2009. The institute supports genetic and genomic research, including the ethical, legal and social implications of genetics research.

National Institutes of Health. Available online. URL: http://www. nih.gov. Accessed June 3, 2009. The NIH posts information on their website that covers a broad range of topics including general health information, stem cell biology, aging, cancer research, and much more.

National Toxicology Program. Available online. URL: http://ntp-server.niehs.nih.gov/. Accessed June 3, 2009. Publishes reports on known or suspected carcinogens and mutagens.

Nature Publishing Group. Available online. URL: http://www. nature.com/nature/supplements/collections/humangenome/ commentaries/. Accessed June 3, 2009. The journal *Nature* has provided a comprehensive guide to the human genome. This site provides links to the definitive historical record for the sequences and analyses of human chromosomes. All papers, which are free for downloading, are based on the final draft produced by the Human Genome Project.

Sanger Institute (United Kingdom). Available online. URL: http:// www.sanger.ac.uk. Accessed June 3, 2009. DNA sequencing center, named after Fred Sanger, inventor of the most commonly used method for sequencing DNA. The institute is also involved in projects that apply human DNA sequence data to find cures for cancer and other medical disorders.

United States Food and Drug Administration. Available online. URL: http://www.fda.gov. Accessed June 3, 2009. Provides extensive coverage of general health issues and regulations.

World Health Organization. Available online. URL: http://www. who.int/en. Accessed June 3, 2009. Extensive coverage of health issues, involving cancer and infectious diseases, throughout the world.

 # Index

Note: *Italic* page numbers indicate illustrations.

A

A antigen 179–181, *181*
abdominal cancer, asbestos and 53
ABO blood group system 179–180, *181*
accelerators, linear 123–124
actin filaments *146,* 148
actinic keratosis 90
adenine 151, 153–154, 156
adenocarcinomas
    colon 76
    definition of 67
    pancreatic 84
adenomas
    colon 76, 133
    definition of 67
adenosine deaminase deficiency 177
adenosine triphosphate (ATP)
    production of 148, 159–160
    storage of 150
    structure of 150
adenoviruses 175–177, *176*
adipocytes 101–105
adjuvant therapy 109, 138
adoptive cell transfer 140–141
adrenal cancer, cadmium and 56
aflatoxins 49
Africa
    aflatoxin exposure in 49
    cancer incidence and types in 92–98, *96,*
        99, *100*
African Americans
    pancreatic cancer among 84
    prostate cancer among 86

age
    and bladder cancer 68
    and brain tumors 71
    and incidence 46
    and leukemia 46, 78
    and multiple genetic mutations 30
    and ovarian cancer 82
    and pancreatic cancer 84
    and prostate cancer 86
AIDS virus 175–177, *176*
alcohol consumption 106
alkylating agents 116
allogeneic bone marrow transplants 113–114
alpha cells, of pancreas 84
amino acids 148–153
    peptide bonds between 151
    structure of 148–150, *149*
anaphase 163
anaplastic astrocytoma 129–130
anaplastic oligodendroglioma 129–130
ancestral prokaryotes 4, *5*
androgen receptors, chemotherapy drugs block-
        ing 111, 118
anemia
    bone marrow stimulants and 110
    from chemotherapy 121
    sickle-cell 175
    symptoms of 121
aneuploidy 26, 33, 37
angiogenesis
    definition of 27, 112
    during development 112
    functions of 112
    in metastasis 27
    targeted in therapy 112–113
angiogenesis blockers 112–113

animal genomes *185*
antibodies, monoclonal 110–111
antigens
    A and B 179–181, *181*
    cell-surface 114
    H 179–180, *181*
    human leukocyte 181–182
    in tissue matching 179–182
apoptosis
    in cell cycle 162
    cell signaling for 166
    chemotherapy drugs and 116
    definition of 27
    lack of, in cancer cells 27, 29–30
    in normal cells 27, 29
    P53 gene in 34–35
    T-cell regulation of 29
archaea 4–6, *5*
areola 74
argon laser 126–127
arsenic compounds, as carcinogens 51–52
arsenic trioxide 52
asbestos
    as carcinogen 52–53, 106
    and lung cancer 53, 80–81
Asia, cancer incidence and types in *97, 98, 100*
Aspergillus 49, 51
aspirin, and colon cancer 133
astrocytes 69
astrocytomas 69–71, 129–130
atoms 143–145, *144*
ATP. *See* adenosine triphosphate
ATP synthase 159
Atsuta, Yoshiko 135–136
Australia, skin cancer in *100*
autogeneic bone marrow transplants 113–114
autoimmunity 139–140
autotrophs 4, 6–10
Avastin. *See* bevacizumab

B
BACs. *See* bacterial artificial chromosomes
bacteria
    communication among 11
    evolution of 4–6, *5,* 145
    gene organization in 186
    human genes obtained from 185–186
    plasmids of *7,* 166–168, 171
    structure of 6, *7,* 145

bacterial artificial chromosomes (BACs) 183
bacteriophage G4 genome 182
bacteriophage lambda 168–169, 183
Balmaceda, Casilda 129–130
B antigen 179–181, *181*
basal cell(s) 87, *88*
basal cell carcinoma 67, 87–90
basal cell papilloma *43*
base-flippers 157–158
bases, nucleotide *149,* 151, 154–155
B cells. *See* B lymphocytes
Belfiglio, Maurizio 131–132
benign tumors
    definition of 65
    switch to malignant from 42–43, 65–66
    warts as *43*
benzene, as carcinogen 53–54
benzopyrene 59–62
Berlin, Jordan 138–139
beta cells, of pancreas 84
bevacizumab 111, 113, *115*
    for breast cancer 131–132
    for pancreatic cancer 138–139
bilirubin, in pancreatic cancer 85
biopsy
    in breast cancer 75
    in colon cancer 77
    in leukemia 79
    in lung cancer 82
    in ovarian cancer 83
    in pancreatic cancer 85
    in prostate cancer 87
    in skin cancer 90
biotechnology xv, 143, 166–174, 175. *See also*
    specific technologies
biotherapies 109–113, *115,* 142
    for brain tumors 130–131
    for colon cancer 134
    for lung cancer 137
    for pancreatic cancer 138–139
Bishop, J. Michael 34
bisphosphonates 117
bladder, anatomy of 68
bladder cancer 68–69
    arsenic compounds and 51
    cadmium and 54–55
    clinical trials on 127, 128–129
    diagnosis of 69
    diet and 68
    gender and 68, 92

incidence of
    by continent 92, *93–97*
    in developed v. undeveloped countries *100*
industrial emissions and 56
mortality rates for *65, 66,* 68
photodynamic therapy for 127
risk factors for 68
stages of 69
superficial (in situ) 69
symptoms of 69
tobacco use and 62, 68
blood cells. *See* specific types
blood clotting, chemotherapy and 122
blood-forming tissues, cancers of. *See* leukemia
blood group system, ABO 179–180, *181*
blood vessels, formation of. *See* angiogenesis
blotting, RNA 172–173
B lymphocytes (B cells)
    biotherapies and 109
    functions of 109
    monoclonal antibodies produced by 111
bone marrow
    biopsy of 79
    cancer arising from. *See* leukemia(s)
    chemotherapy and 121, 122
    stem cell therapy for 124–125, 134–136
bone marrow stimulants 110, 122
bone marrow transplantation 113–116, 134–136
    side effects of 116
    v. stem cell therapy 124–125, 136
    types of 113–114
bone metastases 117, 137
brain, anatomy of 69, *70*
brain metastases, from leukemia 78–79
brain stem 69, *70*
brain tumors 69–73
    clinical trials on 127, 129–131
    diagnosis of *72, 73*
    incidence of
        by continent *93–97*
        in developed v. undeveloped countries
            100
    mortality rates for 64, *65, 66,* 71
    photodynamic therapy for 127
    risk factors for 71
    as secondary tumors 71
    stages of 73
    symptoms of 72–73
Brca1 gene 75, 123
Brca2 gene 75, 123

breast, anatomy of 74
breast cancer 74–76
    bone metastases in, treatment of 117
    clinical trials on 123, 131–133, 134
    diagnosis of *74, 75*
    diet and 105
    estrogen and 45, 75, 102
    estrogen receptor antagonists for 111,
        117–118
    gene therapy for 123
    genetic mutations in 23–26, 75, 123
    incidence of
        by continent 92, *93–97*
        in developed v. undeveloped countries
            100
    mortality rates for *65, 66*
    risk factors for 75
    stages of 75–76
    symptoms of 75
    types of 74–75
bulbs, breast 74
Burn, John 133

C

cadherins *12,* 43
cadmium, as carcinogen 54–56
Caenorhabditis elegans 184–185
calcium arsenate 52
California Environmental Protection Agency
    (Cal/EPA) 48
Camptosar. *See* irinotecan
cancer(s). *See also* specific types
    classification of 66
    common types of 63–90
    discovery of cause of xv–xvi
    incidence of. *See* incidence
    naming conventions for 67
    progression of 41–46, 67–68
    stages of 67–68
    terminology in 65–68
    treatment of. *See* therapies
    worldwide 91–107
        by continent 92–98, *93–97*
        in developed v. undeveloped countries
            98–99, *100*
        WHO report on 91–92
cancer cells xiv–xv, 19–31
    behavior pattern of 29–30
    broken chromosomes and 23–26, *24*

communication failure with 26–27
culture of 20
damage checkpoints in 28–29
disruption of bonds in 43
evolution of 27–28
genome of 23–26, 29, 38–40
immortality of 20–23
malignant 42
motility (movement) of 43–44
multiple genetic mutations in 29–31
single, tumors formed from 41–42
transformation into 65
carbon dioxide laser 126–127
carboplatin 116, *119,* 129
carcinogens 47–62
    definition of 47
    environmental 47, 106–107
    HHS list of 47–48
    in tobacco products 48, 59–62, *60,* 79–80
carcinomas. *See also* specific types
    definition of 44, 66
    in situ 69, 77
    lung cancer as 79
catheters 118
CBE. *See* clinical breast exam
CDC. *See* Centers for Disease Control
Cdkn2 gene 123
cDNA. *See* complimentary DNA
cell(s). *See also* specific types
    basic functions of 155–159
    biology of 143–166
    cancer. *See* cancer cells
    communication of 10–15, 148, 155–156,
        165–166
        and cancer cells 26–27
        direct (paracrine) 13–16
        indirect (endocrine) 13–16
        second messenger in 13, *14,* 165
    division of *11,* 155, 160–165. *See also* meiosis;
      mitosis
        chemotherapy and 116–117
        without controls, in cancer cells 27–29
        sex hormones and 45
    evolution of 4–10, *5*
    macromolecules of 151–155, *152*
    molecules of 148–151, *149*
    as nature's building blocks 143, *144*
    normal 1–18, *10*
    organelles of 6, *9,* 149
    suicide of. *See* apoptosis

cell cycle 160–165, *161*
    damage checkpoints in 28–29, 37, *161,* 162
cell membrane *7, 146,* 155
cell phone radiation, and brain tumors 71
cell-surface antigens 114
cellulose 150
Centers for Disease Control (CDC) 100
central nervous system (CNS) 69, *70*
centromere 163
centrosome *146,* 161–162
cerebellum 69, *70*
cerebrum 69, *70*
cervical cancer vaccine 111–112, *115*
cetuximab 111, *115*
    for colon cancer 134
    for lung cancer 137
    for pancreatic cancer 138–139
chemotherapy 116–122, *119*–120, 142
    administration of 118
    clinical trials on. *See* clinical trials
    FDA approval of 118
    mechanisms of action 116–117
    side effects of 118–122
    types of 116
Chernobyl nuclear accident 59
chickens, sarcomas in xv, 33–34
childbearing, late, and breast cancer 75
children
    brain tumors in 71
    leukemia in 46, 62, 78, 134, 135, 177
    retinoblastoma in 34
    sun protection for 89
China
    aflatoxin exposure in 49
    cancer incidence and types in 61, 99, *100*
chlamydomonas 6, *8*
chondromas 67
chondrosarcomas 67
chromatids 163
chromatin *9,* 164
chromosomes
    bacterial artificial 183
    broken/abnormal, and cancer cells 23–26, *24*
    eukaryotic 147–148
    in meiosis 164–165
    in mitosis 163–164
    in normal karyotype *25*
    Philadelphia 23, *24,* 42
    segregation of, regulation of 30
    telomeres on 21–23

chrysotile 52–53

cigarette and cigar smoking. *See* tobacco use

cisplatin 116, *119,* 136–137

clinical breast exam (CBE) 75

clinical trials 128–142, 187–188

    application procedure for 187

    on bladder cancer 127, 128–129

    on brain tumors 127, 129–131

    on breast cancer 123, 131–133, 134

    on colon cancer 123, 133–134

    on gene therapy 123

    on leukemia 123, 134–136

    on liver cancer 123

    on lung cancer 136–138

    on melanoma 123, 140–141

    on oral cancer 127

    on ovarian cancer 123

    on pancreatic cancer 138–139

    phases of 187–188

    on prostate cancer 123, 139–140

clomiphene citrate, and ovarian cancer 82

cloned DNA labeling 169–170

cloning, DNA 166–168, *167*

cloning vector 168

CNS. *See* central nervous system

coding region of genes, mutations in 33

codons 158–159

coke oven emissions, as carcinogens 56–57

colon, anatomy of 76

colon cancer 76–77

    clinical trials on 123, 133–134

    diet and 101

    gene therapy for 123

    incidence of 76

        by continent 92, *93–97*

        in developed v. undeveloped countries 99, *100*

    mortality rates for *65, 66,* 76

    risk factors for 76–77

    stages of 77

    symptoms of 77

colonies 15–17

colony-stimulating factor (CSF) 110, 122

communication, cellular 10–15, 148, 155–156, 165–166

    and cancer cells 26–27

    direct (paracrine) 13–16

    indirect (endocrine) 13–16

    second messenger in 13, *14,* 165

complementary base pairing 154–155

complimentary DNA (cDNA) 169

computed tomography (CT) scans

    of brain tumors 73

    of colon cancer 77

    of lung cancer 82

    of melanoma 90

    of ovarian cancer 83

    of pancreatic cancer 85

computer-based radiotherapy 124

connective tissue, cancers of. *See* sarcomas

consent, informed, for clinical trials 187

contact inhibition, in cells 26

contigs 183

Cook, Nancy 133

cooking grease, as carcinogen 48

copper arsenate 52

copy number reductions 39

coronaviruses 175–177

cryoprobe 125–126

cryosurgery 125–126

CSF. *See* colony-stimulating factor

CT. *See* computed tomography

CTLA-4. *See* cytotoxic T lymphocyte-associated antigen 4

Cyanobacteria 6

cytochrome b 159

cytochrome oxidase 159

cytokines

    in biotherapy 109–110

    T cell secretion of 109

cytokinesis 164

cytoplasm 6, *7, 146,* 147

cytosine 151, 153–154, 156

cytoskeleton 148

cytotoxic T lymphocyte-associated antigen 4 (CTLA-4) 139–140

D

dATP. *See* deoxyadenine triphosphate

daughter cells, production of

    damage checkpoints in 28–29, 37, *161,* 162

    in meiosis 162, 164

    in mitosis 160, 162, 163–164

    regulation of 30

dCTP. *See* deoxycytosine triphosphate

deamination 157

Denmark, cancer incidence and types in *100*

deoxyadenine triphosphate (dATP) 169–170

deoxycytosine triphosphate (dCTP) 170

deoxyribonucleic acid. *See* DNA
deoxyribonucleotides 116, 169–170
deoxyribose *149*
depurination 157
dermis, anatomy of 87
deSilva, Ashi 177
developed countries, cancer rates in 98–99, *100*
    diet and 100–105
dideoxynucleotides 171–172
diet
    and bladder cancer 68
    and breast cancer 105
    cancer-resistant 106, 107
    and colon cancer 76, 101
    North American 100–105
    and pancreatic cancer 84
    and prostate cancer 86, 105
digestive tract, susceptibility to cancer 63–64
digital rectal exam (DRE) 86
diploid cells 164
disaccharides 155
DNA 148, 155–158
    chemotherapy drugs targeting 116
    cloning of 166–168, *167*
    complimentary 169
    damage checkpoints for 28–29, 34, 37, *161*,
        162
    diet and 107
    enzymes modifying 166–169
    fluorescent in situ hybridization of 172, 173
    foreign, in cancer cells 39
    functions of 155
    lifestyle and 107
    maintenance of 155, 157–158
    noncoding 184
    nucleotides in 151, *152*
    origin of 2
    polymerase chain reaction in 169, 172, 174
    replication of 155, 156–157
        chemotherapy and 116
        and DNA sequencing 171–172
        and labeling cloned DNA 169–170
        mechanics of 22–23
        telomeres in 21–23
    sequencing of 39–40, *167*, 169, 171–172,
        182–184
    structure of 151, *152*, 155
    transcription of 158
DNA adducts 49, *50*, 60–62
DNA helicase 156

DNA libraries *167*, 168–169, 183
DNA ligase 166, 168, 177
DNA polymerase 156, 169–170, 171, 174
DNA primase 156
DNA synthesis (S phase)
    chemotherapy drugs blocking 116
    damage checkpoints in 28–29, *161*
docetaxel 117, *120*, 136
DOE. *See* Energy, Department of
double helix *152*, 155
DRE. *See* digital rectal exam
driver mutations 39–40
drugs, cancer. *See* chemotherapy; specific drugs
ductal carcinoma 74
ducts, breast 74

E
*Eco*RI 166–168
edema, with brain tumors 71
EGFR. *See* epidermal growth factor receptor
Egypt, bladder cancer in *100*
electrons 143
electron transport chain 148, 159–160
embryogenesis 16
emissions, industrial, as carcinogens 48, 56–57,
    57, 81
endocrine cells, of pancreas 84
endocrine signaling 13–16
endocrine system *103*
endoplasmic reticulum (ER) *9*, *146*, 148
endoscopic ultrasound, in pancreatic cancer 85
endostatin 113
Energy, Department of (DOE) 183
engraftment 125
enhancers, gene 169
environment, carcinogens in 47, 106–107
enzymes. *See also* specific enzymes
    pancreatic 83–84
    restriction 166–169, *167*
    role in genes 32
epidermal growth factor receptor (EGFR) 139
epidermis, anatomy of 87, *88*
epithelial cells
    cancers of. *See* carcinomas
    susceptibility to cancer 63–64
ER. *See* endoplasmic reticulum
Erbitux. *See* cetuximab
erythrocytes. *See* red blood cells
erythropoietin 121

Escherichia coli 166–168, 182
estrogen
    age and 46
    and breast cancer 45, 75, 102
    diet and 102–105
    functions of 44–45, 102
    obesity and 102–105
    and ovarian cancer 82–83
    regulation of 102, *104*
    and uterine cancer 102
estrogen receptors, chemotherapy drugs blocking
    111, 117–118
ethnicity. *See* race
eukaryotes
    evolution of 4–10, *5,* 15, 145
    gene organization in 186
    genome of 6, 145
    glycocalyx of 10
    structure of 6, *8,* 145–148, *146*
Europe, incidence of cancer in 92, *95*
Evista. *See* raloxifene
evolution
    of cancer cells 27–28
    of eukaryote cells 4–10, *5,* 15, 145
    of glycocalyx 15
    of multicellular organisms 13, 15–18, 145
    origin of life 1–4, *3,* 145
    of prokaryote cells 4–6, *5,* 145
exons 186

F

fat
    endocrine function of 101–102
    in North American diet 101–105
    storage in adipocytes 101
fatigue, from chemotherapy 120
fatty acids *149,* 150–151
FDA. *See* Food and Drug Administration
fertility drugs, and ovarian cancer 82
fiber, dietary 105
fluorescent in situ hybridization (FISH) 172,
    173
fluorouracil 116
    for colon cancer 134
follicle-stimulating hormone (FSH) 102, *104*
Fong, Lawrence 139–140
food additives, as carcinogens 106–107
Food and Drug Administration (FDA)
    chemotherapy drugs approved by 118

    clinical trial applications to 187
    interferon approved by 109–110
    photodynamic therapy approved by 127
    treatment approval process of 188
FSH. *See* follicle-stimulating hormone
fungal carcinogens 49, 99, 106

G

gain-of-function genes 33. *See also* oncogenes
gametes 164
gamma rays 58–59, 124
Gap 0 (G$_0$) 160
Gap 1 (G$_1$) 37, 160, *161,* 162
Gap 2 (G$_2$) 37, 160, *161,* 162
Gardasil 112, *115*
Gaziano, J. Michael 133–134
GBM. *See* glioblastoma multiforme
gel electrophoresis *167,* 170–171
Gelsinger, Jesse 177
gemcitabine (Gemzar) 116, *119*
    for bladder cancer 129
    for pancreatic cancer 138
gender
    and bladder cancer 68, 92
    and cancer in Africa 98
    and lung cancer 92
    and pancreatic cancer 84
gene(s)
    cancer caused by 32–34. *See also* oncogenes
    codons and 158–159
    eukaryotic 147
    horizontal transfer of 185–186
    human
        content of 184–185
        organization of 186
        origins of 185–186
    naming conventions for 34, 189
    organization of 186
gene amplification 39
gene expression 155–156, 158–159, *167,*
    172–174
gene therapy 122–123, 142, 174–179
    clinical trials on 123
    definition of 122
    first trial of 177
    mechanism of 122
    side effects of 123, 177–178
    vectors used in 175–177, *176, 178*
genetic code 158–159

genetic mutations
    in cancer cells
        multiple 29–31
        types of 39–40
    as cause of cancer xvi, 23–26
    driver 39–40
    passenger 39–40
    point
        in cancer cells 39
        definition of 33, 175
        in oncogenes 33
        in sickle-cell anemia 175
        in tumor suppressor genes 35
genome(s)
    animal, plant and microbial 185
    cancer cell 23–26, 29, 38–40
    eukaryote 6, 145
    human 38, 182–186
    prokaryote 6, 145
genomic libraries 169
Germany, kidney cancer in 100
germ cell(s) 21, 82
germ cell tumors 82
G4 genome 182
Gleditsia sinensis (GSE) 113
Gleevec (imatinib mesylate) 115, 118
glia 69
glioblastoma multiforme (GBM) 129–131
gliomas 69–71, 129–131
glucagon 84
glucose 84, 149, 150
glycerol 148, 149, 150
glycocalyx
    abnormal, in cancer cells 26
    in cellular communication 10–15, 148,
        165–166
    composition of 179
    evolution of 15
    functions of 165
    in immune system response 114, 179
    structure of 12
    in tissue matching 179
glycolipids
    in cellular communication 10–15, 165–166
    in tissue matching 179
glycoproteins
    abnormal, in cancer cells 26
    in cellular communication 10–15, 148, 165–166
    in tissue matching 179
Gnant, Michael 132

Golgi apparatus 146, 148
G-protein-linked receptor 14
Grady, Deborah 133
graft-versus-host disease (GVHD)
    bone marrow transplantation and 114
    stem cell therapy and 124–125, 135
Greece, brain tumors in 100
green tea extract (GTE) 113
growth hormone
    in pituitary cancer 67
    pituitary cell producing 9
GSE. See Gleditsia sinensis
guanine 151, 153–154, 156
GVHD. See graft-versus-host disease

H

hair loss, from chemotherapy 121
H antigen 179–181, 181
haploid cells 164
Health and Human Services, Department of
    (HHS) 47–48
HeLa cells, immortality of 20, 21
helix, double 152, 155
hematopoietic stem cells (HSCs) 134–135
hemoglobin 77, 110, 175
herbicides, as carcinogens 106–107
Herceptin (trastuzumab) 111, 115
heterotrophs 4, 6, 8
HHS. See Health and Human Services,
    Department of
hierarchical shotgun sequencing 183
HIF-1. See hypoxia-inducible factor 1
hippocampus 70
histones 162
HIV 175–177, 176
HLA. See human leukocyte antigens
homologous chromosomes (homologs) 25,
    164–165
horizontal transfer, of genes 185–186
hormone(s). See also specific hormones
    age and 46
    in endocrine signaling 13–16
    regulation of 102–105, 103, 104
    sex
        diet and 102–105
        and production of cancer 44–45
    steroid, and production of cancer 45
hormone receptors, chemotherapy drugs blocking
    111, 117–118

hormone replacement therapy (HRT) 45, 82–83
Hras gene, point mutation in 39
HRT. *See* hormone replacement therapy
HSCs. *See* hematopoietic stem cells
human genome 38, 182–186
Human Genome Organization (HUGO) 183
human genome project 182–186
human leukocyte antigens (HLA) 181–182
hybridization 172, 173
hybridomas 111
hydrocephalus 71
hyperacute immune response 182
hypothalamus *70*, 102, *103*, *104*
hypoxia-inducible factor 1 (HIF-1) 112

I

ICGC. *See* International Cancer Genome Con-
    sortium
IL-2. *See* interleukin-2
imatinib mesylate *115*, 118
immune system
    age and 46
    bone marrow stimulants and 110
    glycocalyx in 114, 179
    hyperacute response in 182
    stem cell therapy and 124–125, 135
    in transplantation
        bone marrow 114
        tissue matching for 179–182
    white blood cell function in 78
immunotherapies. *See* biotherapies
incidence of cancer
    age and 46
    by continent 92–98, *93–97*
    in developed v. undeveloped countries 98–99,
        100
    diet and 107
    environment and 106–107
    lifestyle and 105–106, 107
    WHO on 98
India, cancer incidence and types in *100*
industrial emissions, as carcinogens 48, 56–57,
    57, 81
infections, from chemotherapy 121–122
informed consent, for clinical trials 187
insertional mutagenesis 33, 123, 184
in situ hybridization, fluorescent 172, 173
insulin 84
integrin *12*

interferon 109–110
interleukin 13, 110
interleukin-2 (IL-2) 110
International Agency for Research on Cancer 48
International Cancer Genome Consortium
    (ICGC) 40
International Committee on Standardized Genetic
    Nomenclature 189
interphase 160, *161*, 161–162
intervening sequences 169, 184, 186
intravenous administration, of chemotherapy 118
introns 169, 186
ion channels 15, *16*
ionizing radiation
    as carcinogen 57–59
    in radiotherapy 123–124
Iran, lung cancer in *100*
irinotecan *119*, 134
irradiation. *See* radiotherapy
islet cell carcinomas 84
islets of Langerhans 84
Izumoto, Shuichi 130–131

J

Japan, cancer incidence and types in *100*, 106
jaundice, in pancreatic cancer 85
jumping genes 185
junk DNA 184

K

karyotype
    abnormal, in cancer cells 23, 24, 30
    normal *25*
keratin
    in basal cell carcinoma 67
    functions of 67, *88*
keratinization *88*
keratosis, actinic 90
kidney cancer
    arsenic compounds and 51–52
    cadmium and 54–55
    incidence of
        by continent *93–97*
        in developed v. undeveloped countries *100*
    industrial emissions and 57
    tobacco use and 62
kinetochores 163
Krebs cycle 159

L

labeling, of cloned DNA 169–170
Lacks, Henrietta 20
lambda bacteriophage 168–169, 183
Langerhans, islets of 84
laser therapy 126–127
lead arsenate 52
leptin 101–102, 105
leptons 143, *144*
leukemia(s) 77–79
 acute v. chronic 78
 age and 46, 78
 arsenic exposure and 52
 benzene and 53–54
 bone marrow transplants for 113–116,
  134–136
 cadmium and 55
 clinical trials on 123, 134–136
 definition of 67
 diagnosis of 79
 incidence of 78
  by continent 92, *93–97*
  in developed v. undeveloped countries *100*
 metastases from 78–79
 mortality rates for *65, 66,* 78
 Philadelphia chromosome in 23, *24,* 42
 risk factors for 78
 stages of 79
 stem cell therapy for 124, 134–136
 symptoms of 78
 tobacco use and 62
 types of 78
 vector-induced 177–179
leukocyte antigens, human 181–182
leukocytes. *See* white blood cells
Levi, Julia 127
libraries
 DNA *167,* 168–169, 183
 genomic 169
life, origin of 1–4, *3,* 145
lifestyle, and incidence 105–106, 107
ligand 15, *16*
linear accelerators 123–124
liposomes *176,* 177
liver, tobacco use and function of 59–60
liver cancer
 arsenic compounds and 51
 cells of *44*
 clinical trials on 123
 cryosurgery for 126

diet and hormones in 105
fungal carcinogens and 99
fungal toxins and 49
incidence of
 by continent 92–98, *93–97*
 in developed v. undeveloped countries
  99, *100*
lifestyle and 106
mortality rates for *65, 66*
tobacco use and 62
lobes
 of breast 74
 of lung 79
lobular carcinoma 74
lobules, breast 74
Locatelli, Franco 135
loss-of-function genes 33. *See also* tumor suppressor genes
lung
 anatomy of 79, *80*
 function of 79
 susceptibility to cancer 63–64
lung cancer 79–82
 arsenic compounds and 51–52
 asbestos and 53, 80–81
 benzene and 54
 cadmium and 54–55
 clinical trials on 136–138
 diagnosis of *81,* 82
 diet and hormones in 105
 gender and 92
 incidence of
  by continent 92–98, *93–97*
  in developed v. undeveloped countries
   100
 industrial emissions and 56–57, 81
 lifestyle and 106
 metastases from 71
 mortality rates for 61–62, 64, 79
 photodynamic therapy for 127
 risk factors for 79–80
 symptoms of 81–82
 tobacco use and 46, 61–62, 79–80, 106
lymphatic system, breast cancer and 74
lymphocytes 78, 109
lymphocytic leukemia 78, 135–136
lymphoid cells 78
lymphoma
 benzene and 54
 bone marrow transplants for 113–116

mortality rates for 65, 66
stem cell therapy for 124
lysosomes 146, 148
lysozyme 153

M

MAbs. See monoclonal antibodies
macromolecules 2, 144
  of cell 151–155, 152
  in origin of life 145
  types of 148
magnetic resonance imaging (MRI) 73
  of brain tumors 72, 73
  of colon cancer 77
  of lung cancer 82
  of melanoma 90
malignant cancer cells, definition of 42
malignant tumors
  definition of 66
  spread of. See metastasis
  switch from benign to 42–43, 65–66
mammography 75
MAO. See monoamine oxidase
MAO gene 186
Mart-1 antigen 141
maturation promoting factor (MPF) 162
measures 190
meiosis 160, 162, 164–165
meiosis I 164
meiosis II 164
melanin 67, 87
melanocytes 87–88, 88
melanoma 67, 87–90, 89
  clinical trials on 123
  diagnosis of 90
  gene therapy for 123
  incidence of 88–89
    in developed v. undeveloped countries
      99
  lifestyle and 106
  mortality rates for 65, 66, 89
menopause 46, 82, 102
mesothelioma 53
messenger RNA (mRNA) 147–148, 158, 169,
  186
metallothionein (MT) 55
metals, as carcinogens 48, 54–56
metaphase 163
metaphase checkpoint 37, 161
metaphase plate 163

metastasis
  angiogenesis in 27
  bone 117, 137
  conditions for 42
  definition of 44, 66
  genes involved in 23, 30, 36, 37, 42–44
  lack of apoptosis and 27
  from leukemia 78–79
  movement of cancer cells in 44
  in stage IV cancer 68
microtubules 146, 161–162, 163
Miller, Kathy 132, 134
mitochondria 9, 146, 148, 159, 183
mitosis (cell division) 160, 162, 163–164
  chemotherapy and 116–117
  damage checkpoints in 161
  meiosis compared to 164
  sex hormones and 45
  uncontrolled, in cancer cells 27–29
mitotic spindle 163
  chemotherapy drugs damaging 116–117
  duplication of 161–162
mixed-function oxidases 60
molecules 144
  of cell 148–151, 149
  in origin of life 145
  types of 148
Mongolia, cancer incidence and types in 99, 100
monoamine oxidase (MAO) 186
monoclonal antibodies (MAbs) 110–111
monocytes 109
monolayer, cells in 26
monosaccharides 150, 152, 155
Montie, James 129
mortality, by type of cancer 64, 65, 66
motility, of cancer cells 43–44
motor proteins 163
MPF. See maturation promoting factor
M phase 160, 161, 162. See also mitosis
MRI. See magnetic resonance imaging
mRNA. See messenger RNA
Msh1 gene, and colon cancer 123
Msh2 gene, and colon cancer 123
MT. See metallothionein
multicellular organisms, evolution of 13, 15–18,
  145
muscles, cancers of. See sarcomas
mutagenesis, insertional 33, 123, 184
mutations. See genetic mutations
Myc oncogene 33–34, 35, 36, 189
myelin 71

myeloablation 135
myelocytoma 33
myelocytomatosis 67, 189
myelogenous leukemia 23, 78, 135–136
myeloid cells 78

N

NAD. *See* nicotinamide adenine dinucleotide
NADH dehydrogenase 159–160
NAG. *See* neodymium aluminum garnet
National Cancer Institute (NCI) 128–129,
    140–141
National Institutes of Health (NIH) 82–83, 187
National Research Council, on human genome
    project 183
National Toxicology Program (NTP) 48
natural killer (NK) lymphocyte 109
nature's building blocks 143–145, *144*
nausea, from chemotherapy 120–121
NCI. *See* National Cancer Institute
neoadjuvant therapy 109
neodymium aluminum garnet (NAG) laser
    126–127
neoplasm. *See* tumor
nervous system, central 69, *70*
neurons *8, 69*
    chemotherapy and 121
neurotransmitters 15
neutrons 143
neutropenia 129
nickel, as carcinogen 54, 55–56
nickel acetate 56
nickel salts 56
nicotinamide adenine dinucleotide (NAD)
    159–160
NIH. *See* National Institutes of Health
nitrogen, liquid, in cryosurgery 125
nitrogenous bases 151
NK. *See* natural killer
noncoding DNA 184
nonlymphocytic leukemia 78
non-melanoma skin cancer 88
non-small-cell lung cancer (NSCLC) 136
normal cells 1–18, *10*
North America
    cost of treatment in 98
    incidence of cancer in
        diet and 100–105
        by type of cancer 92, *93*
NSCLC. *See* non-small-cell lung cancer

NTP. *See* National Toxicology Program
nuclear envelope 163
nuclear explosions 58–59
nuclear pore *146*
nucleic acids 150. *See also* DNA; RNA
nucleolus *146*
nucleotide analogs 116
nucleotides 116, *149,* 151, *152, 154*–155
nucleus 6, *9,* 145, *146,* 147
nutrient broth 2–4

O

obesity
    and cancer rates 100–105
    and ovarian cancer 82
    and pancreatic cancer 84
O blood type 180, *181*
Oettle, Helmut 138
oligodendrocytes 69
oligodendrogliomas 69–71, 129–130
oligosaccharides 155
oncogenes 33–34
    deadliness of 35, *36*
    definition of 33
    discovery of xv, xvi, 33
    functions of 33–34, *35*
    naming conventions for 33–34
    production of 33
oncogenesis 27–28
oral cancer
    benzene and 54
    photodynamic therapy for 127
    tobacco use and 62
organelles 6, *9,* 147
origin of life 1–4, *3,* 145
osteoblast 117
osteoclast *8,* 117
ovarian cancer 82–83
    clinical trials on 123
    diagnosis of 83
    incidence of 83
        by continent 92, *93–97*
        in developed v. undeveloped countries
            100
    mortality rate for 64, *65, 66,* 83
    risk factors for 82
    sex hormones and 45, 82–83
    stages of 83
    survival rate in, five-year 83
    symptoms of 83

ovarian cycle
    diet and 102–105
    regulation of 102
oxidases, mixed-function 60

P

paclitaxel 117, *119*
    for bladder cancer 129
    for breast cancer 131–132
PAHs. *See* polycyclic aromatic hydrocarbons
pain, from chemotherapy 121
pancreas
    anatomy of 83
    functions of 83–84
pancreatic cancer 83–85
    clinical trials on 138–139
    diagnosis of 85
    diet and hormones in 105
    endocrine tumors of 84
    exocrine tumors of 84
    incidence of 84
        by continent *93–97*
        in developed v. undeveloped countries
            100
    industrial emissions and 57
    mortality rates for 64, *65, 66*, 84
    risk factors for 84
    stages of 85
    symptoms of 85
    tobacco use and 62, 84
papillomavirus (PMV) 111–112, *115*
paracrine signaling 13–16
passenger mutations 39–40
PCR. *See* polymerase chain reaction
pemetrexed 136
peptide bonds 151
peripheral neurons, chemotherapy and 121
peroxisomes *146*, 148
pesticides, as carcinogens 106–107
PET. *See* positron emission tomography
P53 gene
    functions of 34–35, *35, 36*
    in gene therapy 123
    in skin cancer 58
p53 protein *38*
phase I clinical trial 187
phase II clinical trial 188
phase III clinical trial 188
phase IV clinical trial 188

Philadelphia chromosome (Ph) 23, *24*, 42
phosphate 148, *149*, 150, 151
phospholipid(s) 148, 155
    and origin of life 2–4
    structure of *152*, 155
phospholipid bubbles 2–4, *3*
photodynamic therapy 126, 127
Photofrin (porfimer sodium) 127
photosynthesis 4, 6
pipe smoking. *See* tobacco use
Pirker, Robert 137
pituitary cancer, growth hormone in 67
pituitary gland *70*
    growth hormone-producing cell from *9*
    hormone release by 15, 102, *103, 104*
    regulation of 102, *103, 104*
plant genomes *185*
plasmids *7*, 166–168, 171
platelets 77–78
    chemotherapy and 122
    stem cell therapy and 125
PMV. *See* papillomavirus
point mutation
    in cancer cells 39
    definition of 33, 175
    in oncogenes 33
    in sickle-cell anemia 175
    in tumor suppressor genes 35
pollution, atmospheric, and cancer 48, 56–57,
    57, 81
polycyclic aromatic hydrocarbons (PAHs) 57
polymerase chain reaction (PCR) 169, 172, 174
polyploidization 155
polyps, of colon 76
polysaccharides 148, *152*, 155
porfimer sodium 127
positron emission tomography (PET)
    of pancreatic cancer 85
    radiation exposure in 59
post-mitotic cells 21, 28, 118, 160
potassium arsenate 52
precancerous conditions 90
preclinical research 187
primary transcript *186*
progesterone, functions of 44–45
progression 41–46, 67–68
prokaryotes
    evolution of 4–6, *5*, 145
    gene organization in *186*
    genome of 6, 145

glycocalyx of 10
structure of 6, *7*, 145
promoters, gene 33, 169
prophase
of meiosis I 164–165
of mitosis 163
prostate cancer 85–87
cadmium and 54–55
clinical trials on 123, 139–140
cryosurgery for 126
diagnosis of 86–87, 140
diet and 86, 105
genetic mutations in 23–26
incidence of
by continent 92, *93–97*
in developed v. undeveloped countries
99, *100*
industrial emissions and 57
mortality rates for *65, 66,* 86
risk factors for 86
sex hormones and 45, 105
stages of 87
symptoms of 86
testosterone antagonists for 111, 118
prostate gland, anatomy of 85–86
prostate-specific antigen (PSA) 86–87, 140
proteins 2, 4, 148. *See also* specific types
complexity in humans 185
defective, production of 43
motor 163
naming conventions for 34, 189
structure of 151–153, *152*
synthesis of 147–148, 155, 158
protons 143
proto-oncogenes 33–34
conversion to oncogenes xvi, 33
definition of 33
naming conventions for 34
protozoans
cancer effects lacking in 28
cell division without controls in 27–29
evolution of 4, *5,* 6–10
PSA. *See* prostate-specific antigen
P21 gene, functions of 34, *35*
purine *149,* 151
pyrimidine *149,* 151

Q

quarks 143, *144*

R

RAC. *See* Recombinant DNA Advisory Committee
race
and bladder cancer 68
and colon cancer 76
and pancreatic cancer 84
and prostate cancer 86
radiation
as carcinogen 48, 57–59
cell phone, and brain tumors 71
ionizing, risks of 57–59
ultraviolet, and skin cancer 57–58
radiotherapy 59, 123–124, 142
bone marrow transplantation with 113
radiation exposure in 59
side effects of 124
radon, and lung cancer 80–81
raloxifene *115,* 118, 131, 132–133
random primer labeling 170
Ras oncogene 33–34, *35, 36*
Ras protein *37*
RBC. *See* red blood cells
Rb gene, functions of 34, *35, 36*
rearrangements, genetic 39
receptors 165
chemotherapy drugs targeting 111, 117–118
monoclonal antibodies targeting 111
tumor cell 141
Recombinant DNA Advisory Committee (RAC)
187
recombinant DNA technology. *See* biotechnology
red blood cells (RBC)
antigens on 179–181, *181*
bone marrow stimulants and 110
chemotherapy and 121
functions of 77, 110
sickle-cell anemia and 175
stem cell therapy and 125
Report on Carcinogens (RoC) 47–48
reproductive cycle
diet and 102–105
regulation of 102, *104*
respiratory chain. *See* electron transport chain
restriction enzymes 166–169, *167*
retinoblastoma, *Rb* gene in 34
retroviruses
in gene therapy 122, 175–177, *176*
in oncogenes 33–34
reverse transcriptase 169

Rho gene, in cell motility 44
ribonucleic acid. *See* RNA
ribonucleotides 116, 153–154
ribose *149,* 150, 151
ribosomal RNA (rRNA) 158
ribosomes *7, 9, 146,* 147–148, 158
risk estimation 48
risk factors
    for bladder cancer 68
    for brain tumors 71
    for breast cancer 75
    for colon cancer 76–77
    for leukemia 78
    for lung cancer 79–80
    for ovarian cancer 82
    for pancreatic cancer 84
    for prostate cancer 86
    for skin cancer 89
rituximab (Rituxan) 111, *115*
RNA 148, 153–154
    chemotherapy drugs targeting 116
    DNA transcription to 116, 158
    functions of 155
    messenger 147–148, 158, 169, 186
    nucleotides in 151, *152*
    origin of 2
    ribosomal 158
    structure of 151, *152,* 153–154, *154*
    synthesis of, chemotherapy drugs targeting
        116
    transfer 158
    translation of 158
RNA blotting 172–173
RNA polymerase 158
RoC. *See* Report on Carcinogens
Rosenberg, Stephen 141
rRNA. *See* ribosomal RNA

S

Sanger, Fred 171
Sanger sequencing method 182–183
Santillan, Jesica 180, 182
sarcomas
    in chickens xv, 33–34
    definition of 67
seborrheic keratosis *43*
sebum 87
secondary tumors 71
secondhand smoke 62, 77, 80
second messenger 13, *14,* 165

sequencing, DNA 39–40, *167,* 169, 171–172,
    182–184
sex chromosomes *25*
sex hormones
    age and 46
    diet and 102–105
    and production of cancer 44–45
    regulation of 102–105, *104*
Shh gene 189
shotgun sequencing, hierarchical 183
sickle-cell anemia 175
side effects. *See* specific therapies
single base substitutions 39
sister chromatids 163
skin
    anatomy of 87, *88*
    susceptibility to cancer 63–64
    warts as benign tumor of *43*
skin cancer 87–90
    arsenic compounds and 51–52
    benzene and 54
    clinical trials on 123, 140–141
    diagnosis of 90
    diet and hormones in 105
    gene therapy for 123
    incidence of 88–89
        by continent *93–97*
        in developed v. undeveloped countries
            99, *100*
    industrial emissions and 56
    lifestyle and 106
    mortality rates for *65, 66,* 88–89
    risk factors for 89
    symptoms of 89–90
    types of *67,* 87–89
    ultraviolet radiation and 57–58, 64, 89
smoking. *See* tobacco use
somatic cells, chromosomes in 164
somatotroph *9*
South America, incidence of cancer in 92, *94*
Southeast, U.S., aflatoxin exposure in 49
S phase 28–29, 116, 160, *161*
spinal cord compression 137–138
squamous cell(s) 87
squamous cell carcinoma 87–90
Src oncogene xv, 33–34, *35, 36*
stages, of cancer 67–68
stem cell(s)
    cancer-causing xvii
    functions of 124
    gene therapy and 179

hematopoietic 134–135
lifespan of 21
stem cell therapy 124–125, 142
    v. bone marrow transplantation 124–125,
        136
    for leukemia 124, 134–136
    side effects of 125
steroid hormones, and production of cancer 45
Stevenson, Robert Louis 19
stomach cancer
    diet and hormones in 105
    incidence of
        by continent 92–98, 93–97
        in developed v. undeveloped countries
            99, 100
        in Japan 100, 106
    tobacco use and 62
The Strange Case of Dr. Jekyll and Mr. Hyde
    (Stevenson) 19
stroma cells, ovarian 82
subatomic particles 143
sugar(s) 145, 149, 150
sugar polymers. See polysaccharides
suicide, cellular. See apoptosis
sun exposure, and skin cancer 89
surgery 125–127
SV40 virus 183
sweat 87
synergistic cancer risk 53
syngeneic bone marrow transplants 113–114

T

Taiwan, arsenic exposure in 51
tamoxifen 111, 118, 119, 131–133
Taxol. See paclitaxel
Taxotere. See docetaxel
T cells. See T lymphocytes
TCR. See tumor cell receptor
telomerase 22–23, 35, 36
telomeres 21–23
telophase 163–164
temozolomide (Temodar) 116, 120, 129–130
terminology, cancer 65–68
testicular cancer
    cadmium and 55
    incidence of
        by continent 92, 93–97
        in developed v. undeveloped countries
            100
testicular metastases, from leukemia 78–79

testosterone
    age and 46
    functions of 44–45
    in prostate regulation 86
testosterone receptors, chemotherapy drugs
        blocking 111, 118
therapies, cancer 108–127
    angiogenesis blockers as 112–113
    biotherapies 142
    bone marrow transplants as 113–116
    chemotherapy 116–122, 142
    cost of, in North America 98
    cryosurgery 125–126
    future of 141–142
    gene 122–123, 142
    laser 126–127
    photodynamic 126, 127
    radiotherapy 123–124, 142
    stem cell 124–125, 142
    surgery as 125–127
thymine 151, 155, 156
TILs. See tumor-infiltrating T lymphocytes
tissue matching 179–182
T lymphocytes (T cells)
    in apoptosis 29
    biotherapies and 109
    CTLA4 inhibitors and, in prostate cancer
        139–140
    functions of 109, 114
    tumor-infiltrating, in skin cancer 140–141
tobacco use
    asbestos exposure and 53
    and bladder cancer 62, 68
    carcinogens in 48, 59–62, 60, 79–80
    and colon cancer 76–77
    and lung cancer 46, 61–62, 79–80, 106
    and pancreatic cancer 62, 84
    secondhand smoke from 62, 77, 80
transcription 116, 158
transfection 166
transfer RNA (tRNA) 158
transformation, of cells 65
translation 158
transplantation
    bone marrow 113–116, 134–136
    tissue matching in 179–182
transposable elements 185
trastuzumab 111, 115
treatment. See therapies
trials. See clinical trials
tRNA. See transfer RNA

TSGs. *See* tumor suppressor genes
tumor(s). *See also* specific types
   benign 65
   cancer cells in 41–42
   malignant 66
   secondary 71
   from single cancer cell 41–42
   surgical removal of 125–127
tumor cell receptor (TCR) 141
tumor-infiltrating T lymphocytes (TILs)
   140–141
tumor suppressor genes (TSGs) 34–35
   definition of 33
   functions of 34–35, *35*
tumor suppressor protein *38*

U

ultrasonography
   in breast cancer 75
   in colon cancer 77
   in cryosurgery 125
   endoscopic, in pancreatic cancer 85
   in pancreatic cancer 85
   in prostate cancer 87
   transvaginal, in ovarian cancer 83
ultraviolet radiation
   and skin cancer 57–58, 64, 89
   types of 58
umbilical cord blood 124–125, 134–136
undeveloped countries, cancer rates in 98–99,
   100
United Nations, WHO established by 91
United States
   cancer incidence and types in 99, *100*
   diet and cancer rates in 100–105
universal blood donors 180
uracil 151, 153–154
uterine cancer
   estrogen and 102
   sex hormones and 45
   tobacco use and 62

V

vaccines 111–112, 130–131
Van Cutsem, Eric 134
Varmus, Harold 34

vascular endothelial growth factor (VEGF)
   112–113, 138–139
vectors
   cloning 168
   in gene therapy 175–177, *176, 178*
   leukemia induced by 177–179
VEGF. *See* vascular endothelial growth factor
viruses
   associated with chicken sarcomas xv
   DNA, in cancer cells 39
   in gene therapy 122, 175–177
vitamin C, and colon cancer 133–134
vitamin E, and colon cancer 133–134
Vogel, Victor 132–133
vomiting, from chemotherapy 120–121

W

warts, as benign tumors *43*
WBC. *See* white blood cells
weights and measures *190*
white blood cells (WBC)
   biotherapies and 109
   bone marrow stimulants and 110, 122
   cancer of. *See* leukemia
   chemotherapy and 121–122, 129
   communication among 13
   functions of 78, 109
   gene therapy and 177, 179
   stem cell therapy and 125
   types of 78
WHO. *See* World Health Organization
Wilms, Max 130
Wilms tumor 1 peptide vaccine 130–131
Women's Health Initiative 82–83
wood preservation, arsenic in 52
World Cancer Report 91–92
World Health Organization (WHO) 48, 91–92, 98
Wt1 gene 130–131

X

X-ray(s), risk from 58–59
X-ray therapy. *See* radiotherapy

Z

zoledronic acid (Zometa) 117, *120,* 131–132